Search Engine Optimization

Your visual blueprint™ for effective Internet marketing, 3rd Edition

by Kristopher B. Jones

D1472605

Visual™

A Wiley Brand

Search Engine Optimization: Your visual blueprint™ for effective Internet marketing, 3rd Edition

Published by
John Wiley & Sons, Inc.
10475 Crosspoint Boulevard
Indianapolis, IN 46256

www.wiley.com

Published simultaneously in Canada

Copyright © 2013 by John Wiley & Sons, Inc., Indianapolis, Indiana

No part of this publication may be reproduced, stored in a retrieval system or transmitted in any form or by any means, electronic, mechanical, photocopying, recording, scanning or otherwise, except as permitted under Sections 107 or 108 of the 1976 United States Copyright Act, without either the prior written permission of the Publisher, or authorization through payment of the appropriate per-copy fee to the Copyright Clearance Center, 222 Rosewood Drive, Danvers, MA 01923, (978) 750-8400, fax (978) 646-8600. Requests to the Publisher for permission should be addressed to the Permissions Department, John Wiley & Sons, Inc., 111 River Street, Hoboken, NJ 07030, 201-748-6011, fax 201-748-6008, or online at www.wiley.com/go/permissions.

Wiley publishes in a variety of print and electronic formats and by print-on-demand. Some material included with standard print versions of this book may not be included in e-books or in print-on-demand. If this book refers to media such as a CD or DVD that is not included in the version you purchased, you may download this material at http://booksupport.wiley.com. For more information about Wiley products, visit www.wiley.com.

Library of Congress Control Number: 2013933933

ISBN: 978-1-118-55174-5

Manufactured in the United States of America

10 9 8 7 6 5 4 3 2 1

Trademark Acknowledgments

Wiley, the Wiley logo, Visual, the Visual logo, Visual Blueprint, Read Less - Learn More and related trade dress are trademarks or registered trademarks of John Wiley & Sons, Inc. and/or its affiliates. All other trademarks are the property of their respective owners. John Wiley & Sons, Inc. is not associated with any product or vendor mentioned in this book.

LIMIT OF LIABILITY/DISCLAIMER OF WARRANTY: THE PUBLISHER AND THE AUTHOR MAKE NO REPRESENTATIONS OR WARRANTIES WITH RESPECT TO THE ACCURACY OR COMPLETENESS OF THE CONTENTS OF THIS WORK AND SPECIFICALLY DISCLAIM ALL WARRANTIES, INCLUDING WITHOUT LIMITATION WARRANTIES OF FITNESS FOR A PARTICULAR PURPOSE. NO WARRANTY MAY BE CREATED OR EXTENDED BY SALES OR PROMOTIONAL MATERIALS. THE ADVICE AND STRATEGIES CONTAINED HEREIN MAY NOT BE SUITABLE FOR EVERY SITUATION. THIS WORK IS SOLD WITH THE UNDERSTANDING THAT THE PUBLISHER IS NOT ENGAGED IN RENDERING LEGAL, ACCOUNTING, OR OTHER PROFESSIONAL SERVICES. IF PROFESSIONAL ASSISTANCE IS REQUIRED, THE SERVICES OF A COMPETENT PROFESSIONAL PERSON SHOULD BE SOUGHT. NEITHER THE PUBLISHER NOR THE AUTHOR SHALL BE LIABLE FOR DAMAGES ARISING HEREFROM. THE FACT THAT AN ORGANIZATION OR WEBSITE IS REFERRED TO IN THIS WORK AS A CITATION AND/OR A POTENTIAL SOURCE OF FURTHER INFORMATION DOES NOT MEAN THAT THE AUTHOR OR THE PUBLISHER ENDORSES THE INFORMATION THE ORGANIZATION OR WEBSITE MAY PROVIDE OR RECOMMENDATIONS IT MAY MAKE. FURTHER, READERS SHOULD BE AWARE THAT INTERNET WEBSITES LISTED IN THIS WORK MAY HAVE CHANGED OR DISAPPEARED BETWEEN WHEN THIS WORK WAS WRITTEN AND WHEN IT IS READ.

FOR PURPOSES OF ILLUSTRATING THE CONCEPTS AND TECHNIQUES DESCRIBED IN THIS BOOK, THE AUTHOR HAS CREATED VARIOUS NAMES, COMPANY NAMES, MAILING, E-MAIL AND INTERNET ADDRESSES, PHONE AND FAX NUMBERS AND SIMILAR INFORMATION, ALL OF WHICH ARE FICTITIOUS. ANY RESEMBLANCE OF THESE FICTITIOUS NAMES, ADDRESSES, PHONE AND FAX NUMBERS AND SIMILAR INFORMATION TO ANY ACTUAL PERSON, COMPANY AND/OR ORGANIZATION IS UNINTENTIONAL AND PURELY COINCIDENTAL.

Contact Us

For general information on our other products and services please contact our Customer Care Department within the U.S. at 877-762-2974, outside the U.S. at 317-572-3993 or fax 317-572-4002.

For technical support please visit www.wiley.com/techsupport.

Sales | Contact Wiley at (877) 762-2974 or fax (317) 572-4002.

Credits

Senior Acquisitions Editor
Stephanie McComb

Project Editor
Kristin Vorce

Technical Editor
Vince Averello

Copy Editor
Lauren Kennedy

Editorial Director
Robyn Siesky

Business Manager
Amy Knies

Senior Marketing Manager
Sandy Smith

**Vice President and Executive
Group Publisher**
Richard Swadley

**Vice President and Executive
Publisher**
Barry Pruett

Project Coordinator
Sheree Montgomery

Graphics and Production Specialists
Joyce Haughey
Andrea Hornberger
Jennifer Mayberry

Quality Control Technician
Melissa Cossell

Proofreading and Indexing
Penny L. Stuart
BIM Indexing & Proofreading Services

About the Author

Kristopher B. Jones is considered one of the top Internet marketing experts in the world. Kris is a frequent keynote speaker, presenter, and moderator at major national and international marketing conferences, including Search Engine Strategies (SES), Pubcon, and Radio Ink Convergence. Since 2008 Kris's book, *Search-Engine Optimization: Your visual blueprint for effective Internet marketing*, has sold nearly 50,000 copies and was ranked on Amazon.com as the best-selling book within the search-engine marketing category more times than any other SEO book. Kris is a sought-after motivational speaker and frequently speaks to corporations and nonprofit organizations, as well as colleges and universities around the world. Kris has delivered inspirational lectures to thousands of college and graduate students at schools such as Penn State University, the University of Pittsburgh, and Villanova University.

Kris was the founder and former President and CEO of Pepperjam, a full-service Internet marketing agency and affiliate network sold to eBay in 2011 (after being acquired by GSI Commerce in 2009). During Kris's tenure at Pepperjam, the company was recognized for three consecutive years by *Inc.* magazine as one of the fastest-growing companies in the United States and was celebrated as one of the best places to work in the state of Pennsylvania. The company currently powers affiliate marketing programs for more than 2,000 major Internet retailers, including Toys "R" Us, Dick's Sporting Goods, and the NFL.

After selling Pepperjam, Kris founded an angel investment firm called KBJ Capital (www. kbjcapital.com), which he has leveraged to invest in and advise a growing portfolio of early-stage technology companies, including ReferLocal.com, where he serves as founder and CEO; Highlighter.com; APPEK Mobile Apps; Pathmapp.com, VigLink; Internet Media Labs; LavCup.com; and Yumm.com, among others. KBJ Capital has also made several alternative financial investments, including in Doc Magrogan's Oyster House, Rapid Recovery, and a fast-growing real estate investment firm Kris cofounded with his entrepreneurial brother Rick.

In addition, in 2012 Kris joined the #1 SEO firm in the United States, Internet Marketing Ninjas, as Chairman. As Chairman, Kris advises the company on its overall business strategy, including mergers and acquisitions, growth into new markets and products, and executive recruitment and retention. Kris has worked closely with CEO Jim Boykin on recent Ninja investments and acquisitions of WebmasterWorld, DevShed, Cre8asite, and Threadwatch, as well as the talent acquisitions of Chris Boggs, Joe Hall, Kim Kopp Krause Berg, and Ann Smarty.

In 2013 Kris was selected by the Online Marketing Institute as one of the "Top 40 Digital Strategists in Marketing." Kristopher was also recognized as an Entrepreneur of the Year by Bank of America (2005), as a finalist for the prestigious Ernst & Young Entrepreneur of the Year (2008), and twice as one of the "Top 20 Business Leaders" in northeastern Pennsylvania under the age of 40 (2006, 2010).

An avid reader, traveler, public speaker, entrepreneur, and business leader, Kristopher truly defines a spiritually motivated individual dedicated to the community in which he lives. Kris is a former senior staff member to former Congressman Paul E. Kanjorski (PA-11).

Kristopher has participated on numerous technology, educational, and nonprofit boards of director and advisory committees, including the Misericordia University Board of Trustees, the Great Valley Technology Alliance (past cochair), WVIA Public Broadcasting, Penn State University (WB) Department of Information Science and Technology, Albany Law School Alumni Association, Pennsylvania Keystone Innovation Grant Committee (KIG), CAN BE Business Incubator, Greater Wilkes-Barre Chamber of Commerce Strategic Planning Committee, Luzerne Foundation Millennium Circle, and the United Way of Wyoming Valley, among others.

Kristopher received a bachelor of arts from Pennsylvania State University, a master of science from Villanova University, and a juris doctorate from Albany Law School.

Learn more about Kris on his personal website, located at www.krisjones.com.

Connect with Kris:

Facebook www.facebook.com/kbjcapital

Twitter www.twitter.com/krisjonescom

LinkedIn www.linkedin.com/in/internetceo

Contact Kris at kris@krisjones.com.

"I have always had the deepest respect for Kris's extensive knowledge of how search engines work and how you get the most out of your search-engine marketing efforts. In this book Kris proves that he is also an excellent writer with the rare ability to explain even complex things in such a way that everyone can understand it. I can highly recommend this book to anyone interested in search-engine marketing!"

Mikkel deMib Svendsen, SEO Expert and Founder, deMib.com/Redpitt.com

"As marketing dollars continue to shift from offline to online, competition for the limited real estate available on a search results page is increasingly fierce. Companies need to embrace SEO as a viable and profitable marketing strategy. Kris's book lays out a step-by-step approach that is an excellent launch point to the competitive world of search-engine optimization."

Todd Friesen, Director of SEO, Salesforce.com

"This book provides valuable information on search-engine optimization and Internet marketing from one of the thought shapers of the business. Kris Jones offers specific instruction on how to improve your website ranking through proven strategies in SEO and social media optimization."

Marcus Tandler, SEO Expert and Blogger, Mediadonis.net

"When is the last time YOU used the Yellow Pages or card catalog? Right!! Search has changed the game, and if you are not in it, your competitors are! If you are looking to rank better, with proven strategies then Kris's book is a must read!"

Wil Reynolds, SEO Expert and Founder, SEER Interactive

"Kris Jones is a true pioneer in the Internet marketing space. His knowledge of search-engine optimization can help any business, small or large, maximize its exposure on the Internet's most critical channel. If you are looking for Internet success, then look for guidance from people who have already succeeded. Kris Jones is one of those people."

Michael C. Jones, GM of Pepperjam Exchange, an eBay Company

"I've been reading everything I could get my hands on in search marketing since the '90s, and I've noticed one constant: most books on search are authored by pretenders or professional writers that research the topic. Kris is the real deal, a search innovator from the trenches. When he talks, search marketers better listen."

Shawn Collins, Cofounder, Affiliate Summit

"With clear, concise writing, Kris Jones builds a bridge between SEO theory and real-world business results. If you know where you want your website and your business to go, but aren't sure how to get there, this book is the map you've been looking for."

Scott Lynett, Publisher & CEO, Times-Shamrock Communications

"Written by an experienced master practitioner, this book is an updated step-by-step guide to dominating search engine results. Get it now and use it like a club to beat up your online competition!"

Tim Ash, Author of Landing Page Optimization, CEO of SiteTuners, and Chair of Conversion Conference

"Let me let you in on a little secret . . . SEO is not magic. It is a fundamental process by which smart marketers structure their online content to achieve maximum visibility with an interested audience. Nobody knows that process better than Kris — the good news is that he's elected to share his expertise in such a format that everyone—from marketer to coder, creative to executive—can understand."

Jeffrey K. Rohrs, Vice President of Marketing, ExactTarget

Author's Acknowledgments

The third edition of this book is dedicated to my loving family, including my wife Robyn, children Kris Jr., Lauren, and Jackson, my mother Charlotte, my father "Harvey," my brother Rick, and my sister Jennifer. I'd also like to recognize the unconditional love, friendship, and continued support I receive from my mother-in-law Terry and father-in-law "Lenny" Martin, as well as my brother-in-law Jonathan Runquist and sister-in-law Melanie Jones. My family is everything to me and my amazing wife is my #1.

The completion of the third edition of this book would not have been possible without the hard work of my editorial team at Wiley, including Stephanie McComb, Kristin Vorce, Lauren Kennedy, and Vince Averello. The professional suggestions and expertise I received throughout the writing process helped make this book a reality and the finished product something to be proud of.

I'd also like to thank Bonnie Stefanic of Internet Marketing Ninjas and Christian Wenzel of Wenzel PPC for offering considerable editorial assistance and support throughout all stages of this publication. Christian was my former director of Pay-Per-Click (PPC) at Pepperjam and is one of the top subject matter experts in the world on optimizing quality scores and driving more business leads at the lowest possible cost per acquisition via PPC. Bonnie is a leading thought shaper in the SEO space and is considered a world authority on SEO tools and link building.

Finally, I'd like to acknowledge my good friend Mike Averto, founder and CEO of web design firm Otreva.com, for building KrisJones.com into what I believe is one of the coolest personal websites on the Internet. Mike overdelivered and exceeded my expectations for modern web design. Mike's use of HTML5 and the latest technologies available in social media integration are pretty breathtaking. Note that KrisJones.com provides readers of this book with a venue to ask follow-up questions and to share suggestions for future editions.

How to Use This Book

Who This Book Is For

This book is for advanced computer users who want to take their knowledge of this particular technology or software application to the next level.

The Conventions in This Book

① Steps

This book uses a step-by-step format to guide you easily through each task. Numbered steps are actions you must do; bulleted steps clarify a point, step, or optional feature; and indented steps give you the result.

② Notes

Notes give additional information — special conditions that may occur during an operation, a situation that you want to avoid, or a cross reference to a related area of the book.

③ Icons and Buttons

Icons and buttons show you exactly what you need to click to perform a step.

④ Extra or Apply It

An Extra section provides additional information about the preceding task — insider information and tips for ease and efficiency. An Apply It section takes the code from the preceding task one step further and allows you to take full advantage of it.

⑤ Bold

Bold type shows text or numbers you must type.

⑥ Italics

Italic type introduces and defines a new term.

⑦ Courier Font

`Courier font` indicates the use of scripting language code such as statements, operators, or functions, and code such as objects, methods, or properties.

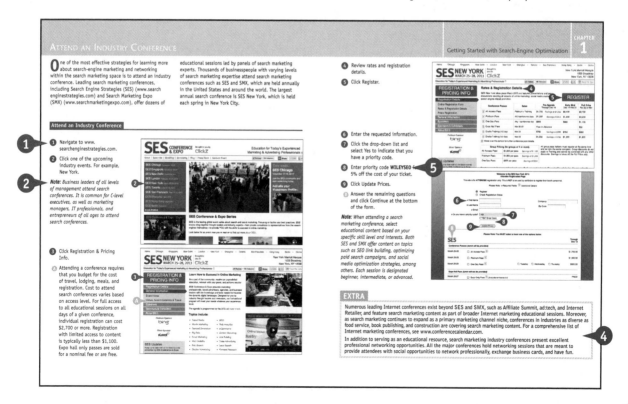

Table of Contents

Chapter 1	Getting Started with Search-Engine Optimization

Chapter 2	Keyword Generation

Chapter 3 — Creating Pages

Chapter 4 — Basic Website Structure

TABLE OF CONTENTS

Chapter 8 Building Links

Chapter 9 Using Google Analytics

TABLE OF CONTENTS

Chapter 12   Optimizing PPC Campaigns through Quality Score Optimization

Chapter 13   Optimizing for Other Search Engines

TABLE OF CONTENTS

Foreword

For many companies, the work performed on their online marketing campaigns can spell the difference between becoming a success or failure for their entire business. In *Search Engine Optimization: Your visual blueprint for effective Internet marketing, 3rd Edition,* Kris Jones gives away some of the most amazing tips and tools to guide you in getting the most out of your online marketing efforts.

This book can help you like no other book on online marketing can. I know this because several of these tools and techniques listed in this book helped Kris to build up his former company, Pepperjam, into one of the largest and most respected Internet marketing firms in the world, and these tools and techniques have also helped my own company (Internet Marketing Ninjas) grow from a one-man company in 1999 to more than 100 in-house employees today.

Kris has outlined what to do, and how to do it, and if you follow the blueprint within, you will possess knowledge far beyond your competitors', giving you the edge to take on your biggest competitors. I have seen what works, and what does not work, via working with countless websites since 1999. I have also read numerous books on the topic of Internet marketing, but this is the only book I have ever seen that outlines the best tools to use and the best techniques to drive major traffic to your website. You can pay a company like mine thousands of dollars every month, or you can get the knowledge passed down from one of the best minds in the industry (Kris) and have the knowledge and the tools to do the work yourself.

I've known Kris for over ten years now, and I have always been impressed by Kris's knowledge of so many facets of Internet marketing. I recall in 2008 when I drove to Pennsylvania to meet with Kris and Pepperjam and I was blown away at the growth his company had recently had. Kris had grown his company by 2,447.5% over the previous year, and his company was taking over the building they occupied, blowing through walls on his floor to accommodate the growth he was seeing. That was also the year that the first edition of Kris's book was published. The following year Kris sold Pepperjam to GSI, which later was sold to eBay.

Clearly this was a man who knew what he was doing. In 2012 I was lucky enough to bring Kris on at my company (Internet Marketing Ninjas) as our Chairman.

That's really what Kris has done in this book. By taking a visual approach to teaching SEO, Kris allows us to visualize not just where we are, but where we could be . . . where we need to be. Reading this book can do for you what walking into Pepperjam did for me. It can open your eyes to a world of possibilities and the full realization of the potential that you never even knew you had. Thank you, Kris, and happy reading to you, the new generation of Internet marketers.

James Boykin

Jim Boykin

Founder & CEO

Internet Marketing Ninjas
www.internetmarketingninjas.com
@jimboykin on Twitter
@seojim on Facebook

An Introduction to Search-Engine Optimization

Search-engine optimization, or *SEO,* is the process of setting up your website so that it ranks well for particular keywords within the organic search results of major search engines, including Google, Yahoo, and Bing. Unlike paid search marketing, which requires you to pay for every click sent to your website from a search engine, traffic sent to your site from a search engine's organic results is free.

In the early days of SEO, gaining top rankings for keywords was much easier than it is today. In those "good old days," search-engine algorithms were easy to crack. All you had to do was include the keyword you wanted to rank for in the title tag of your web page and sprinkle that keyword throughout the content of your page, and chances were you would rank within the top ten results of your favorite search engine. Not surprisingly, over the years search-engine algorithms have become increasingly complex, which has resulted in website owners either outsourcing SEO to professional firms or educating themselves using books like this one.

Dating back to 1996 or so, search engines started to become a very popular tool for web surfers looking for all sorts of information. Long before Google and Yahoo became popular, search engines such as AltaVista and InfoSeek were pioneers at providing search results to users within a fraction of a second. Search results in the early days were nowhere near as relevant as they are today. However, search-engine users in the millions began relying on websites like AltaVista more and more frequently to retrieve information about everything from health abnormalities to pricing on the latest gadget.

Search-engine optimization first began in 1997 through public reports and commentary provided by search-engine experts, including Danny Sullivan and Bruce Clay, among others. Early reports about SEO looked at search-engine algorithms and how the various search engines ranked search results. Inspired entrepreneurs and website owners began studying these reports and testing strategies for how they could rank well within the search results. Before long the SEO profession emerged, and individuals were offering services to help rank websites on major search engines.

As the World Wide Web grew at a remarkable pace, the popularity of AltaVista and Infoseek started to wane. Other search engines came and went, but no company has had more of an impact on search-engine marketing than Google.

Google: The Birth Child of Larry and Sergey

Google was cofounded by Larry Page and Sergey Brin while they were students at Stanford University. Although the company was officially incorporated in 1998, the idea of creating a search engine that would "organize the world's information and make it universally accessible and useful" began as part of a doctoral research project Larry and Sergey began in 1996.

The key to Google's early success was that the algorithm behind the Google search engine was different from the algorithms before it. Based on Larry and Sergey's experience with academic research, they believed that web page authority and relevance could be derived algorithmically by indexing the entire web, and then analyzing who links to whom. This idea came from the fact that in academia authority is derived when researchers advance their own research by citing one another as part of the research process. Indeed, each piece of published scholarly work (including Larry and Sergey's dissertation) has a works-cited page at the end of each finished piece of written research, which includes a list of resources that were cited as relevant to the work being advanced.

Larry and Sergey thought about the process of citing in academic research and hypothesized that those web pages with the most links to them from other highly relevant web pages must be the most relevant pages associated with a particular search. To further bolster this concept, Larry and Sergey created PageRank (named after Larry Page), which not only counts how many links point to any given page but also determines the quality of those links.

The Google algorithm is more complex than just analyzing who links to whom, and algorithmically analyzing links is a great idea that has separated Google from its competition. In fact, today Google is the leading search engine with nearly 70% market share in the United States and has quickly become the preferred search engine in most other parts of the world.

SEO: Beware of Snake Oil Salesman

Search-engine optimization is a critical component of a well-rounded Internet marketing strategy. Having a great website is simply not enough. Hundreds of millions of people use search engines every day to scour the Internet and find information from relevant websites just like yours. In order to appear alongside your competition in the search results, your website must be search-engine-friendly. Moreover, to be competitive within the search results, you need to take steps that convince search engines that your website is an authority and that your content is relevant for particular keywords related to your business or enterprise.

If you are reading this book, you do not need convincing that SEO is integral to your online marketing success. However, the profession of SEO has taken significant criticism for being nothing more than a spammy attempt to manipulate search-engine results. Unfortunately, criticism has come primarily as a result of so-called SEO experts who sell guaranteed top ten placements and instant success formulas for achieving front page search-engine rankings. Fortunately, such unethical, get-rich-quick, snake oil salesmen represent a very small percentage of SEO professionals.

The majority of SEO experts are ethical professionals who understand the complex dynamics of search-engine algorithms and offer assistance and counsel on how to maximize your placement on search engines. The truth is that there are no guarantees in SEO. In fact, if an alleged SEO professional offers guaranteed placement within Google's top ten organic rankings, you need to decline the offer. SEO requires great skill and is not quick. You must have patience. You should look at SEO as an ongoing process that is necessary for you to maintain and maximize your position in the organic search results in the long term. You should set your expectations accordingly and educate other website owners of the process so they do not waste money based on hollow pitches from unethical SEO professionals.

Get Started

The first step to getting started with your SEO campaign is to select a topic. If you already have a website covering a topic that you are satisfied with, then you may want to skip this step. However, keep in mind that you need to set realistic expectations based on your chosen topic. Increasing your website rankings for competitive topics is much more difficult than increasing rankings for less competitive topics.

To get the most from your SEO efforts, you must carefully consider your target audience. Your target audience includes the specific people you are trying to put your website in front of. Understanding who your target audience is and what they are searching for can greatly increase the effectiveness of an SEO campaign.

Prior to beginning your SEO efforts, you should set goals, including how much money you want to dedicate to your efforts. If you are going to conduct SEO internally, you need to set a budget only for the tools you need and the amount of money you must allocate to pay your internal SEO team. If you intend to outsource your SEO, you should set aside a minimum of $3,000 to $5,000 monthly for a dedicated SEO professional. Elite SEO professionals may charge in excess of $10,000 per month.

Putting together an internal team of people to help with your SEO requires you to select one or more individuals with varying proficiency in HTML writing, knowledge of CSS, data analysis, graphical design, server administration, copywriting, link building, social media, and blogging. Although the scope of your project dictates how many people you need to fill out your team, you can always consider outsourcing one or more components of the job. Companies like Internet Marketing Ninjas, located at www.internetmarketingninjas.com, can help you train your internal team and put together an SEO strategic plan for the team to follow.

Although writing large amounts of original content may seem like a daunting task, there are countless professional copywriters who can provide you with well-written content at a reasonable price. Moreover, online services such as Elance allow you to hire copywriters and other service providers through an auction system. The auction system allows you to post your work so that multiple service providers compete for the job. You have the option of comparing multiple vendors and ultimately choosing one or more based on skill level and past performance within the Elance network.

One of the best places to keep up-to-date with what is happening in the search-engine marketing industry is to read blogs and other online news sources. Blogs such as SearchEngineLand.com, SERoundTable.com, and SEOmoz.com provide current perspectives and tips, and news websites including DMNews.com, ClickZ.com, and WebProNews.com provide breaking news and commentary on search-engine marketing.

Another way to increase your knowledge about the search-engine marketing space is to attend an industry conference. Leading search marketing conferences, including Search Engine Strategies (SES) and Search Marketing Expo (SMX) offer dozens of educational sessions led by panels of search marketing experts. See www.search enginestrategies.com and www.searchmarketingexpo.com for more information.

Keyword Generation

Effective keyword generation is one of the most critical elements of successful SEO. All keywords are not created equal; some keywords are easier to rank for than others, and some keywords tend to be almost impossible to rank for. Broad or general keywords tend to be highly competitive and therefore should represent only a small portion of your overall SEO efforts. Specific keywords, which include those keywords that describe your specific product or service and are more than three keywords in length, are less competitive and therefore should make up the bulk of your keyword generation efforts.

For example, if you own an e-commerce website, you stand a better chance of ranking within the top search results for product-level keywords than you do for broad keywords that generally describe your business. Although broad keywords tend to generate higher levels of search volume, product-level terms can generate significant search volume and tend to convert at higher rates than broad terms.

There are numerous useful keyword generation tools that can help you discover effective keywords for your website. Keyword generation tools such as Keyword Discovery, Wordtracker, and Google's Keyword Suggestion Tool allow you to carefully research, analyze, and filter potential keywords. It is not enough to just generate massive lists of keywords. Instead, your keyword lists should represent a cross section of broad and specific terms that your website stands a legitimate chance of ranking for. Because keyword generation is so critical to your SEO success, consider making a modest financial investment by purchasing subscriptions to tools such as Keyword Discovery and Wordtracker even though Google, Bing, and other companies offer tools for free.

Keep in mind that although keyword generation tools can quickly generate thousands upon thousands of keywords, each page of your website should be search-engine-optimized for only one or two keywords. Therefore, focus less on generating massive lists of keywords and more on

generating keyword lists that directly relate to your website and give you the best shot at ranking well on search engines.

One of the most effective ways to generate target keywords beyond basic keyword generation is through competitive research. Readily available competitive research tools such as SEMrush, KeywordSpy, and Compete provide various data about your competition, including what keywords your competitors rank for in the organic search results, as well as what keywords your competitors are using on pay-per-click search engines such as Google. Armed with competitive research information, you can compare your success to your competition and use the information to devise a plan of attack to improve your own ranking within the organic and paid search results.

Create Pages

Keep in mind that search engines do not actually rank websites; instead, search engines rank individual web pages. Therefore, in order to succeed with SEO, each and every page of your website must be optimized for search engines. The most important element of each of your web pages is substantial unique content. However, you can optimize numerous other important structural and technological factors on your web pages to ensure that you position yourself to rank well within the search-engine results.

For example, optimizing technical on-site web page factors, such as adding correct filenames, title tags, meta description tags, meta keyword tags, and meta robots tags, is crucial to making sure the search-engine spiders can determine the relevance of your website. Besides your domain name, the first things search engines discover when spidering through the pages of your website are your filenames. Every single page of your website resides in a different file. By titling your pages with SEO in mind, you have a powerful opportunity to establish relevance to a certain topic or keyword.

Each page of your website should contain a unique title tag that includes the target keywords you want to rank for. Search engines place great importance on the text contained within your title tag and use it as a primary indicator of what your web page is about. Therefore, your title tag should include your target keywords and also provide a concise statement summarizing the content of your web page.

Although search engines rarely use description and keyword tags for ranking purposes, each page of your website should include unique description and keyword tags. Description tags can be especially important because search engines often use them as the display text shown when a search query triggers your web page. Therefore, your description tag should include a call-to-action marketing message so that your listing stands out among other listings and gets clicked.

Optimizing your content with header tags and other text modifiers allows you to stress the main ideas and topics that your content covers. Header tags are HTML tags used to apply significance to keywords or phrases within a web page. Placing a selection of text within a header tag tells the search-engine spiders that the text is of a certain level of importance. Using text modifiers, you can emphasize certain blocks of text by bolding, italicizing, or underlining keywords or phrases.

Taking care to optimize web page images is important for those web browsers that do not support images, and because search-engine spiders are unable to accurately read the content of an image, doing so presents an extra opportunity to add keyword-rich content to your page. Links provide the pathways that search-engine spiders need to find your web pages. Creating links with SEO in mind is necessary for optimal results.

Throughout the process of creating web pages you should try to adhere to the standards set forth by the World Wide Web Consortium (W3C), which works to create standards in web design and development to ensure Internet-wide compatibility.

Basic Website Structure

A well-optimized website design and structure help improve the overall performance of your website, making it easier for users to navigate and for search engines to find and index all your content. You want to balance your website design between the needs of your users and the needs of the search engines. To be successful, your website should not only provide a superior user experience but also include an optimal structure so that search engines index your content.

One way to ensure that search engines find all your content is by submitting a sitemap. Think of your sitemap as an outline of your entire website. A sitemap displays the inner framework and organization of your website's structure to the search engines. A sitemap should reflect the entire navigational structure of your website so that search-engine spiders can find and index all your content. As you add new content to your website, you should submit your sitemap to the search engines regularly, every 24 hours or so.

To establish trust and credibility in the eyes of your visitors and search engines, your website should include both a company information and a privacy page. A company information page helps strengthen your reputation in the eyes of both your website visitors and the search engines. Adding a company information page helps build trust with your visitors by explaining who you are and where you come from; you can provide company biographies, company history, staff photos, and links to social media profiles.

In addition to a company information page, your website should also contain a page explaining your privacy policy. A privacy policy page helps establish trust by declaring that you are committed to protecting the privacy of your visitors' personal information. Try to keep your privacy policy simple and make it easy to read, easy to understand, and easy to find on your website. You should consider adding a link to your privacy policy next to a link to your company information page. This way, your visitors can see that you are a trustworthy and legitimate entity.

Advanced Website Structuring

Once you have the basic structure of your website in place, you can implement several additional advanced structural considerations to optimize your site for search engines. For example, beyond setting up your website so that it is indexed, you may want to instruct the search engines not to index a particular page. A robots.txt file allows you to tell the spiders what they may and may not do when they arrive at your domain. Robots.txt files also provide you a means to prevent both potential copyright infringements and search-engine spiders from consuming excessive amounts of bandwidth on your server.

One primary example of advanced website structuring includes the use of the `nofollow` attribute. The `nofollow` attribute instructs search-engine spiders that they should not follow a particular link or view that link as anything of significance when determining rankings. Because search engines count links from your website to another website as a vote for search-engine ranking purposes, you can add `nofollow` if you do not want the search-engine spider to credit the link.

A second advanced website structural consideration is the way you structure your URLs. URLs must be structured so that they are easily spidered and organized and create a user-friendly website navigation system. For example, search engines as well as people prefer URLs that are simple and that include the keywords describing the page within the URL string.

A third structural consideration is the use of an .htaccess file. An .htaccess file is the Apache web server's configuration file. It is a straightforward yet powerful text file that can accomplish a wide variety of functions that allow you to protect your website from content-stealing robots. Moreover, .htaccess is useful in that it allows you to dynamically rewrite poorly formed URLs that shopping cart or blog software generate.

Other advanced website structural considerations include using `mod_rewrite` to rewrite URLs, redirecting non-www traffic to your www domain, and using 301 redirects whenever you change or redesign your website. Each advanced structuring technique provides you with procedures to ensure that search engines recognize your website and that each of your web pages is correctly indexed.

Content Creation

Creating well-written, original content is absolutely critical to your long-term SEO success. Content is what visitors use to determine value, and it is one of the primary factors that search engines use to rank your website. Whether your website ends up on the first page or the one-hundredth page of Google largely depends on the quality and relevance of your content.

Although you should keep SEO principles in mind when you create content, the key to building long-term rankings on search engines is to write content for people, not search engines. Original and naturally flowing content provides your readers with a positive, enjoyable user experience and greatly improves your chances of top search-engine rankings. Avoid writing content solely for SEO purposes and you can greatly increase your likelihood of long-term SEO success.

When you write content, you must avoid duplicate content. Duplicate content occurs when your website contains content that already exists on the web. Duplicate content issues can have a detrimental effect on your SEO success and should be avoided at all costs. Writing original content is the most obvious way to avoid duplicate content. If you feel that you do not have the time to build large amounts of unique content, you can employ tools on your website, such as user reviews, that allow for user-generated content. User-generated content allows your content to remain fresh, which is one of the factors search engines use to rank one website over another with similar authority.

Writing original content and adding user-generated content does not entirely protect you from duplicate content issues. You must protect yourself from others stealing your content because Google cannot algorithmically detect who owns content. Fortunately, tools such as Copyscape are available to help you avoid and prevent duplicate content issues.

Although you should write content for people and not search engines, you should also use proper keyword density throughout each page of your website. First, you want to optimize each page of your website for no more than one or two target keywords, while at the same time making sure that you do not inadvertently repeat nontarget keywords. By using available tools to maximize optimal keyword density, you can incorporate a substantial number of target keywords throughout your content without compromising the naturally flowing aesthetics of the writing.

You should keep in mind a few important content creation principles as you build your website. First, search-engine algorithms cannot read text that is included in images. Therefore, always include important text and target keywords that appear in images in text form. You can still use images, but search engines cannot read the text contained within them. Second, when drafting your content, you can use a powerful content creation principle called *latent semantic content,* which involves using keywords very similar to your target keywords to enhance the theme and relevance of your page. For example, if your target keyword is "Old Spice," you can also use words like "deodorant" and "cologne" to enhance the thematic relatedness and relevancy of your page for your target keyword "Old Spice."

Create Communities

Creating a community such as a blog or forum on your website is one of the most effective ways to keep your content fresh, while helping to establish your site as an authority for your given area of business. Search engines such as Google favor websites with fresh content over similarly authoritative websites that do not update content as often. Starting a community is easy and inexpensive.

A clear benefit of creating a community on your website is the fact that communities promote interaction and content creation among your users. User-generated content from blogs and forums is a great way to build a reputation as an authority and provides you with opportunities to gain additional, unanticipated search-engine rankings.

A *blog* is an online journal or diary that is frequently updated by an author and typically allows readers to interact by providing comments after each blog post is published. Regardless of what kind of website you own, having a blog is a good idea. First, a blog provides clear SEO benefits through controlled content creation and user-generated content via user comments. Second, a blog helps establish you as an expert. As an expert, other websites will link to your content, which helps improve your search-engine ranking. Third, blogs are sticky. In other words, your users will want to join your RSS feed and come back to your website frequently to check for new content and learn about your products and services.

Blogs are a great tool for communicating special offers and deals to loyal readers, and they allow you to go into detail about specific products that might require detailed explanation. For example, if you are about to launch a new product that includes a new, revolutionary way of doing something, a blog allows you to make the case for the benefits and usefulness of the product versus older-generation products.

Unlike a blog, a *community forum* is a discussion board where members and forum moderators interact by posting questions and answers and discussing common problems. A forum encourages your visitors to return again and again by allowing interaction and information sharing.

Because forums are ultimately message boards where people ask and answer questions, a forum can be a great place to refer a customer who has a question that may be shared by other members of the community. If a visitor has a question about the durability of a particular product or is unsure about one product over another, a forum provides a venue to get feedback and to generate interest in your products.

Having a forum on your website allows you to understand more about your visitors by reading the conversations and discussions among them. You can use this type of information to minimize the demand placed on your customer service by addressing a customer concern before it spreads. Additionally, you can use a forum to ask your customers about what products they want that you do not currently have.

Regardless of whether it is good or bad, consumer feedback can be invaluable and can help you market your products or services more effectively. Keep in mind that a forum on your website does not solely have to be about promoting your products and services. Equally valuable is the information that you can get from your customers to improve your overall website initiatives.

Build Links

If creating large amounts of original, well-written content is considered king for SEO purposes, building quality links back to your website might be considered the Holy Grail. Although times are changing and Google has become very particular about link quality, links remain the most important algorithmic factor in search ranking. It remains true that you must have more than just quality content because Google and other major search-engine algorithms evaluate the number and quality of websites that link to your web pages as a primary and fundamental component of ranking your website over another.

In general, search engines conclude that websites with more backlinks must be more popular and authoritative than websites with fewer backlinks. Keep in mind that search-engine algorithms not only evaluate the number and quality of backlinks going to your website but also what those links say in the form of anchor text. *Anchor text* is the text contained in front of a hyperlink from one page to another.

Building links is sort of like trying to answer the age-old question of what comes first, the chicken or the egg. Should you just build great content and wait for other websites to link to you, or should you proactively recruit others to link to your site?

If you are serious about SEO, you should proactively and aggressively build links. It is true that if you build original, compelling content, others are likely to link to your website, and over time Google might conclude that you are an authority. However, gaining and maintaining search-engine ranking is very competitive, and if you want to rank well in the search results, you need to have not only great content but also quality, relevant backlinks.

All links are not created equal. Although quantity is important, focus on trying to build quality and relevant links. Relevant links come from websites related to your line of business and content. For example, if you have a gourmet food website, getting a link from *Gourmet Retailer* magazine is better than getting a link from an equally popular celebrity gossip website. Quality links tend to come from popular websites that are generally trusted sources. Two of the main measures of popularity are Google's PageRank and the Alexa ranking system. PageRank gives you a rough idea of how authoritative Google thinks the website is, and Alexa provides a measure to compare the traffic volume of potential linking partners. In general, you should look for quality and relevant linking partners that have PageRank scores and Alexa rankings as good as or better than your own. A popular tool for helping you evaluate the quality of links is SEOmoz's Open Site Explorer, which includes both free and paid versions.

Building links can be extremely time-consuming and may even cost money if you decide to use a link broker or a pay-per-post network. One of the more time-consuming forms of link building includes requesting one-way or reciprocal links directly from other websites. The process usually involves reaching out to potential link partners via e-mail and asking politely for a link or suggesting a barter situation where you link to them if they link to you.

Another way of building links is through blog and forum participation. However, in many cases, search engines such as Google either devalue or do not count blog and forum comments as links toward your PageRank and other metrics they may use to calculate your relative authority to other websites. Despite this, other search engines use links from blogs and forums for ranking purposes.

An increasingly effective way to build links is through content marketing on blogs, social media websites, and other content aggregators, such as press release distributors. For example, you can guest blog or hire guest bloggers to write interesting content about your business with links back to your website. Another content marketing strategy is to design infographics. Content marketing using infographics is a method of brand and link building that uses graphically represented information in the form of an infographic as a linkable asset that you can promote to attract mentions and build links to your website. Infographics also serve as a useful tool to convey complex information or to provide summary visual data on specific topics in your particular field of expertise or profession. While the goal of an infographic is to summarize information and not to directly promote your business there are various ways that you can leverage infographics to promote your brand and generate backlinks. Finally, numerous content aggregation websites exist to help you distribute your content, including popular press release distributors such as PRWeb and PR Newswire. When drafting content for content marketing purposes, SEO best practices apply. However, your primary goal outside of best practices should be to create content that people find interesting, appealing, funny, engaging, and worthy of being shared with others.

An increasingly high-risk strategy when building links is to actually buy them through link brokers and pay-per-post networks. However, consider carefully before you use link brokers and pay-per-post networks because search engines such as Google have strict policies against the use of paid links as a way of increasing PageRank. If Google concludes that one of your links is not natural, the link is likely to be devalued for PageRank purposes. Keep in mind that despite Google's policies against buying links to boost PageRank, purchasing links from high-quality, relevant websites has other benefits, including branding and traffic generation.

Google Analytics

Google Analytics is a free analytics solution that was designed to give you a complete view of every aspect of activity on your website. Understanding how to properly analyze and implement the numerous types of data Google Analytics provides gives you a considerable edge over your competition in the quest for top organic search rankings. Moreover, Google Analytics gives you a high-level view of your website traffic and user interaction, which allows you to analyze the various traffic sources coming to your website. You can take this information to improve your overall traffic-generation strategies, including pay-per-click, SEO, affiliate marketing, and any other traffic sources.

Google Analytics is free and easy to install. The most important detail in the installation process is making sure that your tracking code is correctly placed on every single page of your website. This ensures that all your Google Analytics reports are as accurate and reliable as possible. After you have Google Analytics in place, you can analyze your traffic data in various ways. Looking through your traffic sources in Google Analytics is a simple way of finding out which keywords are sending you traffic.

Another way to use Google Analytics is to set and track conversion goals. For example, if your website tracks orders through a shopping cart or leads in the form of a newsletter subscription, e-mail submit, or catalog request, goal tracking allows you to evaluate the number of transactions that occurred and the keyword that triggered the conversion. Goal tracking is especially useful when targeting keywords in your SEO efforts. Knowing ahead of time what keywords are already converting for your site and targeting those keywords until you reach the top organic positions is a very effective SEO strategy.

Google Analytics allows you to not only track traffic that is coming to your website but also any traffic that may leave in the form of an external click. For example, if you are setting up any traffic trades or promoting any affiliate offers on your website, you will want to keep track of how many clicks you are sending to external sites.

A key benefit of Google Analytics is that you can send yourself or colleagues e-mail reports. You can also provide others with access to your Analytics account with full or restricted access. Moreover, reports can be sent and downloaded in multiple popular formats, including PDF and CSV, which make it very easy to combine or compare reports across different online and offline sources.

Social Media Optimization

Social media optimization, or *SMO,* is a form of online marketing that focuses on participating on various social media websites to generate traffic, buzz, and links back to your website. Social media websites include social discovery websites such as StumbleUpon and Pinterest; industry forums and online communities such as SEOmoz and WebmasterWorld; video-sharing websites such as YouTube; and social network websites such as Facebook, Twitter, Google+, and LinkedIn. Various recognized SEO and SMO pundits have referred to SMO as "the new SEO" because SMO is often used as an effective and powerful method to quickly build large numbers of links back to your website, which can lead to improved organic search-engine rankings. In addition, innovative start-up technology providers such as Klout provide relative measures of social media influence. Search engines like Google and Bing have

begun to use similar social media indicators to influence search rankings.

Leading social networks contain hundreds of millions of active members. People of all ages from around the world use social networks to stay in touch with old and new friends and interact by sharing pictures, videos, and more. In fact, an increasing number of businesses are currently using Facebook, Twitter, and most recently Pinterest as a vehicle to manage the company's reputation, build brand recognition, promote products, and generate buzz.

Facebook is a popular social networking site that allows you to build lists of friends and interact with people all over the world through profile pages, pictures, videos, message boards, and various technology applications. Facebook is one of the top ten most trafficked websites in the United States, boasting more than 1 billion active members and growing quickly. You can use Facebook to interact with current and prospective business associates while generating considerable traffic to your website and buzz about your business. Facebook is a service used by businesses of all sizes and people of all ages to network and communicate in real time.

Facebook allows you to create dedicated pages, commonly referred to as Business Pages, to promote your business. With Facebook's large and active member base, it is essential that you create a dedicated Business Page for your business. A dedicated Facebook Business Page allows you to provide fans with your company overview, website(s), contact info, press releases, videos, blog RSS, Twitter updates, company news, and status. You can also interact with your fans by responding to comments they post to your Business Page, as well as through other social networking tools made available through Facebook. "Like" my Facebook Page at www.facebook.com/kbjcapital.

StumbleUpon is a peer- and social-networking technology that includes a toolbar that you install in your web browser. The StumbleUpon toolbar allows you to discover and rate web pages, videos, photos, and news articles. Getting your web pages, videos, photos, and news articles submitted to StumbleUpon is an effective way to generate buzz, traffic, and build backlinks to your website. Follow me on StumbleUpon at www.stumbleupon.com/stumbler/krisjonescom.

Twitter is a free social networking service that allows you to microblog by sending short updates, or *tweets,* of

140 characters or less to others via a text message from your mobile phone, by typing a message from the Twitter site, or using instant messaging from Jabber or Google Talk. Twitter is a great way to build a list of followers. For business purposes, you can quickly send messages to your Twitter friends when a popular item comes back into stock or as a means to share a special offer or deal. Follow me on Twitter at @krisjonescom.

Twitter Search is Twitter's powerful and increasingly popular real-time search engine. Unlike major search engines like Google and Bing that update their search indexes every few days or weeks, Twitter Search updates its entire database of news and tweets as they occur. The most powerful way to use Twitter Search and build the amount of people who follow you on Twitter is to type keywords into Twitter Search that relate to your specific product or service. Once Twitter delivers search results, you should follow those users who mention the target keyword.

LinkedIn is a popular business-oriented social networking site that allows you to network with like-minded business professionals and build a list of contacts. By building a database of contacts with people you know and trust in business, you have access to a large network of friends with whom you can conduct business, offer jobs, and promote your business. LinkedIn is an effective network for sharing professional information and news about your business-related activities. Connect with me on LinkedIn at www.linkedin.com/in/internetceo.

Video-sharing websites like YouTube allow users to upload, view, and share video clips. Videos are a great way to promote your business or to generate buzz and interest in your website. The most effective videos either tend to make people laugh or are extremely creative and unusual. For example, some of the most viral videos on YouTube are homegrown videos that contain something outrageous or embarrassing. In addition, videos put a face on an otherwise faceless business pitch. Videos build trust in your users and can even result in a "celebrity" or "cult" following if people find your videos interesting.

Pinterest is a social networking and photo-sharing website that allows users to create and manage theme-based image collections, such as events, interests, hobbies, and more. Users can browse other collections of images called *pinboards,* *repin* images to their own collections, or *like* photos. Pinterest is one of the top 50 websites in the world with nearly 50 million users and is especially popular with the female demographic.

Uploading images from your website and creating pinboards allows you to generate traffic to your website and may improve your SEO. Pinterest is of particular benefit to websites that are rich with colorful and interesting images.

WebmasterWorld is the oldest and most authoritative Internet marketing and webmaster forum community in the world. WebmasterWorld features thousands of discussions on a range of topics, including SEO, social media, and affiliate marketing. Specific forum threads exist on Google, Facebook, and Twitter and often include breaking news and analysis from experienced webmasters.

WebmasterWorld is a great resource for learning more about online marketing and networking with web users with similar interests. WebmasterWorld is also a great place to establish yourself as a web expert by offering insights and expertise in your particular discipline. Basic membership is free.

Create Pay-per-Click Campaigns

With SEO, your goal is to rank for free within the organic search results for target keywords related to your website. In contrast, with pay-per-click (PPC) your goal is to pay for placement by competing with other advertisers for top rankings within the sponsored results section of search results. There is no charge when someone clicks your organic listing, but you are charged every time someone clicks your PPC listing. PPC listings are typically designated as sponsored listings and appear above and to the right of the organic results.

Regardless of your SEO success, you should also use PPC as a primary method to promote your website. In fact, research suggests that having both a high-sponsored and high-organic ranking greatly increases the credibility of your website and, therefore, increases the traffic to your website. If you think of the search results page as a piece of real estate, a powerful strategy is to get your website onto that piece of property as many times as you can. This book was written to help you do just that.

The largest and most popular PPC advertising platform is Google AdWords, but a competitive and growing platform is Microsoft's Bing Ads. Before you open a PPC account on Google and start spending money, familiarize yourself with the structure of various components of an AdWords account. You should also study the various free educational resources Google provides and visit community forums such as WebmasterWorld.

Google and Bing allow you to target your ads in various ways. The most common form of targeting is *geo-targeting,* which allows you to display your PPC ads in specific geographic regions. Geo-targeting is especially effective for regional businesses and can be used as a strategy to test various regional markets.

Another popular form of targeting is called *remarketing,* which involves showing your PPC ads only to people who have visited specific pages on your website as they visit other sites on the Google Display Network. Because the remarketing tag can be installed on every page of your website, it allows you to develop specific audiences. Examples of these audiences include home page visitors, visitors of specific product categories, and visitors to your shopping cart.

Writing effective ad copy, using available keyword-matching options, and setting effective bid strategies are important components of a successful PPC advertising campaign. Each of the major search engines allows you to draft multiple advertisements. The search engines test each of your advertisements and serve the ads with the highest CTRs most often. Writing effective ad copy means using compelling language that separates your ads from the competition, entices people to click them, and contains a high conversion rate.

Keyword matching options are important because they tell the search engine how broadly or specifically you want to advertise based on the keywords you bid on. For example, using a broad-match option on the keyword "cheese" might trigger your advertisement when a user types the popular keyword "Chuck E. Cheese" into a search engine. On the other hand, using an exact-match option on the keyword "cheese" triggers your advertisement only when the exact word "cheese" is typed into a search engine.

Understanding basic and advanced PPC account reporting is critical to maximizing your advertising spend and analyzing your PPC advertising success. A major benefit of PPC advertising is robust, real-time, keyword-level PPC reporting. If you choose, you have the option of digging as deep as you want into the efficacy of your PPC initiatives.

In addition, you can select to use conversion tracking, which allows you to set conversion goals and monitor your *return on investment,* or *ROI,* at the keyword level.

Once you have spent a reasonable amount of time getting to know the inner workings of a PPC account, you are ready to deposit money and begin generating targeted website traffic. Keep in mind that you will be charged for all clicks in real time. Make sure you set strict budget limits at first and go slow. Your methodology and diligence will determine your ultimate success, not how many keywords and campaigns you have active at any given time.

Quality Score Optimization

Quality score optimization, or *QSO,* is a set of strategies for improving your quality score. Quality score is a principal ranking factor that search engines use to determine your relative ranking and pricing for a particular keyword listing. In today's PPC advertising environment, the highest bidder does not always win. Instead, Google and other leading search engines rank websites based on numerous quality factors and use your designated maximum cost-per-click (CPC) as only one of many factors that determine whether you achieve a given keyword placement. The goal of QSO is to understand the factors that Google and others use to calculate quality score so that you can maintain PPC advertisements at the highest possible position and the lowest CPC.

The primary factors that search engines consider for calculating quality score are the click-through rate, ad group and campaign structure, ad copy, landing page quality, and keyword bid. Note that many of the quality score factors influence one another. For example, the quality of your ad copy almost certainly affects your click-through rates, and your ad group and campaign structure is likely to influence your perceived landing page quality.

Click-through rate refers to the percentage of times your ad was clicked compared to how many times it was shown. The higher your click-through rate is for any given keyword-ad combination, the higher quality the search engines are likely to rate your advertisement, and the lower the price you will have to pay for placement. One way of quickly improving your click-through rates is to remove keywords with low click-through rates from your ad groups. Another way to improve click-through rates is to write more-appealing ad copy.

The structure of your ad groups and campaign can influence the quality score. For example, ad groups that have large numbers of unrelated keywords are likely to have low quality scores because the search engines conclude that the advertisements do not accurately reflect each keyword in the ad group. Similarly, the search engines might perceive campaigns that contain numerous unrelated ad groups as less relevant. Ad groups that contain keywords that are tightly related and include well-written ad copy tend to have higher quality scores. Moreover, making sure that your campaigns are closely related is likely to improve your quality score.

Writing multiple advertisements and making sure that your ad copy is well written and appealing is one of the most effective ways to improve your quality score. As mentioned earlier, your ad copy must directly relate to the keywords in your ad group. One way of doing this is to use advanced methods that allow you to dynamically insert your target keyword into the advertisement.

Google and the other search engines allow you to test multiple advertisements. Therefore, you should submit numerous advertisements, making sure that you include enticing ad copy that contains the keywords you want to rank for. The search engines show each of the advertisements until one or more of the ads emerge with the highest click-through rate.

Landing page quality refers to the perceived value and relevancy of the page that you send your PPC traffic to. Landing page quality is so important that a low landing page score can be disastrous to your overall PPC advertising initiatives. In fact, if you have a poor landing page score, you may be required to pay as much as $10 per click for placement on a keyword, whereas another advertiser deemed to have a high landing page score pays only 35 cents for the same keyword placement. Some of the factors that affect your landing page score are the relatedness of your ad copy and landing page and whether the keyword you are bidding on is included on the landing page. Google also appears to take into consideration the PageRank of your website, as well as how many people link to the landing page in question.

Your *keyword bid* is the maximum that you are willing to pay for a click on a particular keyword or ad group of keywords. Your quality score directly and significantly affects the amount you pay for a given click. In general,

the more you are willing to pay, the more likely it is that your ad will appear. However, as an overall ranking factor, your keyword bid is much less of a primary indicator of position that it was in the past. The more effective you are in increasing your quality score based on the factors mentioned earlier, the less you have to pay per click and the higher your ranking is likely to be.

This approach to QSO is not exhaustive. Quality score is a very dynamic and complex algorithm and is likely to be tweaked and changed as Google and the other search engines constantly strive to improve search quality and make more money.

Optimize for Other Engines

Internet search allows you to retrieve information at lightning speed. Although search engines such as Google, Yahoo, and Bing are the most common forms of search sites, many websites specialize in organizing very specific types of websites rather than trying to index the entire Internet. Getting your site exposure on these more-targeted search engines can send extra traffic or allow you to target a niche that may be too competitive to rank for in the major search engines.

Technorati is a popular search engine for searching blogs. If you can get your blog to rank well on Technorati, you can gain considerable exposure and traffic. Moreover, other bloggers use Technorati to look for stories to write about. In this way, getting your blog ranked on Technorati can be used as an effective link-building strategy.

Google Images is a popular service for searching images. Getting Google Images to index your images can potentially lead to significant traffic, especially because Google shows their image results at the top of their regular organic listings.

If you sell products, chances are you can benefit from having your products listed in shopping search engines, such as Shopping.com, Shopzilla, and BizRate.com. Shopping search engines accept product feeds from online retailers and allow users to search and sort these lists by various criteria. Keep in mind that most shopping search engines require you to pay them on a cost-per-click or cost-per-action basis.

Whether potential customers find your products on auction services such as eBay and classified services such as

Craigslist, ReferLocal Classifieds, or eBay Classifieds greatly depends on whether your listings are optimized for the eBay, ReferLocal, and Craigslist search engines. Your title and description for both services should include keywords that someone looking for your product is most likely to use. Moreover, you should include text to describe each of the images you use to promote your products.

Optimize for Local Search

In October 2010 Google began displaying blended search results for local businesses. Blended local search results include a snippet of text about the business along with links to your business website and your Google+ Local business page. Google+ is Google's social network that is growing in popularity. Google displays the number of reviews and average ranking you receive from your Google+ Local page, which makes it imperative for your business to have a Google+ Local page. Also, keep in mind for local search purposes that you need to optimize not only your website but also your Google+ Local page.

Google+ Local makes it easy for people to review and share your business with friends and around the web. Google+ Local provides a hosted, interactive profile page of your business and allows you to interact with existing customers and prospects alike. With Google+ Local you can easily upload pictures and videos of your business and interact with customers and fans through a conversation wall similar to Facebook's Timeline. Google+ provides business owners with a number of features to improve your SEO. Google has publicly disclosed that it may use Google+ data to influence its search results. The key to maximizing the SEO benefits of Google+ is to actively engage with the platform. In this way you will grow your following while also providing Google with many positive signals about you and your business.

One of the most important factors that Google uses to determine relevance and authority for ranking websites in search is the number and velocity of consumer reviews you receive about your website. While there are a number of places you can get reviews, including Yelp, Merchant Circle, and Foursquare, the most important place to receive reviews for ranking better on Google is on your Google+ Local Page.

Social media continues to play an increasingly important role across all forms of digital marketing, including local search. Social media signals such as the amount of followers you or your business has on sites like Twitter, Google+, and Facebook appears to be an important ranking factor considered by search engines like Google. Keep in mind that it is not enough to just grow your following; you must also focus on acquiring followers who have social influence. Level of social media engagement is another signal considered by search engines. The more engaged your business is on sites like Facebook and Google+, the more likely that engagement will have a positive influence on your search rankings.

It is not enough to simply have an optimized Google+ Local Page. You also need to optimize your website and take into consideration multiple geographic signals that search engines look for to rank websites in blended local search. For example, when you optimize for local search, make sure to place your business contact information in the footer or header of each page. Adding your geographic information ensures that search engines identify your content with a specific geography. In addition, if you sell a product or service that is targeted or limited to a specific geographic location, you should add geographic information such as the city, state, and zip code to the title and meta description tags on each relevant page of your site.

Search engines also look at how many and the quality of links that point to your website. One way to increase the number of links you have for your website is to make sure you are listed in local online business directories, such as Local.com and ReferLocal.com. However, it is equally important that the information you provide across all your citations is accurate and consistent. Search engines penalize you for inaccurate or inconsistent information.

Optimization for local search is most appropriate for local business owners or for businesses that target specific geographic areas. Regardless, local search tactics may be used on a case-by-case basis for any website looking to rank well in specific geographies for specific keywords and topics.

Use SEO Tools and Plug-ins

As outlined in this book, SEO is often a tedious job and requires you to perform numerous tasks over and over. Fortunately, SEO tools and plug-ins exist to help you work more efficiently.

SEO tools and plug-ins have become increasingly popular because of the sheer amount of time they save you during the SEO process. For example, instead of browsing to several different websites to research your information, you can view all the data right from one spot in your web browser. By using SEO browser plug-ins, you can quickly access a website's PageRank, its age, indexing and backlink information, and even mentions of it in the social media space. Plug-ins can generate a list of topically related websites that can serve as your gateway to the online community for any given topic.

The SEO plug-ins commonly used for WordPress have been created out of necessity. The standard installation of WordPress is by far the most popular blogging software; however, it does not support commonly known best practices for on-page SEO. For this reason, SEO-savvy developers have taken the time to produce powerful plug-ins that make doing SEO for your blog far more effective and efficient. From custom title tags to automatic sitemap generation, SEO plug-ins for WordPress are essential if you manage your website content using WordPress.

A powerful tool for improving on-page optimization is the Internet Marketing Ninjas Side-by-Side SEO Comparison Tool, which provides website meta tag information. It also shows keyword density information for your website and your competitors' websites for head phrases and tail phrases. The Side-by-Side SEO Comparison Tool also provides information on the ratio of linked text to nonlinked text, as well as internal linking information for the page selected for you and each of your competitors' web pages.

CHOOSE A TOPIC

If you are starting from scratch and do not have a previously developed website to optimize, choosing a topic for your website is the first step in starting a successful search-engine-optimization plan.

To get started, narrow your topic and stay focused. If you are developing a website about mortgages, consider focusing on a specific topic within the overall topic of "mortgages," such as "Pennsylvania mortgages" or the even more specific "Wilkes-Barre mortgages." Although less traffic exists for sites targeting these more specific terms such as Wilkes-Barre mortgages, there is also less competition and a higher likelihood of achieving top search-engine ranking.

Choose a Topic

1 Navigate to www.google.com.

2 Search for a popular topic, such as "mortgages."

A Notice approximately 135,000,000 results. Note that getting your website ranked high for highly competitive terms, such as mortgages, is much more difficult than getting it ranked for less competitive topics.

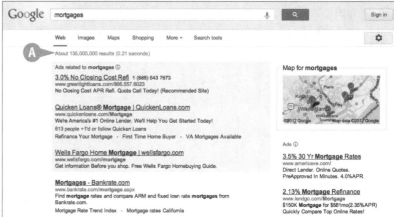

3 Search for "pennsylvania mortgages."

B Notice approximately 28,200,000 results. It is easier to get ranked the more specific the topic.

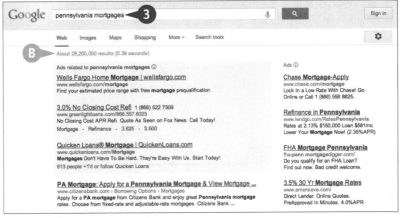

4 Search for "wilkes barre mortgages."

C Notice approximately 932,000 results. Fewer results imply less competition within a particular niche. You stand a much greater chance of getting ranked high for Wilkes-Barre mortgages than broader mortgage topics since fewer websites compete.

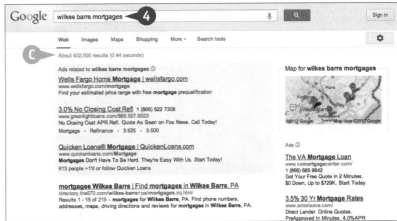

EXTRA

Most general terms are very competitive and extremely difficult to rank for. Keywords and phrases span from very general to very specific. An example of this progression would be pets, dogs, large dogs, Great Danes, brown Great Dane puppies.

The term "pets" is very general, and although the traffic for such a term is enormous, that traffic may not translate into a large number of sales. If you are creating a website or marketing a website about breeding Great Danes, the website is more likely to achieve top search-engine ranking if specific terms are targeted.

FIND YOUR TARGET AUDIENCE

To get the most from your search-engine-optimization efforts, you should design and optimize your website for your target audience. Your target audience is the group of people whom you are trying to reach through your online marketing efforts. Target audiences are often defined by demographics such as age groups, nationalities, or specific interests.

Conduct research to uncover the key terms and phrases that your target audience is searching for. Are people searching for "seo" or "search engine optimization"? You can use a tool like Google Trends to discover trends in the popularity of different search queries.

Find Your Target Audience

1 Navigate to www.google.com/trends.

2 Type **seo, search engine optimization**.

A Notice the traffic trend from 2005 through 2012. The term "seo" is increasing in popularity.

B Results are separated by regional interest and related terms.

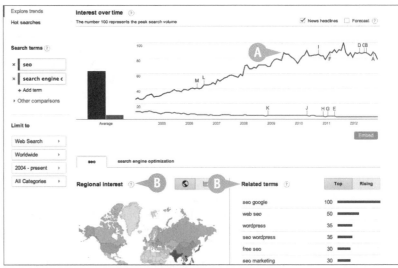

3 Change Worldwide to United States.

C Results are limited to traffic from the United States.

4 Click a specific state to see Google Trends results. For example, Pennsylvania.

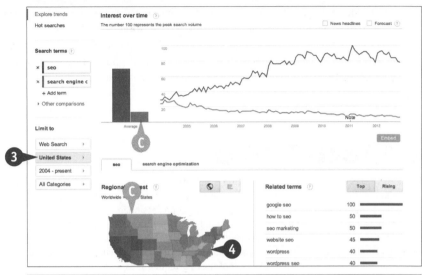

D Note the ability to see related terms and rising terms. This information may help you better understand your target audience.

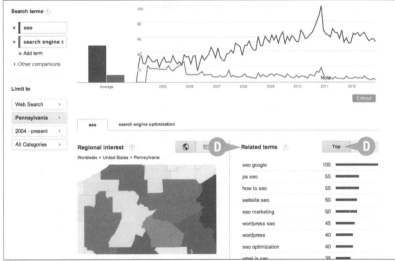

EXTRA

Optimizing for your target audience involves allocating time and resources to customize your website design. Make a point to study your successful competition before you move forward with website design and content development. Try to stay original, but do not feel the need to reinvent the wheel. Take advantage of proven designs and content strategies from the competition you most admire, since much of the costly research has already been done for you. Your mission is to improve upon products or services already available while keeping your target audience in mind.

Set a Budget

If you decide to do your own search-engine optimization, more than just your time is required. Set aside a budget for your search-engine optimization as if it is any other form of marketing. Certain tasks involved in a comprehensive search-engine-optimization plan require a financial investment. You may not need to hire a company to do your search-engine optimization, but you should give yourself the best opportunity to improve your rankings, increase your traffic, and beat your competitors. To give yourself that opportunity, a budget is required.

Web Design and Development Costs

Numerous costs are involved in just getting a website running. Free web hosting should be avoided, a domain name is required, and unless you are adept at website design, having a professional website developed can cost a significant amount of money. These are necessary costs that cannot be avoided. Generally, web hosting can cost anywhere from $10 per month to hundreds of dollars per month, depending on the type of hosting required. Selecting a web host and a domain name are discussed in more detail in Chapter 4.

You can purchase a domain name for roughly $10 depending on where you look, but professional website design can cost

hundreds, thousands, or more depending on the complexity of design required. High cost does not necessarily translate into great results, and a redesign of a website can positively or negatively affect your search-engine rankings. Website design can not only affect search-engine rankings, but it also can directly affect your site's conversion rates. The *conversion rate* of your site is the percentage of visitors who are converted into a sale. A difference in only a fraction of a percentage point can have an enormous impact on whether a search-engine-optimization campaign is profitable or a drain on financial resources.

Keyword Research Costs

Other costs may arise. Quality keyword research and analysis tools can be a necessity depending on the size of the project, and these tools normally cost between $50 and $100 per month. These tools are reviewed in detail in the next chapter. A quality keyword research and analysis tool is often one of the first investments that any search-engine-optimization specialist makes.

Content Development Costs

Your content creation is also a consideration. You may decide to outsource content creation to skilled copywriters who write content at an hourly rate. These rates vary depending on the skill and experience of the writer. You should expect to pay between $15 and $75 per hour for content writing. As Chapter 3 discusses, a website's content is a highly influential factor in search-engine rankings. To compete with other websites in competitive markets, your site has to contain a substantial amount of unique, relevant content. If you want your visitors to trust your website as an authority source in your field, make sure your content is well written and factually correct.

Link-Building Costs

Also, be sure to have a budget for link building. If you choose to pay for building links, the cost can range from a few dollars per link to upwards of a few hundred dollars per link, depending on the quality of that link. As Chapter 3 discusses, both the number and the quality of inbound links to your website are possibly the

most influential factors on your search-engine rankings. At the same time, buying links is highly risky and alternative link-building strategies should be carefully considered. See Chapter 8 for more information on building links.

Setting realistic goals for your search-engine-optimization project ensures that you stay on task and keep focused despite the many mountains and valleys you are sure to encounter. Search-engine optimization is not an exact science, and even if you follow best practices, there are no guarantees. Many search-engine-optimization companies guarantee front-page rankings or even place time frames on when success is likely to be realized, but ultimately, the search engines decide your fate. Set realistic goals for the project, and you are less likely to be disappointed and distracted throughout the process.

Progress Steadily

Search-engine optimization is much like exercise and diet. You may not notice immediate results from doing a single workout or cutting out a single fatty meal, but over the course of weeks, months, and years, the effects accumulate. Similarly, with search-engine optimization, you can rest assured knowing that your efforts build over time to produce results. Also, much like with exercise and diet, working slowly and steadily over time is much more likely to produce results than trying to cram all the work into a few weeks or months. Spread out your search-engine-optimization work over time or risk a penalty from the search engines for trying to manipulate their ranking algorithms.

Spammers have historically manipulated search engines by programming content generators capable of building websites with thousands of pages of text in minutes or less. At one time, these websites almost immediately gained high rankings in the

search engines due to their large quantity of "unique" content. Upon closer inspection, though, this content was very evidently machine-generated garbage.

The same holds true in your efforts to build inbound links back to your website. Spammers have historically manipulated the search engines by programming link generators capable of building thousands of links back to their websites in a very short period. Most of the time, these programs target online guest books and message boards, and automatically generate entries on the guest books or posts on the message boards that include a link back to a selected website. In a time when quantity of links was considered much more important and easier to measure than quality of links, this practice, especially in combination with an automatic website generator, fed the search engines with the ingredients considered important for a high-ranking website.

Focus on Natural Growth

Now search engines want to see a slow, steady, natural growth of your website. They realize that a single person or even a group of people are unlikely to have the ability to generate hundreds of pages of content as soon as a website goes live. This type of growth is the fingerprint that a machine-generated website leaves behind. The engineers behind the search-engine ranking algorithms work hard to ensure that machine-generated content and links are penalized appropriately. Penalties may include decreased search rankings or temporary or permanent removal from search-engine rankings.

As you learn different search-engine-optimization techniques in this book, think about how they fit into your overall goals. Are you trying to build more traffic to your website overall? Are you trying to increase sales of a certain product? Are you trying to establish your brand? Your specific goals determine how you should approach the project. Plan out which strategies you are going to implement, how you are going to implement them, and when you plan to have the projects completed.

Put a Team Together

Not everyone is an expert at every aspect of search-engine optimization. To take full advantage of what search-engine optimization has to offer your website, many skills are required, including HTML writing, knowledge of CSS, data analysis, graphical design, server administration, copywriting, link building, and blogging. Do not hesitate to put together a team of people skilled in these different areas to assist in the project. You do not need to hire a team of people to work at your side; you can outsource some of the work to others through popular outsourcing websites such as Elance.

Put a Team Together

1 Navigate to www.elance.com.

2 Enter a description of the service that you want.

3 Click Go.

Note: *You are sure to find that you excel at some search-engine-optimization tasks and lack the knowledge or motivation to excel in others. In this case, consider hiring a freelancer or leverage someone that has the particular skill set necessary to execute the task.*

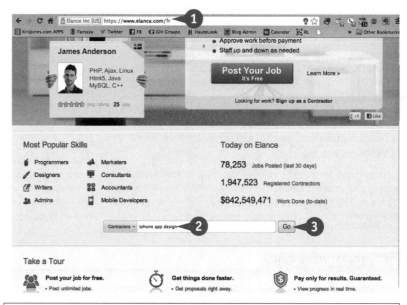

A You see a list of service providers, their geographic place of business, rates, total jobs completed, and overall rating on the Elance platform.

B You can click a provider from the list to see their portfolio, feedback, and contact information.

4 Click Post Your Job and sign in with your Elance account.

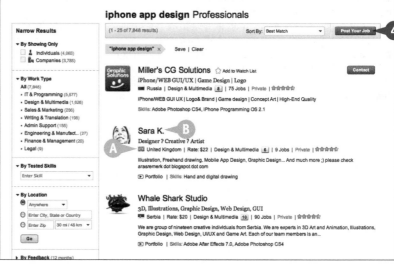

⑤ Enter pertinent details about your project.

⑥ Click Continue to post your project.

Elance providers can now view your project and choose to bid.

Note: *As you read through the rest of this book, you are going to encounter many techniques that you feel uncomfortable performing due to lack of knowledge or simply lack of time. Just about everything can be outsourced, so do not hesitate to explore that option if necessary.*

EXTRA

Another popular place to outsource SEO work is oDesk (www.odesk.com), which has more than 2.5 million registered contractors available for hire. oDesk has an advanced and very friendly user interface. It has a unique online platform that enables you to supervise your workers and track their time worked and tasks performed. You can view and verify their time logs to create detailed bills that can be paid by credit card. One of the benefits of oDesk is that you can pay contractors by the hour, which eliminates the challenge of coming up with a fixed fee based on a project description.

KEEP UP WITH INDUSTRY NEWS

The web is full of informative blogs and forums where industry experts freely share their knowledge and experiences in search-engine marketing. Keep up with the pulse of the Internet marketing industry by reading these blogs and forums daily. Search-engine optimization is not an exact science. Ranking algorithms constantly change, and though the optimization techniques generally remain the same, new tips and tricks become available daily.

Respected industry blogs such as Search Engine Land (www.searchengineland.com), SEOmoz (www.seomoz.org), Internet Marketing Ninjas (www.internetmarketingninjas.com/blog), BlueGlass (www.blueglass.com/blog), SEO Book (www.seobook.com/blog), and others are updated frequently, sometimes numerous times per day.

Keep Up with Industry News

1 Navigate to www.internet marketingninjas.com/blog.

Note: *This book provides you with a framework upon which true industry expertise can be built. Much like other industries, continuing education is a must if you plan to excel at search-engine optimization. Take advantage of every free resource that is available. Unlike many other industries, search-engine marketing experts are generally not afraid to share some of their best secrets.*

2 Click Like us on Facebook.

Note: *If you do not already have a Facebook account, click Sign Up on the Facebook site and follow the instructions.*

3 Click the Facebook Like button.

Note: *Once you like the page, you will begin to receive updates in your News Feed every time Internet Marketing Ninjas updates its Facebook page.*

④ Navigate back to www.internet marketingninjas.com/blog.

⑤ Click Signup for our News.

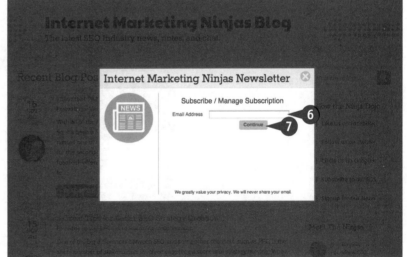

⑥ Enter your e-mail address.

⑦ Click Continue.

Note: *You are now signed up to the Internet Marketing Ninjas news e-mail newsletter and will receive regular updates on industry news.*

EXTRA

Some very influential SEO professionals maintain blogs where they share a tremendous amount of information about their trade. The following blogs are highly recommended:

- www.mediadonis.net — Owned by Marcus Tandler (aka Mediadonis), an internationally known SEO professional with nearly 15 years of experience, Mediadonis.net covers a range of current and advanced issues related to SEO and Internet marketing. Marcus also runs the popular SEO conference SEOktoberfest (www.seoktoberfest. net), which is held each year in conjunction with Oktoberfest.

- www.davidnaylor.co.uk — David Naylor, owner of Bronco (www.bronco.co.uk), a UK-based web development firm, is one of the most influential SEO experts in the world with more than a decade of SEO experience.

ATTEND AN INDUSTRY CONFERENCE

One of the most effective strategies for learning more about search-engine marketing and networking within the search marketing space is to attend an industry conference. Leading search marketing conferences, including Search Engine Strategies (SES) (www.search enginestrategies.com) and Search Marketing Expo (SMX) (www.searchmarketingexpo.com), offer dozens of educational sessions led by panels of search marketing experts. Thousands of businesspeople with varying levels of search marketing expertise attend search marketing conferences such as SES and SMX, which are held annually in the United States and around the world. The largest annual search conference is SES New York, which is held each spring in New York City.

Attend an Industry Conference

1 Navigate to www. searchenginestrategies.com.

2 Click one of the upcoming industry events. For example, New York.

Note: *Business leaders of all levels of management attend search conferences. It is common for C-level executives, as well as marketing managers, IT professionals, and entrepreneurs of all ages to attend search conferences.*

3 Click Registration & Pricing Info.

A Attending a conference requires that you budget for the cost of travel, lodging, meals, and registration. Cost to attend search conferences varies based on access level. For full access to all educational sessions on all days of a given conference, individual registration can cost $2,700 or more. Registration with limited access to content is typically less than $1,100. Expo hall only passes are sold for a nominal fee or are free.

4 Review rates and registration details.

5 Click Register.

6 Enter the requested information.

7 Click the drop-down list and select Yes to indicate that you have a priority code.

8 Enter priority code **WILEYSEO** for 5% off the cost of your ticket.

9 Click Update Prices.

B Answer the remaining questions and click Continue at the bottom of the form.

Note: *When attending a search marketing conference, select educational content based on your specific skill level and interests. Both SES and SMX offer content on topics such as SEO link building, optimizing paid search campaigns, and social media optimization strategies, among others. Each session is designated beginner, intermediate, or advanced.*

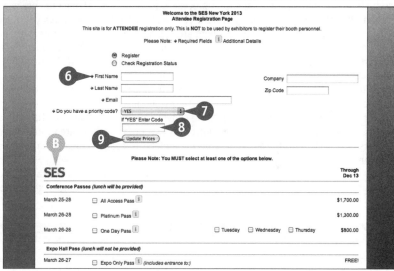

EXTRA

Numerous leading Internet conferences exist beyond SES and SMX, such as Affiliate Summit, ad:tech, and Internet Retailer, and feature search marketing content as part of broader Internet marketing educational sessions. Moreover, as search marketing continues to expand as a primary marketing channel niche, conferences in industries as diverse as food service, book publishing, and construction are covering search marketing content. For a comprehensive list of Internet marketing conferences, see www.conferencecalendar.com.

In addition to serving as an educational resource, search marketing industry conferences present excellent professional networking opportunities. All the major conferences hold networking sessions that are meant to provide attendees with social opportunities to network professionally, exchange business cards, and have fun.

After you select a website topic, keyword generation is the first and arguably most important step of the search-engine-optimization (SEO) process. The bulk of your website, including directory structure and filenames to title tags and page copy, is built around keywords and phrases chosen during the keyword-generation phase. Keyword generation is very important to a successful SEO campaign and is something you should never rush or take lightly.

Initially, you want to generate a potential keyword list that is as large as possible, with the keywords organized by search volume. *Search volume* refers to the number of searches performed on a unique keyword over a period of time. You can also use cost-per-click (CPC) as an indicator of the relative value of a keyword. *CPC* is an approximation of the cost advertisers pay for a click on an ad for a specific keyword phrase. A large keyword list ensures that you have a healthy mix of keyword phrases. Selecting only keywords with little search volume or keywords with rankings dominated by established authority sites could spell disaster for your SEO efforts before they even get off the ground. In this chapter, you learn about tools that help make your keyword research and generation process efficient and highly successful. Moreover, you learn numerous tips about competitive research that can save you time and money.

Select Keywords

The first step in the keyword-generation process is to strategically select keywords that you want your website to rank for on the major search engines. There are two kinds of keywords: head terms and tail terms. *Head terms* are short keywords, usually one to two words, that tend to have a high search volume. *Tail terms* are longer keywords, typically three or more words, that tend to have a much lower search volume than head terms but are also more specific. They sometimes suggest that a visitor is further along in the conversion process. An effective SEO strategy sets out to generate large amounts of quality website traffic by targeting a blend of head terms and tail terms.

Analyze Your Competition with Compete.com

Compete.com is a competitive analysis tool that identifies keywords your competitors rank for in search engines, as well as how website users interact with your competitors' websites. Despite only giving you rough estimates, Compete.com data provides incredibly useful intelligence for your SEO campaigns. The tool provides a glimpse into the actual value of a keyword in terms of visitor interaction and site usage. After all, simply getting users to your website is only the first step in a larger process. Having users interact with your website, digest your content, and eventually follow your call to action to buy or do something such as submit a lead form is the ultimate goal. Knowing which keywords can send relevant active users to your website can provide you with a powerful advantage during the keyword-generation process.

Analyze Your Competition with SEMrush

SEMrush is a competitive research tool that allows you to easily determine the top keywords your competitors rank for organically on Google or Bing. SEMrush offers three options for accessing competitor keywords. Users who are not registered can view up to 10 free domain searches per day. Users with a paid subscription can view up to 5,000 domain searches per day and have access to a much larger feature set.

Research Keywords with KeywordSpy

KeywordSpy is a competitive keyword research tool that identifies keyword ideas based on keywords your competitors are bidding for in pay-per-click (PPC), as well as keywords your competitors rank for organically on major search engines like Google or Bing. KeywordSpy's real-time keyword tracking technology allows you to easily assess the effectiveness of your keyword ranking, which in turn can influence your keyword research strategy. The keyword list of your organic rankings should serve as an excellent reference for your ongoing keyword research and generation efforts.

Using the Wordtracker Keyword Tool

Wordtracker, an exploratory keyword research tool, offers a free version of its subscription keyword suite, which is ideal for doing quick keyword research. The Wordtracker Keywords tool provides you with a list of terms related to your base keyword as well as the estimated daily search volume for each individual keyword. The paid version of Wordtracker is a more robust tool suite and allows you to save keyword lists for later use and editing and includes features for planning campaigns.

Using the Google AdWords Keyword Tool

Google offers a free exploratory keyword research tool from the largest search engine in the world, Google.com. The Google AdWords Keyword Tool provides powerful keyword research data, including an individual keyword search volume, as well as a comparative evaluation of how much competition exists for a given keyword within Google's PPC product AdWords. Although the Google AdWords Keyword Tool does not give exact numbers in terms of search volume, it does provide useful at-a-glance information on how competitive a given term will be in AdWords PPC advertising.

Using the Google Trends Tool

Google Trends is a free tool that allows you to research seasonal and geographic information about keywords. Google Trends provides contextual information about the seasonality and variance in the amount of searches by location, which can provide important strategic information for planning SEO campaigns and PPC strategies.

Research Keywords with Keyword Discovery

Keyword Discovery is a subscription-based exploratory keyword research tool that allows you to examine the estimated search volume for thousands of keywords. Keyword Discovery pulls data from more than 180 search engines and has an extensive keyword database with considerable historical information dating back several years. Keyword Discovery also has several other databases beyond search engines, which include searches from eBay, as well as other popular shopping sites and foreign search engines.

Filter Keywords with Keyword Discovery

Keyword Discovery has a filter tool for identifying keyword variations. You will find filter tools very useful when expanding on existing keyword lists. With a filter tool, you can quickly add common prefixes and suffixes to large keyword lists in seconds. You can also use a filter tool to do a mass find-and-replace with common synonyms. Filter tools are ideal for adding "buying" words like *buy, order,* and so on to your keyword list. Filter tools can also instantly double the size of your keyword list by swapping your main keyword with a common synonym.

Research Keywords with Bing Keyword Tool

Bing Keyword Tool is a free keyword research tool that is part of the Bing webmaster tool set. The Bing Keyword Tool is useful for finding additional keyword ideas that may have been missed by other keyword sources. Also, the Bing Keyword Tool is different from the Google AdWords Keyword Tool in that it pulls organic keyword data directly from Bing rather than providing estimates.

Research Keywords with Übersuggest

Übersuggest is a keyword research tool that allows you to find additional keyword ideas to add to your keyword list that are closely related to a given search term. Übersuggest is a valuable tool for finding phrase variations because it gathers data from Google Suggest, a highly authoritative source for identifying similar search terms.

SELECT KEYWORDS

Selecting general and specific keywords that are relevant to the products, services, or content of each page of your website is an essential component of SEO. General or generic keywords are one or two words in length and are commonly referred to as *long-tail* or *head terms;* specific keywords are three or more words in length and are commonly referred to as *tail terms.* For example, the keyword "cheese" could be considered a head term; the keyword "gourmet cheese gift basket" could be considered a tail term.

Head terms tend to generate substantially more traffic than tail terms, but do not necessarily lead to more revenue or repeat visitors. Tail terms typically send much less traffic, but often convert more often than head terms. Therefore, you should select a blend of both head and tail terms to incorporate into each of the pages of your website.

Choose Between Head and Tail Terms

Regardless of whether you are optimizing an existing website or building a new one, you should select keywords that are consistent with the content of each unique web page, as well as the overall theme of the website. In general, you should select tail terms when optimizing web pages with specific content and head terms when optimizing web pages with more general content.

Select head keywords for your home page that represent the overall theme of your website. For example, if your website is about gourmet cheese, for SEO purposes you want to target the

keyword term "gourmet cheese" for your home page. Typically, your home page has the highest number of *backlinks* — links that point to your website from other websites — out of all the pages on your site. Home pages are also generally viewed as the most important page of a website and are meant to tell both readers and search-engine spiders what the overall website is generally about. For this reason, your home page has the highest chances of ranking for the competitive head terms, and your subpages should target less-competitive head terms, as well as tail terms.

Select Head Terms Sparingly

It is difficult to rank for head terms, especially head terms that define your particular industry or website category. In fact, only the top ten websites within any particular industry or category rank on the front page of a search engine for a general head term. Unfortunately, even if you take and apply all the suggestions in this book, there is no guarantee that you will rank for one or more competitive head terms.

In many cases, the websites that rank high for competitive head terms use manipulative tactics that are inconsistent with the terms and conditions of the major search engines. As a

result, websites using shady SEO practices tend to enjoy top rankings for only a limited time prior to being banned from the search engines temporarily or indefinitely. Although you may be tempted to use manipulative practices that may allow your website to be competitive for head terms in the short term, know that an increased risk exists with undertaking unsavory practices and tactics. Instead, focus on building great content with an emphasis on providing your readers with a great user experience.

Select Tail Terms for Most Web Pages

Your primary SEO strategy should focus on building content that ranks well in the search engines for long-tail terms. Too often the SEO efforts of website owners fail because of an overemphasis on ranking for head terms. Although the search volume for head terms is greater, you stand a much greater chance of ranking well for specific tail terms. Moreover, ranking well for just a few tail terms is much better than not ranking at all for a head term. Always keep in mind that you need to set long-term goals for SEO. Over time, as you build out content on your website and optimize each page for selected keywords, you will notice that your website traffic will have grown substantially.

Optimize Every Page of Your Website

When you select keywords to incorporate into your website, remember that your goal is not to optimize your website all at once, but to optimize each page of your website. You should never optimize for more than one or two main target keywords per web page because doing so dilutes your optimization in too many directions and decreases your overall effectiveness and ranking potential. However, it is acceptable to include a small number of synonymous phrase variations with the same user intent, as long as your content looks natural and does not present a poor user experience.

The approach you take to optimizing each page of your website is different depending on whether you are optimizing existing web page content or building new content. If you are optimizing existing web page content, you should select one or two keywords that best summarize that page. In addition, you may need to manipulate the content a bit to make sure that your target keywords are emphasized and stand out from the rest of the content. If you are building new content, you should have one or two target keywords in mind before you start writing. For example, if your target keyword is "Extra Double Aged Gouda," your web page content should focus specifically on gaining ranking for that keyword. See Chapter 6 for more information about building optimized web page content.

Add Target Keywords to Meta Tags

When optimizing your website, you should strategically place one or two target keywords in the title tag and meta description of your web page. Also, since your meta description is often used as copy in search-engine results, you should use effective sales copy in your meta description tag to increase the click-through rate (CTR) and drive greater traffic to your website. Your selected keywords should ideally be the starting point used to generate the content for each web page you construct. If not, you should make sure that your target keywords are strategically sprinkled throughout the page. When you are building backlinks to your pages, keep the target keywords for each page in mind. If your page is about storing gourmet cheeses, building links with the anchor text "storing gourmet cheese" produces the optimal results. See Chapter 8 for more about backlinks and anchor text.

Be realistic when you select your head terms, and evaluate the competition. Picking head terms that rank within the top few search results for established websites is setting yourself up for failure if you are starting from scratch with an unestablished domain. Although ranking within the top few organic results for the keyword "mortgage" could lead to significant revenue generation, a newly established website with no authority in the eyes of search engines stands little chance of gaining top placement for such a competitive head term. And even though you cannot immediately rank for a general head term like "mortgage," you can break down the general term "mortgage" into smaller, more specific topics, and optimize for those tail terms throughout your website.

Compete.com, www.compete.com, is a competitive analytics tool that provides information on where your competition is generating search-engine traffic on pay-per-click and organic searches. Compete.com also provides information on user interactions after arriving on your site from a search engine, which other popular keyword research tools do not provide. Compete.com is able to include this information due to its unique data gathering method.

Compete.com subscriptions range from $199 monthly for a basic account to more than $500 monthly for an enterprise account. To access user interaction data, you must create a Compete.com account and upgrade to a paid subscription level.

Analyze Your Competition with Compete.com

1 Navigate to www.compete.com and enter a competitor's site in the field on the home page.

2 Click Go.

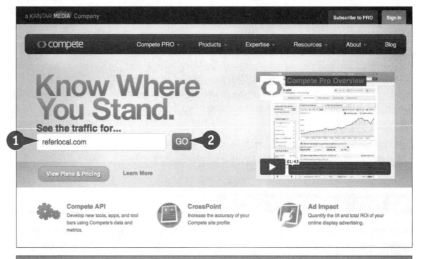

3 Click Signup under MyCompete Free and fill out form that requests e-mail address, password, and CAPTCHA code. Once the form is complete, click Signup.

A After signing up for free Compete Site Analytics account, you will be redirected to historical traffic trend data for your competitor.

4 Click Save Graph Image or Export CSV.

B Note that below the graph Compete provides unique visitor data for your competitor's site.

5 If you want to access additional keywords, click View Plans & Pricing to upgrade your account.

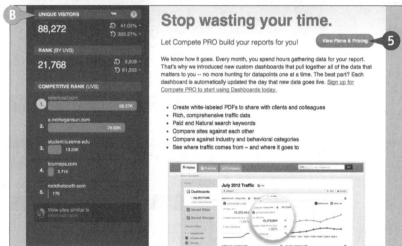

EXTRA

The advanced competitor data that Compete.com offers is broken down into a few categories. They are as follows:

- Volume Rank is the rank of keywords in terms of what keyword is sending the most volume. This provides a look at the top-performing keywords.
- Keyword Engagement is a measure of the average time a user spends on the site and can be used to gauge user interaction.
- Keyword Effectiveness combines Volume Rank and Keyword Engagement. It is a basic measure of which keywords are valuable in terms of referred users who navigate beyond one page after they hit the site.

To create an effective keyword-generation strategy, you should analyze competitors' organic search-engine rankings for keywords you are targeting. Tools such as SEMrush, located at www.semrush.com, help determine how well you rank for specific keywords versus competitors.

SEMrush offers a free account that allows you to determine the top keywords your competitors rank for organically on Google or Bing. Once you register, you receive ten free domain searches per day, which you can use to analyze your organic onsite rankings as well as those of competitors. SEMrush offers data visualization tools that provide at-a-glance competitor information for organic search and PPC.

SEMrush allows you to generate keywords based on competitor keywords lists using both basic and advanced, more granular search techniques.

Analyze Your Competition with SEMrush

1. Navigate to www.semrush.com.

2. Enter a domain into the domain field. For example, bradsdeals.com.

3. Click Search.

A. Note the results that appear under Organic keywords. Search results represent the top five organic search listings on Google for the domain bradsdeals.com.

B. Note the results that appear under Ads keywords. Search results represent the top five search listings on Google AdWords for the domain www.bradsdeals.com.

④ Click Positions in the Organic Research drop-down list.

Ⓒ Note the results that appear under Organic keywords. Search results represent the top organic search listings on Google for the domain www.bradsdeals.com.

⑤ Click Competitors in the Organic Research drop-down list.

Ⓓ Note the results that appear. Search results represent a list of competitors within the organic search results on Google for the domain bradsdeals.com.

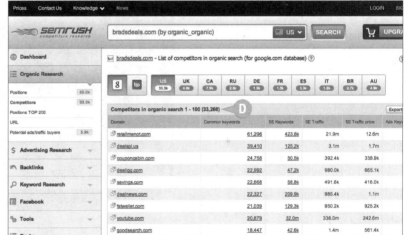

EXTRA

In addition to organic rankings, SEMrush provides you with important information on keyword popularity, including metrics such as search volume and CPC. Observing competitors' keyword popularity is important because it can be used to determine the approximate amount of traffic your competition is receiving from a given keyword placement. The SEMrush keyword popularity metrics also provide a rough idea of how much traffic you can possibly gain by increasing rankings for your keywords. For example, if your site is ranked between spots 7 and 10 for two keywords, but one receives double the monthly searches, you stand to gain the most from optimizing for the higher search volume keyword.

RESEARCH KEYWORDS WITH KEYWORDSPY

KeywordSpy, www.keywordspy.com, allows you to perform keyword research based on keywords your competition is bidding for in pay-per-click and keywords your competition ranks for organically on major search engines. Moreover, KeywordSpy offers a real-time keyword tracking tool that allows you to monitor keyword performance on your site and competitors' sites.

KeywordSpy's real-time keyword tracking technology allows you to assess the effectiveness of keyword rankings, which in turn influences your keyword research strategy. By typing your domain into the tracking tool, KeywordSpy produces a report of keywords you rank for organically and in pay-per-click. KeywordSpy offers a trial and subscription service.

Research Keywords with KeywordSpy

1 Navigate to www.keywordspy.com and log in using your account.

2 Type in a competitor's domain. For example, type **www.patagonia.com**.

3 Click Search.

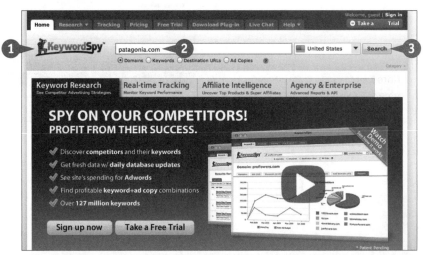

Ⓐ Note the competitor activity with PPC advertising, including estimated daily ad budget and average CPC.

4 Click the PPC Keywords tab.

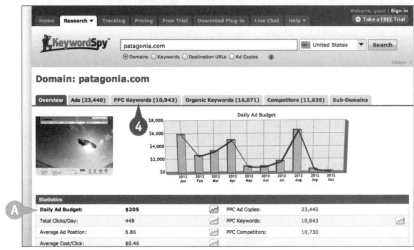

B Note your competitor's various
PPC keywords.

5 Click the Organic Keywords tab.

C Note your competitor's various
organic keywords.

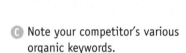

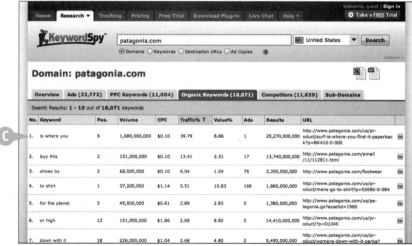

EXTRA

Having real-time access to your organic rankings allows you to discover keywords that you rank for but that were not a primary part of your keyword-generation process. In fact, sometimes you will find that you rank for keywords that you were not even trying to rank for. This insight helps you focus your attention on keywords that search engines have already ranked your website for and modify your keyword research process as appropriate. Analyzing your organic ranking also allows you to find new keywords to add to your pay-per-click campaigns.

Using the Wordtracker Keyword Suggestion Tool

Wordtracker offers a free keyword suggestion tool, located at https://freekeywords.wordtracker.com, which provides a list of related keywords and the estimated search volume for each keyword.

The Wordtracker Keyword Suggestion tool shows search volume estimates as daily figures, which is useful when choosing target keywords for SEO efforts. The keywords with high search volume are the most common words your target audience uses when searching in your vertical. You can organically rank number one in a search engine for a keyword, but if no one is searching for it, you will not receive any traffic from that top keyword ranking. Build your site around the terms customers use.

Using the Wordtracker Keyword Suggestion Tool

① Navigate to https://free keywords.wordtracker.com.

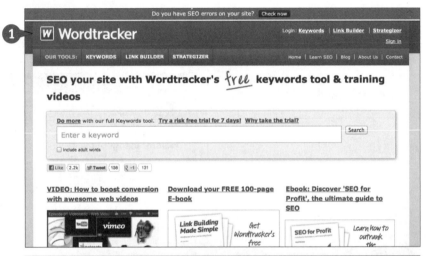

② Enter your base keyword into the keyword field and click Search.

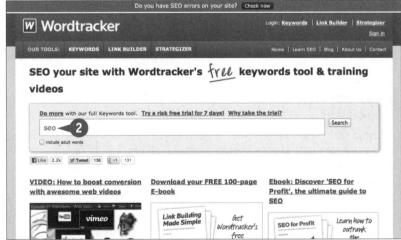

Ⓐ Note that the list of 100 keywords appears.

Ⓑ You can scan the list of keywords, taking note of the estimated search volume of each.

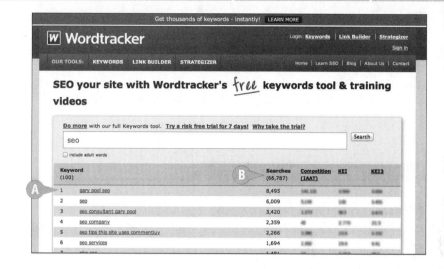

EXTRA

The free version of the Wordtracker Keyword Suggestion tool is limited to 100 results per search. The paid version provides access to thousands of keywords, which is useful for building large keyword lists, running a PPC account, and searching for supplemental keywords for content optimization.

Another benefit of the paid version of Wordtracker is it enables you to import a list of keywords and check their search volume in bulk, whereas with the free version, you need to enter unique keywords one by one.

Using the Google AdWords Keyword Tool

The Google AdWords Keyword Tool, https://adwords. google.com/o/KeywordTool, is a free tool that generates keywords based on a user entering keyword phrases, categories, or a site URL. Because Google data powers the AdWords Keyword Tool, it has the unique advantage of being able to display a measure of advertiser competition. *Advertiser competition* is the amount of advertisers bidding on each term within the Google AdWords program. This helps you find new keywords to use in your PPC account or for SEO. Keywords that have a fairly high search volume with a low competition rating can make perfect additions to your keyword lists.

Using the Google AdWords Keyword Tool

1. Navigate to https://adwords. google.com/o/KeywordTool.

2. Enter one or more keywords into the word or phrase field, placing one on each line.

3. Enter the letters shown in the image. This is to prevent requests from automated tools.

4. Click Search.

Ⓐ Alternatively, you can enter a URL into the Google AdWords Keyword Tool.

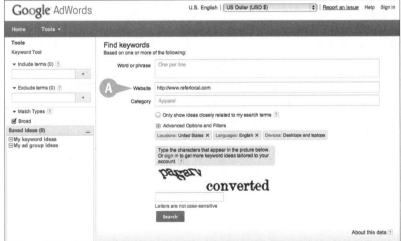

B The list of keywords appears.

C Notice all the additional specific keywords that you can use for search-engine optimization.

D You can sort keywords by Competition, Global Monthly Searches, and Local Monthly Searches.

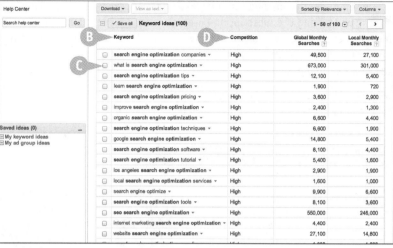

5 Click Download to export keywords.

You can examine the list and select the most appropriate keywords for your website.

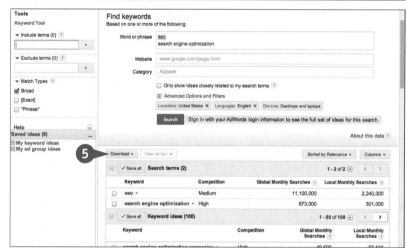

EXTRA

The data from the Google AdWords Keyword Tool is primarily used to add keywords to PPC campaigns; however, it can be valuable when you are generating keywords efforts for SEO. The AdWords Keyword Tool allows you to gauge search volume, approximate CPC, and competition, which help with evaluating the value of keywords. Also, by entering a URL, you can see how Google interprets the content of a given page, which is useful for optimizing site content.

Note that Google provides 100 keyword results and limited features for AdWords Keyword Tool users who are not logged into their AdWords account. It is recommended you create or log in to your AdWords account to see all keyword results and features.

nother effective method for doing keyword research involves using the subscription-based Keyword Discovery tool suite, www.keyworddiscovery.com. Keyword Discovery offers a wealth of information to aid your keyword research efforts.

With Keyword Discovery, you can generate a large list of head and tail terms for any topic you choose, including many industry terms you may not yet be aware of. Keyword Discovery returns a large list of keywords related to the base keyword you use to query. For example, by typing the base keyword **cheese** into Keyword Discovery, you get a list of keywords related to your base keyword "cheese," such as cheese knife and stinky cheese.

Research Keywords with Keyword Discovery

1 Navigate to www.keyword discovery.com and log in to your account.

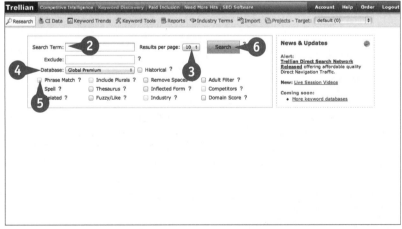

2 Enter your keyword into the Search Term field.

3 Select the number of results you want to view per page.

4 Select your database. Global Premium is the default database. You can also select language-based databases or specialty databases such as Shopping, New, or Questions.

5 Select the appropriate check boxes for options such as Phrase Match or Include Plurals.

6 Click Search.

Ⓐ The defined number of results appears, with their estimated search volume.

⑦ To chart the results, click the bar graph icon to break down the number of searches by month for the previous 12 months. Or click the pie graph icon to break down the market share of the searches by search engine.

Ⓑ Note the bar graph chart that appears, showing seasonal trends in search volume for the keyword you chose in Step 2.

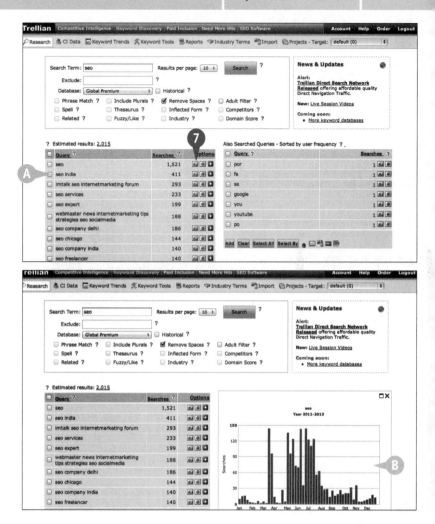

EXTRA

Keyword Discovery aggregates data collected from more than 180 search engines. The large amount of data Keyword Discovery provides is useful for identifying keyword opportunities to guide content strategy. Creating pages and content for relevant keywords and keyword groupings can help increase organic traffic through rankings. See Chapter 6 for more information on creating content.

An added benefit of analyzing the lists Keyword Discovery provides is the analysis of keyword popularity. The keywords "dancewear" and "dance wear" are common variants, yet one is searched nearly 20% more often than the other. The more knowledge you have about keywords and how your audience searches, the greater your chances of gaining more search traffic.

RESEARCH KEYWORDS WITH BING KEYWORD TOOL

Bing Keyword Research Tool is a free keyword research tool that is part of the Bing webmaster tool set. The Bing Keyword Research Tool is useful for finding additional keyword ideas that may have been missed by other keyword sources. Also, the Bing Keyword Research Tool is different from the Google AdWords Keyword Tool in that it pulls organic keyword data directly from Bing rather than providing rounded search volume estimates. This is useful because a more exact search volume value is good for helping you evaluate whether a given keyword or group of keywords may be good organic search targets.

Research Keywords with Bing Keyword Tool

1 Navigate to www.bing.com/toolbox/webmaster.

2 Log in to your Bing Webmaster Tools account.

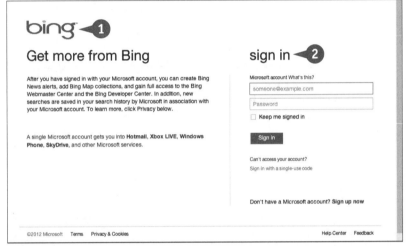

3 Click Diagnostics & Tools in the left sidebar menu.

4 Click Keyword Research in the Diagnostics & Tools submenu.

5 Enter your base keywords into the keyword field.

6 Enter your language in the Language drop-down list.

7 Enter your country in the Country/Region drop-down list.

8 Enter the date range the search volume data will be fetched from.

9 Select the Strict check box if you want results to be strict and not include search volume for keywords containing selected words.

10 Click Search.

A Notice that the output is split between keywords that you search for and additional keyword suggestions based on the keywords you provided.

11 Hover over the dollar sign icon to view CPC data for keyword phrases.

12 Click the Export button to export data.

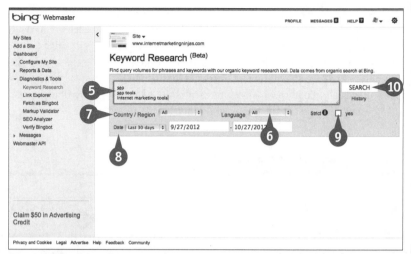

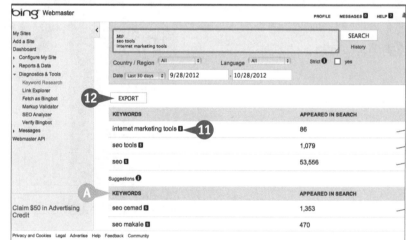

EXTRA

One interesting feature of Bing Keyword Tool is Strict mode. If you select the option for Bing Keyword Tool to return keyword ideas in Strict mode, the tool will return keyword search volumes that are specific to a keyword or key phrase, excluding all phrases that include the specified keyword. For example, if you type in **cheese**, and leave the Strict option unselected, the search volume shown for the keyword phrase "cheese" will be an aggregated number that includes the search volume for all keyword phrases containing the keyword "cheese."

Research Keywords with Übersuggest

oogle Suggest shows Google Search users related search terms when a query is typed. Google Suggest is an excellent source for expanding existing keyword lists because the suggestions provided are what Google has determined are the most related search terms for a particular query. Conducting keyword research by hand using Google Suggest is time-consuming, but you can do it quickly and efficiently using a popular secondary tool called Übersuggest, located at www.ubersuggest.org. Übersuggest provides Google Suggest keywords based on language and search vertical chosen, such as shopping search or news search. By clicking on a specific keyword in the list output by Übersuggest, you can see related keywords.

Research Keywords with Übersuggest

① Navigate to www.ubersuggest.org.

② Enter a keyword.

③ Select a language.

④ Select a search vertical.

⑤ Click Suggest.

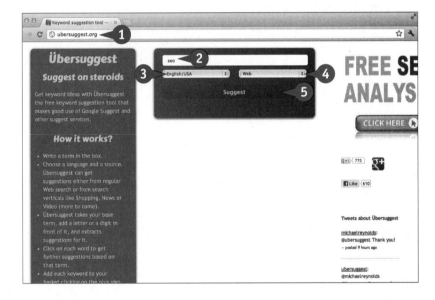

6 Click on a keyword to see additional keyword ideas based on that keyword.

7 Click on green + (plus) button to add a keyword to the master keyword idea list.

8 Click the Get button to view a text version of keyword ideas that you can copy to Clipboard.

A You can examine the list and select the most appropriate keywords for your website.

EXTRA

Übersuggest does not provide search volume and CPC for keyword suggestions. Once you have identified keyword opportunities from Übersuggest, run your list in bulk using the Google AdWords Keyword Tool to identify keyword search volume and CPC, which will help you qualify whether the keywords merit inclusion as part of a PPC or SEO campaign.

You can also use Übersuggest as part of your keyword-based SEO content strategies. By searching keyword groups returned by Übersuggest and clicking keywords for further suggestions, you can find new keyword-based topics for content creation that you may have missed.

The Google Trends Tool, www.google.com/trends, is a free keyword research tool that provides insights into search terms entered into the Google search engine. For a given search term, Google Trends provides information about interest over time and by region. You can adjust time ranges and regional settings, and explore keywords by topical categories. Google Trends also provides information about related search terms, including what the top search terms and rising search terms are at any given time.

Google Trends is useful for understanding yearly and seasonal trends for search terms as well as the variance in search term usage across a geographic area.

Using the Google Trends Tool

1. Navigate to www.google.com/trends.

2. Enter a keyword.

3. Click Explore.

🅐 You can use the graph that shows interest over time to show seasonality.

🅑 View the list of related terms for keyword opportunities in your research.

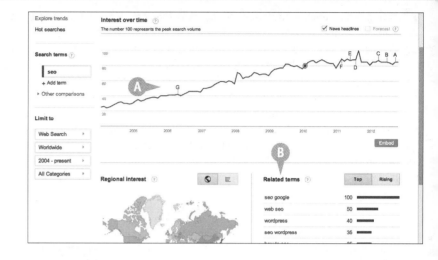

EXTRA

Google Trends is very useful when you are planning your SEO campaigns because it provides authoritative information on seasonal trends. You should always target keywords with a mix of seasonal and nonseasonal search volume. You should also begin your link-building efforts for your targeted seasonal terms at least six months before the period of peak search volume. This ensures that you are ranked as highly as possible for those high-volume periods once the season begins.

Another similar useful tool is Yahoo Search Clues, http://clues.yahoo.com, which provides demographic information, as well as previous search query and next search query information.

Creating search-engine-optimized web pages is the core effort of a successful Internet marketing campaign. Taking care of technical on-site factors such as filenames, title tags, meta description tags, meta keyword tags, and meta robots tags is crucial to making sure the search-engine spiders can determine the relevance of your website. Think of search-engine spiders as robots that read the content of your web pages. Optimizing your content with header tags and other text modifiers allows you to stress the main ideas and topics that your content covers. Optimization of images is important for those web browsers that do not support images, and because search-engine spiders cannot read the content of an image, optimizing images presents an extra avenue to squeeze in more content. Links provide the pathways that search-engine spiders need to find your web pages. Creating these links with search-engine optimization in mind is necessary for optimal results. Throughout the web page creation process, try to adhere to the standards set forth by the World Wide Web Consortium (W3C). The consortium works to create standards in web design and development that ensure Internet-wide compatibility.

Choose Filenames

Every web page that you create is stored in a file. Every file has a name. Using filenames that are relevant to the content of your web page is important for numerous reasons. Besides your domain name, the search-engine spiders see your filenames before anything else. If your filenames are not relevant to the content contained on that page, the search engines can algorithmically detect a disconnect. Taking the extra time to ensure that filenames are properly designed can provide an added boost to your rankings.

Optimize Title Tags

Title tags are extremely influential in search-engine ranking. What you place in your web page title tags has a substantial effect on where, and for what terms, your page ranks. Just as important, the first thing a human visitor sees when finding your page on the search-engine results is your title tag. Title tags should describe what your web page is about and compel potential visitors to go to your site.

Optimize Meta Description Tags

Meta description tags allow you to summarize what a particular web page's content is about. Some search engines use the meta description tags in their results pages directly underneath the web page titles. Your rankings on these search engines are likely influenced by your meta description tags. Writing a brief yet informative description about your web page's content and adding it to your meta description tag is a search-engine-optimization tactic you should not skip.

Optimize Meta Keyword Tags

Meta keyword tags allow you to indicate the relevance of a particular web page to certain keywords and phrases. Although many search engines ignore this tag, some likely still use it in their ranking algorithms. For that reason alone, you want to implement this tag on all your web pages. The keywords and phrases contained in your meta keyword tags work in tandem with the meta description tag to describe the content of a particular web page.

Create a Meta Robots Tag

Sometimes you may not actually want the search-engine spiders to visit certain pages within your website. Although this is often not the case, especially because the goals of search-engine optimization are to increase search-engine-generated traffic, there are situations where the privacy of a particular web page or website is of utmost concern. The meta robots tag allows you to identify which pages the search engines are allowed to index in their results pages, and whether they are allowed to follow links on those pages to other web pages or websites. This is especially useful if certain sections of your website require payment to access. The last thing you want is search engines sending visitors directly to those locations.

Add Emphasis with Header Tags

Optimizing your content includes emphasizing your main topics and ideas. A well-structured web page has a logical hierarchal flow with headings and subheadings fortified with content. These main topics and ideas can be placed within header tags that not only alter the format of the text the web browser displays but also tell the search engines and human visitors that these keywords and phrases are important.

Using Text Modifiers

Beyond just optimizing your main topics and ideas, you want to emphasize appropriate keywords and phrases within your content. Your web page content should speak to visitors, emphasizing words and phrases to express urgency or significance. Using text modifiers, you can emphasize certain blocks of text by bolding, italicizing, or underlining them. The search engines also take modified text into consideration when determining your content's relevance to that text.

Optimize Images

Search-engine spiders are becoming more sophisticated every day, but the spiders still cannot read any images present on your pages. If images make up a large portion of your content, the search engines will have a difficult time understanding the topic of your content. Using alt image tags to describe your images gives the search engines a readable text description of those images and also aids in compatibility with nongraphical web browsers.

Create Links

Your internal linking structure leads the search-engine spiders and human visitors from one web page to another on your website. The structure of your links tells the search engines what the linked web page is about. Your internal linking structure is taken into consideration by the ranking algorithms that determine where your web pages rank for target keywords and phrases. Making it simple for both the search engines and human visitors to find every page on your website is critical for optimal website structure.

Validate HTML

Writing valid HTML is just as important as speaking proper English. Improper HTML can cause web browser incompatibilities that result in your website appearing differently across different browsers. W3C has gone to great lengths to develop standards for web development to ensure compliance across all browsers.

CHOOSE FILENAMES

Strategically choosing filenames is an important first task when you create web pages. Besides your domain name, the first thing search engines discover when spidering through the pages of your website are your filenames. Every single page of your website resides in a different file. These files can be written in HTML, PHP, ASP, or any other web programming language. When you title your pages with search-engine optimization in mind, you have a powerful opportunity to establish relevance to a certain topic or keyword. Make sure your filenames relate directly to the content of the page.

Choose Filenames

① Open a web page in any text editor such as Notepad or a web development program.

② Write the content of your page and select an optimized filename. For example, if your HTML page is about San Francisco hotels, and you are trying to rank well for the search term "San Francisco hotels," consider naming the file sanfranciscohotels.html or san-francisco-hotels.html.

③ Click Save.

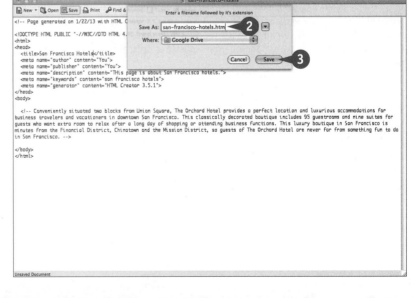

④ Upload the file with the optimized filename to your server.

Ⓐ Note that filenames appear in the search-engine results.

Ⓑ Note that making your filenames relevant to the content contained within the page provides search engines with an additional cue about the relevance of your content to the page in question, which may positively influence your ranking.

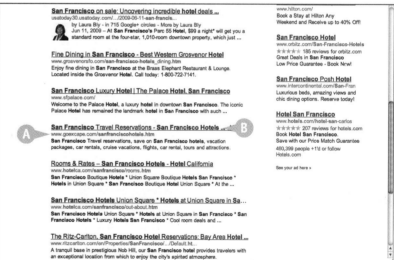

EXTRA

Authorities at the major search engines have stated that hyphens in URLs and web page filenames are viewed as spaces by the search-engine ranking algorithms. This is important because hyphen usage in domain names and web page filenames aids in readability and organization when used in moderation. Overuse of hyphens is considered to be a spamming technique and it can result in a penalty from the search engines if it is done to an unreasonable extent. The search engines do not specify to what extent hyphen usage is acceptable, but try to limit hyphen usage to no more than two hyphens per filename.

OPTIMIZE TITLE TAGS

The title tag is possibly your most important consideration when you try to raise your search-engine rankings for a particular keyword or phrase. Search engines use the text contained within the title tag as a primary factor to determine the content of a certain web page. The text that makes up your title tag is also the clickable link text that typically appears on the search-engine results pages when your site appears in the rankings. Title tag text also appears at the top of a web browser when someone is visiting a particular page on your website.

The title tag is located in the header of an HTML document and its syntax is as follows:

```
<HEAD>
<TITLE>The title of your web page</TITLE>
</HEAD>
```

Optimize Title Tags

1 Open a web page in any text editor such as Notepad, or a web development program and locate the <HEAD> tag.

2 Within your <HEAD></HEAD> tags, type <TITLE>, followed by your optimized title text, and close the title tag with </TITLE>.

Note: *You should limit your title tag to 65 characters or fewer because most search engines do not display any more than that. Your title tag should be a concise statement summarizing the main point of your content, and should be compelling enough to entice search-engine users to click the link text and visit your site.*

3 Save the file, and upload it to your web server.

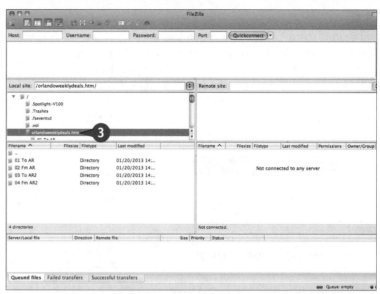

Ⓐ The title appears at the top of your web browser when you visit that page.

Note: *Your title tag must be unique for each and every page of your website and should include the one or two keywords you want the page to rank for. Due to the ranking influence that the title tag possesses, a search-engine penalty is likely to result if the same title tag is repeated across all pages.*

EXTRA

When you link from one page to another on your website, your link text should be closely related to the title tag of the page linked to. The same applies when acquiring links from other websites, which is discussed in more detail in Chapter 8. If those links contain link text that is closely related to the title tag of the page on your website, the major search engines are likely to conclude that your web page is relevant to those terms.

OPTIMIZE META DESCRIPTION TAGS

You should optimize every meta description tag on your website because meta description tags are part of the display information that visitors see when your site is listed in the search engines. The meta description tag contains a brief description of what your web page is about. Although it is not as influential as it once was in search-engine ranking, the meta description tag is important because you can use it to deliver your marketing message and entice search-engine visitors to click your listing versus clicking that of your competition.

The meta description tag is located in the header of an HTML document, and its syntax is as follows:

```
<HEAD>
<META NAME="description" CONTENT="This is
 a brief description of your web page.">
</HEAD>
```

Optimize Meta Description Tags

Create a Meta Description Tag

1 Open a web page in any text editor such as Notepad or a web development program and locate the `<HEAD>` tag.

2 Within your `<HEAD></HEAD>` tags, type `<META NAME= "description" CONTENT="`, your optimized meta description tag, and `">`.

Note: When search-engine users find your page in the search-engine results, the text contained within your meta description tag often appears directly underneath the title tag. Create a few compelling sentences describing your product, services, or website content, and place them in your meta description tag. The description should interest the potential visitor and tempt that person to click your search-engine result link.

3 Save the file, and upload it to your web server.

3

View a Meta Description Tag in Action

1 Navigate to Bing.com. Type **yumm** into the search box.

A The description listed for the yumm.com entry is the meta description tag located on the page.

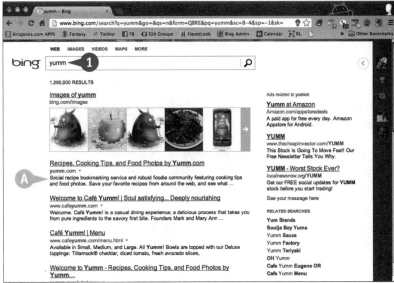

EXTRA

At one time, the meta description tag could be stuffed with keywords and phrases in an attempt to trick the search engines into believing a web page was more relevant for those terms than it actually was. Advances in search-engine ranking algorithms have reduced the impact the meta description tag has on rankings but from a human visitor standpoint, it is still very important. When search-engine users find your page in the search-engine results, the text contained within your meta description tag often appears directly underneath the title tag.

Try the free meta tag generator from SeoBook.com located at http://tools.seobook.com/meta-medic.

OPTIMIZE META KEYWORD TAGS

Perhaps the least important factor in optimizing a website for search-engine rankings is the use of the meta keyword tag. Similar to the meta description tag, the meta keyword tag contains a list of keywords or phrases, separated by commas, that describe the subject matter of a particular web page. Today, the search engines give little consideration to meta keyword tags. Still, you should not skip implementing this tag on all your web pages.

The meta keyword tag is located in the header of an HTML document, and its syntax is as follows:

```
<HEAD>
<META NAME="keywords" CONTENT="a, list, of,
  keywords, describing, your, web, page,
  separated, by, commas">
</HEAD>
```

Optimize Meta Keyword Tags

1 Open a web page in any text editor such as Notepad or a web development program and locate the <HEAD> tag.

```
creatingpages - Notepad
File  Edit  Format  View  Help
<!DOCTYPE HTML PUBLIC "-//W3C//DTD HTML 4.01 Transitional//EN" "http://www.w3.org/TR/html4/loose.dtd">
<HTML>
<HEAD>
<STYLE TYPE="text/css">
<!--
H1 {
Font-size: 25px;
Font-family: Arial, Verdana, sans-serif;
Color: black; }
H2 {
Font-size: 15px;
Font-family: Arial, Verdana, sans-serif;
Color: black;
Padding: 0;
Margin: 0; }
STRONG {
Font-size: 15px;
Font-family: Arial, Verdana, sans-serif;
Color: black; }
-->
</STYLE>
<TITLE>Creating Pages</TITLE>
```

2 Within your <HEAD></HEAD> tags, type <META NAME="keywords" CONTENT=", followed by your optimized meta description tag, and ">.

Note: For each page on your website, generate a short list of no more than ten keywords or phrases and include them in the meta keyword tag. Do not repeat keywords or phrases, and be sure that each web page on your site has a unique meta keyword tag.

```
creatingpages - Notepad
File  Edit  Format  View  Help
<!DOCTYPE HTML PUBLIC "-//W3C//DTD HTML 4.01 Transitional//EN" "http://www.w3.org/TR/html4/loose.dtd">
<HTML>
<HEAD>
<STYLE TYPE="text/css">
<!--
H1 {
Font-size: 25px;
Font-family: Arial, Verdana, sans-serif;
Color: black; }
H2 {
Font-size: 15px;
Font-family: Arial, Verdana, sans-serif;
Color: black;
Padding: 0;
Margin: 0; }
STRONG {
Font-size: 15px;
Font-family: Arial, Verdana, sans-serif;
Color: black; }
-->
</STYLE>
<TITLE>Creating Pages</TITLE>
<META HTTP-EQUIV="Content-Type" CONTENT="text/html; charset=utf-8">
<META NAME="description" CONTENT="Creating search-engine optimized Web pages is the core effort of a suc
<META NAME="keywords" CONTENT="file names,title tags,meta description tag,meta keywords tag,meta robots
<META NAME="robots" CONTENT="index,follow">
</HEAD>
```

③ Save the file, and upload it to your web server.

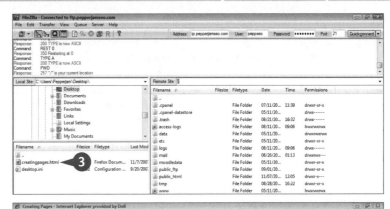

Ⓐ View the source to verify the keywords are placed correctly.

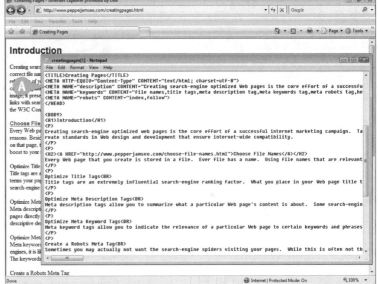

EXTRA

SeoCentro offers an invaluable tool to help analyze meta tags at www.seocentro.com/tools/search-engines/metatag-analyzer.html. The tool analyzes every meta tag of a web page and offers suggestions for improving those tags. It analyzes the length and relevancy of your title, description, and keywords meta tags. It also verifies that all the tags, including the robots tag discussed in the next task, are formatted correctly. Incorrectly formatted tags can render your HTML unreadable by the search engines, causing a ranking penalty, and they could prevent a web browser from loading your page correctly, thus rendering it unreadable to human visitors as well.

CREATE A META ROBOTS TAG

You can use the meta robots tag to tell a search-engine spider whether the web page it visits should be indexed or whether links on that page should be followed. These search-engine "robots" often need to be controlled. The meta robots tag is not used as extensively now as in the past because much more functionality can be obtained through the use of a robots.txt file, which is discussed in Chapter 5.

The meta robots tag is located in the header of an HTML document, and its syntax is as follows:

```
<HEAD>
<META NAME="robots" CONTENT="index,follow">
  or
<META NAME="robots" CONTENT="noindex,follow">
  or
<META NAME="robots" CONTENT="index,nofollow">
  or
<META NAME="robots"
  CONTENT="noindex,nofollow">
</HEAD>
```

Create a Meta Robots Tag

1 Locate a web page on your site that you do not want the search engines to index.

2 Open that web page in any text editor such as Notepad or a web development program and locate the <HEAD> tag.

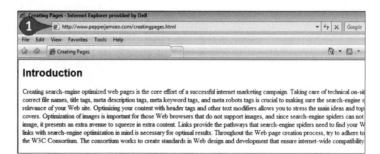

3 Within your `<HEAD></HEAD>` tags, type `<META NAME="robots" CONTENT= "noindex,nofollow">`.

Note: *This meta robots tag prevents the search engines from indexing a page and following any links from that page. The most common use of a* `noindex` *meta robots tag is to avoid search-engine penalties related to publishing duplicate content on your website. For more information on avoiding issues with duplicate content, see Chapter 6.*

4 Save the file, and upload it to your web server.

The search-engine spiders are now directed not to index or follow any links on this page.

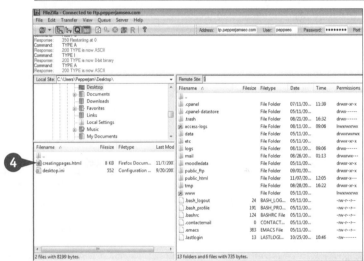

EXTRA

The meta robots tag includes directives for the search-engine spiders. The four directives available are `index`, `noindex`, `follow`, and `nofollow`. Including `index` in the meta robots tag tells the spiders to index that page. `Noindex` tells the spiders not to index that page. Including `follow` tells the spiders to follow links on that page. `Nofollow` tells the spiders not to follow links on that page. Use only one of the four variations at a time. You can also use `CONTENT= "all"` in exchange of `"index,follow"` or `CONTENT= "none"` in exchange for `"noindex,nofollow"`.

ADD EMPHASIS WITH HEADER TAGS

You can use HTML header tags to apply significance to keywords or phrases within a web page.

Header tags are arranged in preset levels of importance ranging from <H1>, the most important, to <H6>, the least important. Unless it is modified through other means, text enclosed within an <H1> tag appears larger than its neighboring text on the web page, and text enclosed within an <H6> tag appears smaller.

Header tags can be used anywhere within the <BODY> tag of an HTML document, and the appearance of the resulting formatting can be altered with Cascading Style Sheets (CSS). Their syntax is as follows:

```
<H1>Text enclosed within a Header 1 tag</H1>
<H2>Text enclosed within a Header 2 tag</H2>
```

Add Emphasis with Header Tags

1 Open a web page in any text editor such as Notepad or a web development program and locate a main topic.

1

creatingpages - Notepad

File Edit Format View Help

```
<!DOCTYPE HTML PUBLIC "-//W3C//DTD HTML 4.01 Transitional//EN" "http://www.w3.org/TR/html4/loose.dtd">
<HTML>
<HEAD>
<STYLE TYPE="text/css">
<!--
H1 {
Font-size: 25px;
Font-family: Arial, Verdana, sans-serif;
Color: black; }
H2 {
Font-size: 15px;
Font-family: Arial, Verdana, sans-serif;
Color: black;
Padding: 0;
Margin: 0; }
STRONG {
Font-size: 15px;
Font-family: Arial, Verdana, sans-serif;
Color: black; }
-->
</STYLE>
<TITLE>Creating Pages</TITLE>
```

2 Find text you want to emphasize.

3 Add an <H1> tag in front of this text and an </H1> tag following the text.

Note: *Placing a selection of text within a header tag tells the search-engine spiders that the text is of a certain level of importance. Search-engine ranking algorithms place emphasis on text enclosed within header tags when determining where pages should be ranked for these terms.*

2

creatingpages - Notepad

File Edit Format View Help

```
<!DOCTYPE HTML PUBLIC "-//W3C//DTD HTML 4.01 Transitional//EN" "http://www.w3.org/TR/html4/loose.dtd">
<HTML>
<HEAD>
<STYLE TYPE="text/css">
<!--
H1 {
Font-size: 25px;
Font-family: Arial, Verdana, sans-serif;
Color: black; }
H2 {
Font-size: 15px;
Font-family: Arial, Verdana, sans-serif;
Color: black;
Padding: 0;
Margin: 0; }
STRONG {
Font-size: 15px;
Font-family: Arial, Verdana, sans-serif;
Color: black; }
-->
</STYLE>
<TITLE>Creating Pages</TITLE>
<META HTTP-EQUIV="Content-Type" CONTENT="text/html; charset=utf-8">
<META NAME="description" CONTENT="Creating search-engine optimized Web pages is the core effort of a suc
<META NAME="keywords" CONTENT="file names,title tags,meta description tag,meta keywords tag,meta robots
<META NAME="robots" CONTENT="index,follow">
</HEAD>

<BODY>
<H1>Introduction</H1>
<P>
Creating search-engine optimized web pages is the core effort of a successful internet marketing campaig
reate standards in Web design and development that ensure internet-wide compatibility.
```

2 **3** **3**

4 Save the file, and upload it to your web server.

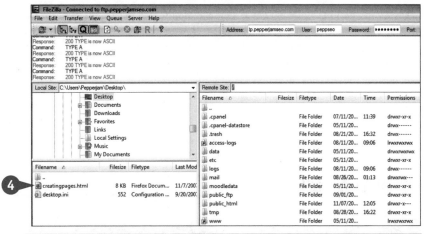

A The text now appears bolded and is considered to be a main heading by the search engines.

Note: Beyond using header tags to highlight text on your pages, you can use them to logically format your content into hierarchal topics and subtopics. For example, if you are writing an information page about personal development, place that key phrase in a header tag like `<H1>Personal Development </H1>`. *If within that same topic there is the subtopic "Tony Robbins Personal Power," place that key phrase in a subheader like* `<H2>Tony Robbins Personal Power</H2>`.

APPLY IT

Although excellent for search-engine optimization, header tags are not always visitor and appearance friendly. Luckily, the appearance of header tag text can be modified while preserving its influence on the search-engine ranking algorithms. It requires using CSS. Add the following code inside your header tag:

```
<style type="text/css">
<! --
H1 {
Font-size: 20px;
Font-family: Arial, Verdana, sans-serif;
Color: blue; }
-- >
</style>
```

Now, any time that you use an `<H1>` tag within your content, the font is Arial, the color blue, and the size 20.

As discussed in the previous task, you can modify text on a web page to emphasize important keywords and phrases to help search engines and human visitors identify the main topic of that page. This can lead to higher rankings for those terms. Besides header tags, you can use other text-modifying tags to place emphasis on certain keywords, phrases, or blocks of text.

These tags include `<STRONG>`, `<EM>`, `<B>`, `<I>`, and `<U>`. They work as follows:

```
<STRONG>Strongly emphasized text</STRONG>
<EM>Emphasized text</EM>
<B>Bolded text</B>
<I>Italic text</I>
<U>Underlined text</U>
```

Whereas header tags should be used to emphasize the main topics that logically break content into different sections, these other text-modifying tags should be used within those bodies of content.

Using Text Modifiers

① Open a web page in any text editor such as Notepad or a web development program.

② Find text you want to modify.

③ Add a `<STRONG>` tag in front of this text and a `</STRONG>` tag following the text.

Note: Use `<B>` and `<I>` tags if your intent is purely to bold or italicize text. These tags differ from the `<STRONG>` and `<EM>` tags in that they are not intended to portray any semantic meaning. They are strictly presentational elements. The `<U>` tag should be used to underline text. Much like the `<B>` and `<I>` tags, it is not intended to portray any semantic meaning.

④ Save the file, and upload it to your web server.

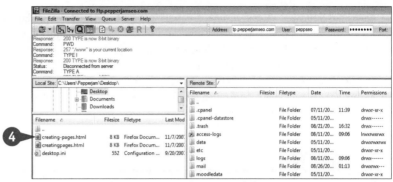

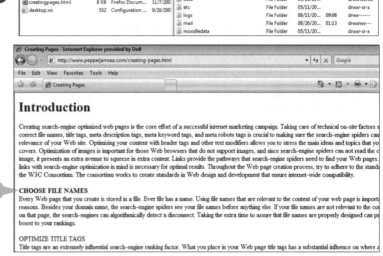

Ⓐ The text now appears bolded and is considered to be strongly emphasized by the search engines.

Note: *Although it is unlikely that the use of these tags is going to provide any serious boost to your rankings, it is important to understand that search-engine optimization is a cumulative effort, and the use of these practices together is what provides results.*

APPLY IT

Much like header tags, all text modifier tags can be altered using CSS while preserving their search-engine ranking influence. Add the following code inside your header tag:

```
<style type="text/css">
<! --
STRONG {
Font-size: 25px;
Font-weight: bold;
Font-family: Arial, Verdana, sans-serif;
Color: red; }
-- >
</style>
```

Now, any time that you use a `<STRONG>` tag within your content, its font is size 25, Arial, red, and bolded. These modifications are useful when you want the header tag text to match the rest of your website.

OPTIMIZE IMAGES

Sometimes you want to use an image in your content instead of a selection of text, and you can use alt image tags to ensure that search engines understand what the image is about. Search engines cannot accurately read images, so unless you explicitly tell the search engines what your images are about, those images provide no overall search-engine-optimization value.

From an SEO perspective, you should limit the use of images on your web page. However, if you use images, you should also use alt image tags. An alt image tag is located within an `<IMG>` tag, and its syntax is as follows:

```
<IMG SRC="yourimage.jpg" ALT="A brief
   description of the image.">
```

Optimize Images

1 Open a web page in any text editor such as Notepad or a web development program and locate an image insertion.

```
creatingpages - Notepad
File  Edit  Format  View  Help
<!DOCTYPE HTML PUBLIC "-//W3C//DTD HTML 4.01 Transitional//EN" "http://www.w3.org/TR/html4/loose.dtd">
<HTML>
<HEAD>
<STYLE TYPE="text/css">
<!--
H1 {
Font-size: 25px;
Font-family: Arial, Verdana, sans-serif;
Color: black; }
H2 {
Font-size: 15px;
Font-family: Arial, Verdana, sans-serif;
Color: black;
Padding: 0;
Margin: 0; }
STRONG {
Font-size: 15px;  |
Font-family: Arial, Verdana, sans-serif;
Color: black; }
-->
</STYLE>
<TITLE>Creating Pages</TITLE>
<META HTTP-EQUIV="Content-Type" CONTENT="text/html; charset=utf-8">
<META NAME="description" CONTENT="Creating search-engine optimized Web pages is the core effort of a suc
```

2 Find the `<IMG>` tag, add `ALT="`, type an optimized image description, and then add a closing quote.

Note: Although images are not necessarily search-engine friendly, they are a vital part of visitor-friendly design. A vibrant, colorful, image-based website compels its visitors to stay longer and browse more pages. It can also increase visitor trust and lead to higher sale-conversion rates.

```
creatingpages - Notepad
File  Edit  Format  View  Help
<!DOCTYPE HTML PUBLIC "-//W3C//DTD HTML 4.01 Transitional//EN" "http://www.w3.org/TR/html4/loose.dtd">
<HTML>
<HEAD>
<STYLE TYPE="text/css">
<!--
H1 {
Font-size: 25px;
Font-family: Arial, Verdana, sans-serif;
Color: black; }
H2 {
Font-size: 15px;
Font-family: Arial, Verdana, sans-serif;
Color: black;
Padding: 0;
Margin: 0; }
STRONG {
Font-size: 15px;  |
Font-family: Arial, Verdana, sans-serif;
Color: black; }
-->
</STYLE>
<TITLE>Creating Pages</TITLE>
<META HTTP-EQUIV="Content-Type" CONTENT="text/html; charset=utf-8">
<META NAME="description" CONTENT="Creating search-engine optimized Web pages is the core effort of a suc
<META NAME="keywords" CONTENT="file names,title tags,meta description tag,meta keywords tag,meta robots
<META NAME="robots" CONTENT="index,follow">
</HEAD>

<BODY>
<H1><img src="header.gif" width="500" height="100" alt="Chapter 3 Logo"></H1>
<H1>Introduction</H1>
<P>
```

③ Save the file, and upload it to your web server.

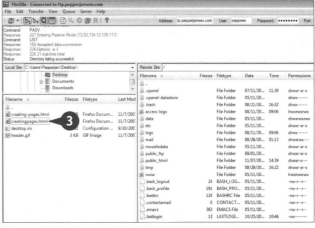

Ⓐ When you position your mouse over an image that includes an alt image tag, the alt image text appears.

Note: *The alt image tag is a textual replacement for an image. If for any reason an image cannot be displayed, the alt image text appears in its place. It also appears when you position a mouse pointer over the image for a certain period.*

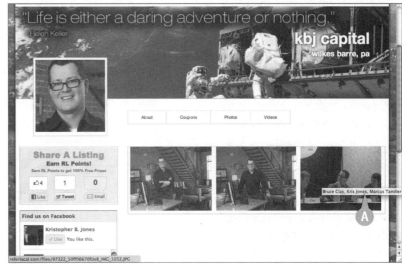

EXTRA

Rather than just filling your alt image tags with lists of keywords or phrases, take the time to write a unique, relevant description of the image being described. Abuse of these tags can lead to a rankings penalty, so be careful when writing your descriptions. Do not repeat the same words over and over again, and never repeat the same alt image tag more than once. Images can increase the usability and improve the appearance of your website, but whenever possible, use actual text within your content instead of images.

CREATE LINKS

You can create an internal link structure that allows search-engine spiders, as well as human beings, to quickly and easily navigate your website. As search-engine spiders crawl from page to page within a single website and then from page to page across multiple websites, each and every link is taken into consideration. Although it can be difficult to control how many links point to your website from other sources, you can easily control how your own internal links are structured. Link creation may be a basic task, but if done correctly, it can be tremendously influential to your overall search-engine rankings.

Create Links

1 Open a web page in any text editor such as Notepad or a web development program and find a location to place a link.

1

```
creatingpages - Notepad
File  Edit  Format  View  Help
<!DOCTYPE HTML PUBLIC "-//W3C//DTD HTML 4.01 Transitional//EN" "http://www.w3.org/TR/html4/loose.dtd">
<HTML>
<HEAD>
<STYLE TYPE="text/css">
<!--
H1 {
Font-size: 25px;
Font-family: Arial, Verdana, sans-serif;
Color: black; }
H2 {
Font-size: 15px;
Font-family: Arial, Verdana, sans-serif;
Color: black;
Padding: 0;
Margin: 0; }
STRONG {
```

2 Type <A HREF=", the URL of the web page you are linking to, and ">.

3 Add descriptive link anchor text and follow it with </A>.

Note: *Creating effective links involves only two elements. First, be sure to always use absolute URLs, even when linking within your own website. Instead of* <A HREF= "page.html">Next Page</A>, *use* <A HREF="http://www.yoursite. com/page.html">Next Page</A>. *If you use relative URLs, links no longer work if you move pages from one directory to another unless the entire file structure moves with it.*

2

```
creatingpages - Notepad
File  Edit  Format  View  Help
<!DOCTYPE HTML PUBLIC "-//W3C//DTD HTML 4.01 Transitional//EN" "http://www.w3.org/TR/html4/loose.dtd"
<HTML>
<HEAD>
<STYLE TYPE="text/css">
<!--
H1 {
Font-size: 25px;
Font-family: Arial, Verdana, sans-serif;
Color: black; }
H2 {
Font-size: 15px;
Font-family: Arial, Verdana, sans-serif;
Color: black;
Padding: 0;
Margin: 0; }
STRONG {
Font-size: 15px;
Font-family: Arial, Verdana, sans-serif;
Color: black; }
-->
</STYLE>
<TITLE>Creating Pages</TITLE>
<META HTTP-EQUIV="Content-Type" CONTENT="text/html; charset=utf-8">
<META NAME="description" CONTENT="Creating search-engine optimized Web pages is the core effort of a
<META NAME="keywords" CONTENT="file names,title tags,meta description tag,meta keywords tag,meta robo
<META NAME="robots" CONTENT="index,follow">
</HEAD>

<BODY>
<H1>Introduction</H1>
<P>
Creating search-engine optimized web pages is the core effort of a successful internet marketing camp
reate standards in Web design and development that ensure internet-wide compatibility.
</P>
<P>
<H2><A HREF="http://www.pepperjamseo.com/choose-file-names.html">Choose File Names</A></H2>
Every Web page that you create is stored in a file.  Ever file has a name.  Using file names tha
</P>
<P>
```

3

4 Save the file, and upload it to your web server.

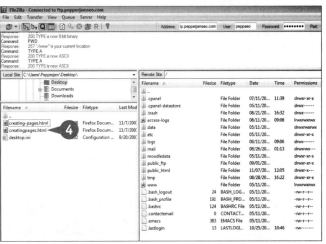

A A hyperlink has been created.

Note: *If possible, avoid using images to link to other pages of your website. As discussed in the previous task, search engines cannot read images, and thus you lose the opportunity to attach descriptive link anchor text to that page. Alt image tag text is not passed as anchor text when linking from an image.*

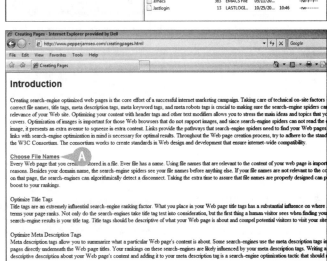

EXTRA

The search engines place more credibility on links assigned to certain locations on a web page. Generally speaking, the higher a link appears on the page, the more it assists the rankings of the web page it links to. Also, links embedded within blocks of content hold more value than isolated links. Your overall website navigation menu should appear on the top of your page in a prominent location. These links to the main categories of your website are of utmost importance for both the search engines and human visitors.

Validate HTML

Valid, properly written HTML allows search engines to easily read your web page content and underlying HTML code. Much like the English language, there is a right way and a wrong way to write the code that structures your web pages. W3C, an international group that works to develop protocols and guidelines that ensure the long-term growth of the web, has developed standards for HTML development. Web browser developers like Google, Mozilla, and Microsoft adhere to these standards to guarantee cross-browser uniformity when displaying web pages.

Validate HTML

1 Navigate to http://validator.w3.org.

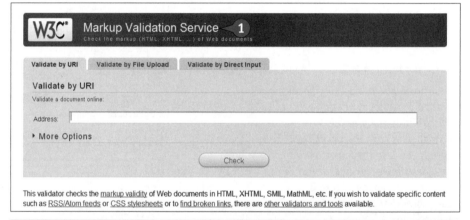

2 In the address bar, enter a URL that you want to test for HTML standard validation.

3 Click Check.

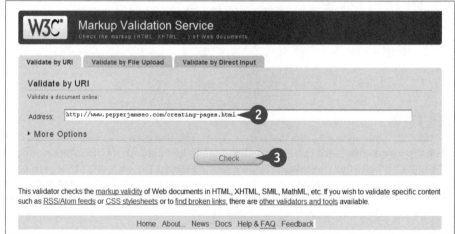

(A) The results of the validation check appear.

(4) Click Validation Output.

(B) All the errors appear with suggestions to fix the problems.

Note: *You should make your best attempt to pass the validation test, but do not spend a great deal of time if it appears to be impossible. Many sites do not pass, including Google, Yahoo, as well as most other heavily visited Internet hot spots.*

EXTRA

Search engines read websites line by line, and errors in your HTML syntax can trigger a penalty if the invalid code prevents the search-engine spider from reading the content. Invalid code can cause websites to look different from browser to browser. Some web developers apply various patches and Band-Aids to minimize browser display problems instead of adhering to W3C standards, and although the end result may be browser compatibility, these patches often involve adding a substantial amount of unnecessary code. Avoid applying patches and Band-Aids by testing your code for standard compliance during development.

An Introduction to Basic Website Structure

Optimizing the basic structure of your website greatly increases the likelihood that search engines will successfully locate and index your content. Search-engine ranking algorithms analyze numerous on-site factors when determining where a web page ranks for particular search terms. Some of these factors include your website content, your domain name, whether your website works on all browsers, your website structure, your navigational linking structure, the accessibility of all your pages, and your credibility. You can do many things to address these factors, including choosing reliable web hosting, choosing an appropriate domain name, optimizing your site for all web browsers, creating a logical site structure and navigational menus, generating a sitemap, and creating an about us page and a privacy policy page.

On-site factors are absolutely critical to search-engine optimization, or SEO. A well-optimized design and structure help improve the overall performance of your website, help users to navigate it, and allow search engines to find and index all your content.

During website design or redesign, ask yourself the following two basic questions: Does my website appeal to visitors? Is my website search-engine friendly? Once you answer those two essential questions, build each page as a balance between the needs of the search engines and the experience of the user.

Find Web Hosting

The first step in on-site optimization is choosing a reliable web-hosting company. Web hosting is required to make your website accessible on the Internet. If you choose an unreliable or poorly maintained web host, your website faces numerous potential issues, such as website downtime and security concerns. Choosing an appropriate web host requires you to carefully evaluate and address all the technical requirements of your website. You must give careful consideration to your hosting package if you require e-commerce functionality or if you expect your website to get a significant amount of traffic. Depending on your needs, you can compare hosting packages based on price, database needs, and bandwidth limitations, among other things.

Establish a Domain Name

Choosing a good domain name has two potential benefits. First, domain names work toward forming impressions about your online credibility. A well-thought-out domain name gives users the impression of value and trust. Second, it is important to choose a relevant domain name because is often the first thing the search-engine spiders see when indexing your website. Written by the software engineers at the search engines, spiders are programs that jump from website to website, reading content and following links. Search engines and potential website visitors view a poor domain name as noncredible and unreliable.

Optimize for Multiple Browsers

It is imperative that your website is viewable to users on all the major web browsers. A web browser enables a user to display and interact with text, images, and other information typically located on a website or local area network. It allows users to easily access information provided through HTML. Popular web browsers, such as Internet Explorer, Safari, Mozilla Firefox, and Google Chrome, enable Internet users to view and interact with websites. Further, millions of people use smartphones and other mobile devices, such as the Apple iPad or Google Nexus, to surf the web, which requires that you optimize your website for multiple types of browsers. Unfortunately, each individual browser does not read HTML code in the same fashion. In fact, you may design a website a certain way and view it in Internet Explorer, only to find out later that it looks much different in Firefox. Because of these potential problems, you should confirm that your website is viewable in all browsers. Fortunately, you can use online tools to test whether your website is compatible with multiple browsers.

Plan and Design a Website Structure

An effective website structure enhances the user experience and allows search engines to determine the subject matter and relevancy of your site. You should create a blueprint of your site before you begin your design and content creation. It is important to keep all related website content grouped together into categories. For example, if your website is about gourmet food, you would have a cheese section, a sauce section, and a section on dry goods. Each category should have a unique directory and filename structure, so when your website is indexed by search engines, it demonstrates a wide breadth of

content related to the subject. By doing this, the search engines can view your website as an *authority* across various areas of gourmet food.

You need to spend time working on your website structure. Failure to have a properly structured site can make it difficult, if not impossible, for search engines to properly index your website. Such a failure may lead search engines to omit your website from the search results and conclude that you are not an authority on the subject matter of your site.

Link within Subject Matter Themes

In order for search-engine spiders to locate and index all your website content, you need to develop a linking structure that allows search engines to find each and every page. However, avoid linking unrelated pages to one another, since search engines favor pages with similarly themed content and tend to dislike pages that are not part of a larger subject or theme. Think of your linking structure as a means to logically progress from one page of your site to the next. By avoiding a haphazard linking structure, you ensure maximum effectiveness for both the search engines and your users.

Design a Sitemap

An effectively designed sitemap increases the likelihood that your site is indexed by search engines. A well-built sitemap displays the inner framework and organization of your website's content to the search engines. A sitemap should reflect the entire navigational framework of your website so that search-engine spiders can find and index all your content.

Create a Company Information Page

Adding a company information or about us section to your website enhances credibility and provides visitors with important information about your business's history, your management team, and any notable accomplishments or awards you have received. The company information portion of your website allows users to get to know the people behind the website and the business. The presence of this page also builds credibility in the eyes of search engines, and they are automated to try to detect the presence of a company information page. Search engines are constantly striving to improve the experience of their users, and providing this type of information can bolster your ranking while gaining credibility with your visitors.

Create a Privacy Policy

Regardless of the type of website you have, creating a privacy policy page adds credibility and authority to your website in the eyes of both search engines and users. Like a company information page, search engines now try to detect the presence of a privacy policy. A basic privacy policy details all your company's marketing information practices and policies. It shows users how seriously you take their personal and private consumer information and that you are committed to protecting it. A privacy policy page informs your website visitors that you will not, under any conditions, sell any personal information, including credit card and contact information, to other companies.

FIND WEB HOSTING

Make sure to choose a hosting provider that has a positive reputation and an established online presence. Select a host with 24-hour support and a 24 hours a day, 7 days a week uptime guarantee. You will benefit from working with some of the more popular hosting service providers, even if they are more expensive; doing so can help you avoid costly downtime.

One effective way of selecting a reliable and trustworthy web-hosting company is to read the reviews from other website owners and designers. Two of the premier web-hosting review forums include Web Hosting Talk at www.webhostingtalk.com and FindMyHosting at www.findmyhosting.com.

Find Web Hosting

1. Navigate to www.findmy hosting.com.

2. Review the list of Best 10 Web Hosting Companies.

A. Note that you can easily read reviews and compare scores for each web hosting company.

3. Click Compare Hosts.

4. Compare web hosting plans.

B. Note the monthly pricing for each plan.

C. Note the features for each plan.

5. Browse the results, and click a package you find appealing.

6. Take note of the company name offering the package you are interested in.

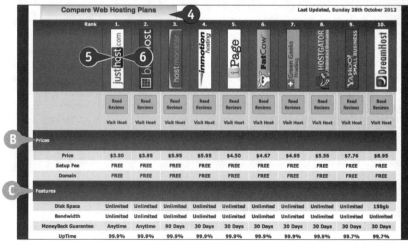

7 Navigate to www.webhosting talk.com.

8 Enter the name of the company you are interested in into the search field.

9 Choose Search Forums from the drop-down list and click Go.

D A list of threads appears. Each of these threads contains a reference to the company name you have searched.

You can browse the provided threads to find more information and reviews of the company before making a purchase.

EXTRA

Some web hosting providers offer free hosting. You should avoid free web hosting if you are looking to build a large-scale website with e-commerce functionality, or if you expect to use a significant amount of bandwidth. Free hosting also tends to be advertisement supported, which can be a real nuisance, especially if you cannot control the advertisements.

For SEO purposes, you should host your own website. Many of the free services limit your ability to control the domain that your website points to, resulting in a poor-quality domain name. Moreover, major search engines are unlikely to attribute authority to websites hosted on free hosting services.

Establish a Domain Name

Your domain name is an important factor search engines use to rank your website. Selecting a domain that relates to the theme of your website increases the likelihood that search engines will rank your website for related keywords. Generally, you have two options: choose a domain name that contains keyword phrases that describe the content on your website, or choose a brandable domain name.

When choosing a domain name, include one or two major keywords your website is attempting to rank for. If your website is aiming to create a new brand or develop a new niche in the market, register a domain name that contains as few characters as possible and avoid hyphens.

Establish a Domain Name

① Navigate to www.godaddy.com.

② Enter a domain name you want to register.

③ Select the top-level domain (TLD) extension.

④ Click Search.

Ⓐ The selected domain has already been registered.

Ⓑ If the domain has already been registered, you may be able to register the name by selecting a different TLD extension.

Ⓒ Alternatively, you can view suggestions from GoDaddy.

⑤ Enter a domain name you want to register.

(D) The selected domain name is available.

6 Select the TLD extension you want to register.

7 Click Continue to Registration.

8 Complete the checkout process.

EXTRA

It is often necessary to secure variations of your primary domain name to prevent cybersquatting. *Cybersquatting* occurs when someone registers variations of your current domain name.

At the same time you register your primary domain name, register the same domain with common TLDs, country extensions, and common misspellings. At the very least, register the .com, .net, and .org extensions, as well as .co.uk and any other country that you may want to conduct business in.

Securing a good domain name is not easy, especially due to *domaining*, which is when domain names are purchased, usually in bulk, and monetized. If the domain you are looking for is unavailable, consider purchasing that domain in the domain secondary market from brokers such as www.sedo.com.

OPTIMIZE FOR MULTIPLE BROWSERS

When you design your website, you must make sure that users can view it on all the major web browsers, including the most recent versions of Internet Explorer, Mozilla Firefox, Chrome, and Safari. It is also important to design it with different screen resolutions in mind. Additionally, because mobile phones and tablets are now widely used, you must optimize your website for those as well. Unfortunately, browsers do not interpret and display the results the same way. It is possible to design a website a certain way and view it in Internet Explorer only to find out later that it looks different in Firefox. One useful free tool for cross-browser testing is Adobe BrowserLab at https://browserlab.adobe.com.

Optimize for Multiple Browsers

1 Navigate to https://browserlab.adobe.com.

2 Click Start using BrowserLab.

3 Create an Adobe ID.

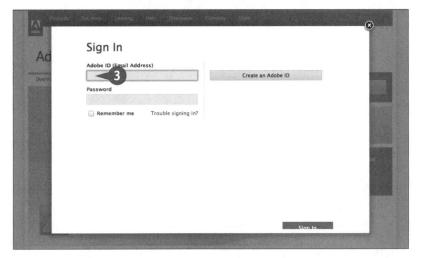

④ Enter the URL you want to view.

⑤ Select the browser version to view in the drop-down list.

Your website appears as it would within the selected browser.

Ⓐ You can adjust the view using the View drop-down list.

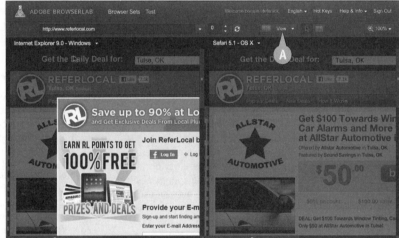

EXTRA

Adobe BrowserLab allows you to see how a given URL looks in multiple different browsers and lets you view a given URL in older versions of those browsers. You can also preview pages in multiple ways, align previews automatically, and use rulers and guides with BrowserLab. BrowserLab has a plug-in for Firefox browsers and can be used as part of the popular Dreamweaver design suite.

In addition to BrowserLab, Screenfly, located at www.quirktools.com/screenfly, is a useful browser testing tool that allows you to quickly check screen resolution and responsiveness of your website design on alternative devices.

When designing your website, approach it with a developed plan for your website structure. A well-structured and organized web design ensures that search-engine spiders will be able to read every page of your website, provides a positive experience for visitors, and makes changing the design or adding pages much easier.

The most significant idea behind choosing a theme for your website is to find one and stick with it throughout the entire website. Nothing draws the ire of the search engines more than a website with no clear focus or real benefit to a user. If you create a website about computers but write content about cars and then link to other websites on gardening, you are preventing the search engines from recognizing that you are an authority on computers.

Start with a Plan

Before you start any design work on your website, decide how best to structure your website. If you sell a variety of products spanning a large number of categories, your website will be structured differently from a single-themed informational website.

Once you have made a decision on the overall theme of your website, your next step is to begin designing the structure of the site. Start by planning all the necessary categories and subcategories that your website will consist of. Think of the planning stage as a blueprint that enables both your visitors and the search-engine spiders to easily navigate your content.

Build Your Website around a Thematic Structure

Once you have planned the layout of your website and decided on its overall structure, your next step is to divide the website into different categories, or themes. A well-thought-out thematic structure helps maintain a clear delineation between the different content areas of a website. To achieve high search-engine rankings, you need to appear as an authority on these main topics. Therefore, it is beneficial to design your website in well-organized and structured themes that do not confuse users or search engines. An additional benefit from organizing your website in this way is that it allows you to target specific keywords and phrases within each particular section.

A website theme represents a group of subject-specific content on your website, much like chapters of a book outline specific content and ideas. The home page describes the overall subject in the introduction of the website and then breaks it down into different subsections that support that major subject.

Take a website dealing with Internet marketing as an example of a website using thematic structures. Each subsection of this website would focus on just one aspect of Internet marketing. Subsection content would link only to similar content. For example, a subsection on paid search would have pages of content dealing only with paid search.

Design your file structure to represent these themes. For example, if your major categories are pay-per-click marketing, search-engine optimization, and online media buying, your file structure should represent this. Use folders for your main categories like www.example.com/pay-per-click, www.example.com/seo, and www.example.com/media-buying.

Although search engines reward websites that have large amounts of unique content, it is important that your content does not dilute the individual thematic categories of your site. By adhering to the structure previously outlined, you ensure that the search engines see you as an authority site for each topic. The purpose of these thematically structured sections is to reinforce the overall subject relevance of your website.

Proper linking between pages on your website enables search-engine spiders to find, index, and rank each page. If the search engines cannot crawl every page of your site, some pages will not be found, and therefore not included in search-engine results. A proper linking structure not only allows search engines to find all your pages but also helps search engines determine the theme or themes of your website.

Link in a Hierarchy

Be sure to link from your home page to all the major themes or categories of your site. Do not link directly from your home page to individual pages within your site's main categories. Instead, link to those documents from your main category pages. Through your linking structure, you should logically guide both users and the search engines from page to page. Your linking should create a hierarchy of your pages from the top-level main categories down through your individual content documents or product pages.

Link Directly

You should avoid linking from one page to another on your site if the pages are not directly related to one another. For example, if you have a site that sells cell phone accessories, try not to link from a page about Verizon headsets to a page about AT&T chargers. When doing this, you tend to dilute your themes. Remember, search engines put a lot of emphasis on links in their ranking algorithms, and not just links to your site but also links from your site. If you link from one page to another page that is not directly related to the first, even if both are located on your own site, you can give the search engines the impression that these pages are directly related. If linking those pages makes sense, you can learn about how to link them properly using the `nofollow` attribute covered in Chapter 5.

Avoid Broken Links

You can use free software like LinkChecker, found at http://wummel.github.com/linkchecker, to check your website for broken links or pages that do not exist. If you link to a page that does not exist, the search-engine spiders may try to crawl and index that page. Search engines can penalize you or give you a negative score if too many of these broken links exist, either as internal or external links, on your website. If you are linking to external pages on other websites, frequently check to make sure they have not been taken down or moved. Although you cannot control the actions of other webmasters, you can at least make sure that you do not link to pages that no longer exist or whose content has changed.

Avoid Error Messages

Most web-hosting packages come with entry-level website statistics. Check these statistics often to see if your visitors are receiving any error messages. The problem may be that other webmasters are linking incorrectly to pages on your website. If so, your visitors may be receiving 404 Page Not Found errors, which should show up in a website statistics package. Incorrect links of this type can be addressed by setting up 301 redirects to the correct pages, which is discussed Chapter 5.

DESIGN A SITEMAP

A sitemap gives visitors a place to find what they are looking for without getting lost in the navigation of the website. Writemaps, at www.writemaps.com, is a useful free sitemap tool that allows you to map out categories and subcategories, create URLs, write notes about specific pages, and share copies of your sitemap using protected URLs. Writemaps is web-based, which allows you to collaborate with others easily during the sitemap creation process. Start off your site structure with your home page and key category pages. Make sure to include your about us and privacy policy pages. Writemaps exports to several formats, including XML. Using the Writemaps XML export feature, you can create an XML sitemap to function as an outline or index of your entire website.

Design a Sitemap

① Navigate to www.writemaps.com.

② Sign up to create a free account.

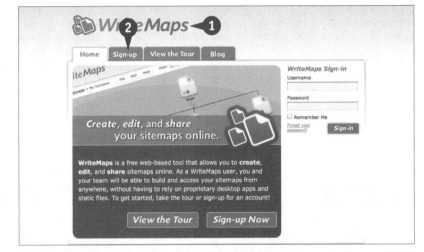

③ Click the i (information) icon.

④ Specify a page URL.

⑤ Add any page notes.

⑥ Click Done.

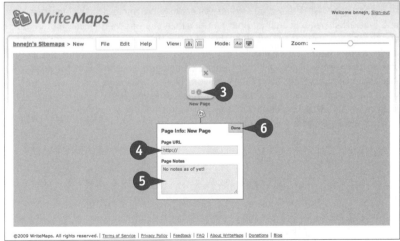

⑦ Click New Page and specify a page label.

⑧ Click the green + (plus) button to add a new page.

Ⓐ Drag and drop pages to adjust locations in the site hierarchy.

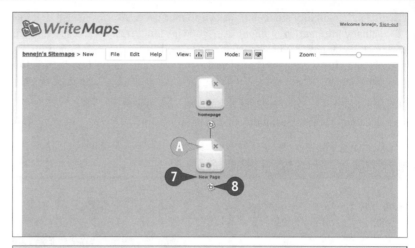

⑨ To create an XML sitemap, click the File menu and choose Export XML SiteMap.

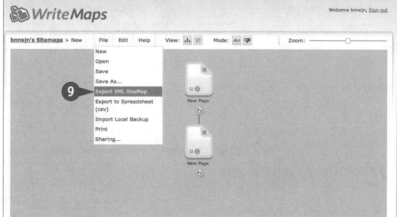

EXTRA

If you have an existing website, the Internet Marketing Ninjas' Find Broken Links, Redirects & Site Crawl Tool at www.internetmarketingninjas.com/seo-tools/google-sitemap-generator) is a free SEO tool that identifies pages returning errors and redirects, displaying them in red. This tool also shows on-site meta tag information and generates an XML sitemap for your website. To use the Find Broken Links, Redirects & Site Crawl Tool, enter your URL, number of web pages to crawl, and click the Ninja Check button. Once the tool is finished, click the Create XML Sitemap button at the top of the page. Alternatively, if you have a large site, you can select to receive results via e-mail.

CREATE A COMPANY INFORMATION PAGE

Trust and credibility are important to Internet users. A company information or about us page helps build trust with visitors by providing company biographies, history, photos, and videos to share your identity, mission, and brand message.

It is important for search engines to see this page during the indexing process to establish that your site is trusted.

Place a link for your company information page on your website home page. Label the link About Us, Company Information, or something similar so that users can easily find it. This link needs to be clearly visible and prominent on your home page.

Create a Company Information Page

Note: *This task uses the website www. seomoz.org as an example.*

Decide Home Page Link Placement

1 Go to the home page of your website.

Ⓐ Notice the About link at the top of the SEOmoz.org home page.

2 Place an About Us link on your home page.

Note: *The most common place to link to an about us page is within the lower section of your website. However, you may also want to add a second link to your primary navigation at the top of your page to generate trust and credibility with your website visitors.*

Write an About Us Section

1. Write an about us section that includes information about you and your company.

2. Include information such as what your business does and its contact information, such as a phone number or e-mail address.

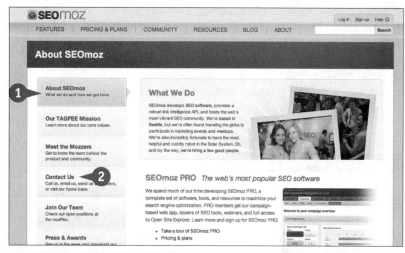

Include a Biography Section

1. Write a brief biography about yourself.

2. Include a few photos of yourself or your company.

Ⓐ Notice SEOmoz employees have their own pages that include information about their personal, educational, and professional backgrounds.

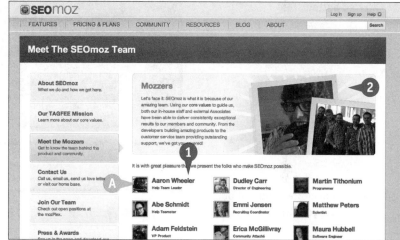

EXTRA

Statistics show that your website's company information or about us page is likely to be one of the pages on your site new visitors click most often. As a result, you should spend ample time creating a compelling and complete profile of both yourself and your business. Consider including a mission statement and biographies of your management team. Additional information can include the history behind your business, what sets you apart from your competitors, and contact information. Provide an address and phone number to help build credibility with your visitors, especially if you run an e-commerce website.

CREATE A PRIVACY POLICY

Create a privacy policy to ensure visitors are aware of your information-collecting policies. A privacy policy page is a best practice for legal reasons and because it notifies visitors how you handle the information you collect on them. A privacy policy page also helps show search-engine algorithms that you are a legitimate business. Organizations such as FreePrivacyPolicy.com and the Direct

Marketing Association, www.the-dma.org, have tools to assist in creating privacy policies.

Privacy policies are important if you collect e-mail addresses or any demographic information about visitors. Avoid copying privacy policies belonging to other websites, and always keep your privacy policy current.

Create a Privacy Policy

1 Navigate to www.free privacypolicy.com.

2 Click the Click Here to Get Started button.

3 Enter the requested information to generate your free privacy policy.

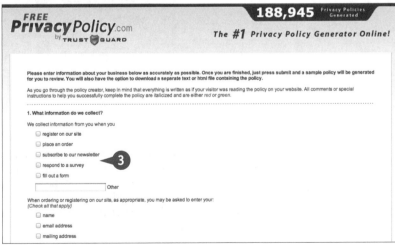

④ Enter your name and e-mail information at the bottom of the page.

⑤ Click Submit.

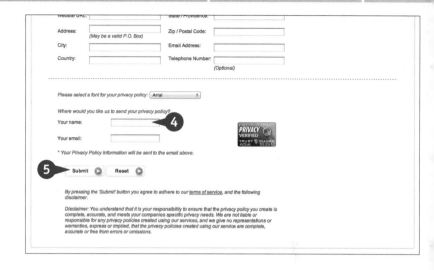

EXTRA

Many consumer group websites offer great advice in putting a privacy policy together, though it is not intended to replace professional advice. The Direct Marketing Association offers a tool for creating privacy policies, available for free to DMA members, at www.the-dma.org/privacy/creating.shtml.

The Direct Marketing Association tool allows you to choose what type of information to state in your privacy policy. It is expected that you will notify users if you collect user-specific information on pages visited, as well as why you collect it and how long you retain it. You can also specify whether your website places cookies and what information the cookies collect.

An Introduction to Advanced Website Structuring

Proper website design and structure is an integral part of any search-engine-optimization campaign. Although the techniques discussed in this chapter are not required for success, having this knowledge in your arsenal allows you to take an advanced, streamlined approach to problems that would otherwise be difficult to solve. Many webmasters are not even aware that these issues exist let alone know how to deal with them when they arise. Mastering these tactics requires the willingness to dig deeper than the surface and delve into some fairly technical tasks. Ultimately, the world's premier search-engine-optimization experts must develop advanced skills and techniques to keep their websites on top of the search-engine results pages.

The search-engine ranking algorithms are constantly evolving. More and more website owners are losing their spots in the rankings as their competition becomes more technically competent and adept at the technical side of search-engine optimization. Consider the tasks in this chapter as stepping stones to an advanced understanding of how you can enhance your search-engine-optimization efforts. You can use the techniques covered here to streamline much of the tedious work involved with search-engine optimization. For example, using the `mod_rewrite` module discussed in the "Using Mod_Rewrite to Rewrite URLs" task can, depending on the size of your website, shave hours or even days off the amount of time normally required to rewrite every URL on your website. Adding a simple line of text to a robots.txt file as discussed in the "Create a Robots.txt File" task can save your web server from an overflow of search-engine spider traffic. This traffic can waste a tremendous amount of server resources and even force your web host to charge you extra money for bandwidth overcharges. These are just a few examples of potentially daunting tasks that can be simplified using these techniques.

Create a Robots.txt File

Creating a robots.txt file is a way of speaking directly to the search-engine spiders when they arrive at your site. These spiders are simply robots programmed to obey certain commands. There are numerous scenarios where such an exchange is useful. Perhaps you would rather the spiders not visit certain sections of your site. Or maybe you want to instruct them to visit every single page. Other times you may want to control the frequency at which the spiders visit your site. A robots.txt file allows you to tell the spiders what they may and may not do once they arrive at your domain.

Specify a Canonical Page

Specifying canonical pages is useful for when your website has a large number of pages that have identical content or very similar content. One way that this occurs is when you have a sorting functionality on your website that creates new URL parameters for each selection. The canonical attribute is a useful tool to tell search engines which of the pages from a set of similar pages you would prefer to show up in organic search results.

Using the Nofollow Attribute

Attaching a `nofollow` attribute to a link is your way of telling the search-engine spiders that they should not follow that link or view that link as anything of significance when determining ranking. Although the `nofollow` attribute was developed to prevent spamming blogs and guest books from influencing search-engine rankings, it can also be used to funnel relevance and authority throughout the individual themes of your website. The `nofollow` attribute can also be used to link to other websites that are not directly related to the content of your own website. At this time, Google has asked that all paid links be tagged with the `nofollow` attribute to indicate that the links should not affect ranking influence.

Structure URLs Correctly

Structuring your URLs correctly is a critical step when developing a search-engine-optimization plan of attack. Both the search engines and search-engine users appreciate descriptive URLs. From a mechanical standpoint, descriptive URLs are easily spidered, and from a user's standpoint, they are easily understood. The search engines also take into consideration the keywords and phrases contained within your URLs and use these to influence your rankings. Properly designed URLs provide a solid foundation upon which to build more pages while maintaining an efficient organizational structure. Make a strong effort to create your URLs correctly the first time through because changing URLs later can be a daunting task.

Protect Yourself with an .htaccess File

It is possible to modify your web server's functionality by using an .htaccess file. An .htaccess file is the Apache web server's configuration file. It is a straightforward yet powerful text file that can accomplish a wide variety of functions. It enables you to protect your website from content-stealing robots and allows you to dynamically rewrite poorly formed URLs generated by shopping cart or blog software. Most website owners have never seen an .htaccess file or know of its existence. Although normally left to expert server administrators, an .htaccess file can help you avoid several potential problems.

Using Mod_Rewrite to Rewrite URLs

You will find many references to the importance of proper URL structure for search-engine optimization throughout this book. The `mod_rewrite` module of the Apache web server gives you the power to rewrite poorly formed URLs on the fly as well as manipulate the appearance of any filename you choose. Using the `mod_rewrite` module may appear difficult at first, but tools are available to simplify the complex parts, and the benefits of using this module to its fullest extent far outweigh the steep learning curve.

Redirect Non-WWW Traffic to WWW

You may be amazed to learn that some search engines see the example.com and www.example.com variations of your domain name as two totally separate websites. This is called a *www/non-www canonical issue* because there is confusion as to which version is standard. This technical weakness can lead to less-than-optimal rankings — one version of your domain name may rank alongside another version of your domain name even though they share the same content. The search engines may believe you are proliferating duplicate content and penalize your website's rankings. It is important to set up your server to redirect all traffic to one variation using a 301 redirect to prevent any confusion by the search engines.

Redirect with 301 Redirects

If you move pages around or even decide to move your entire website from one domain to another, you need a method of alerting the search engines to this move. If not, you lose all your previous rankings, and the time and effort put into achieving them becomes a waste. 301 redirects provide you with the means to tell the search engines that not only have you moved your site, but you want all your rankings to move with it. This is a very important and often overlooked issue.

CREATE A ROBOTS.TXT FILE

Depending on the content of your website, you may have a large number of images stored on your server, which can lead to an unwanted increase in server bandwidth if your images are found through a search engine. Prevent this by creating a robots.txt file that disallows search-engine spiders from crawling and indexing your /images directory.

If you sell a copyrighted informational product or piece of software on your website, the search engines may be able to find and index your intellectual property. Prevent this by creating a robots.txt file that disallows search-engine spiders from crawling and indexing the directory or file where your product is located.

Create a Robots.txt File

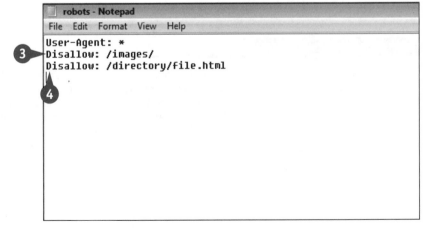

① Open a text editor such as Notepad.

② Type `User-Agent: *`. This line describes which search-engine spiders should obey this rule. The * refers to all robots.

③ To disallow all robots from crawling your /images directory, add this text: `Disallow: / images/`. You can also add any other directories that you would prefer not be crawled.

④ To disallow a certain file from being crawled and indexed, add this text: `Disallow: / directory/file.html`.

5 Save the file, and name it
robots.txt.

6 Upload the file to your web root
directory.

The robots.txt file now prevents
search-engine spiders from
entering the /images directory
and indexing /directory/file.html.

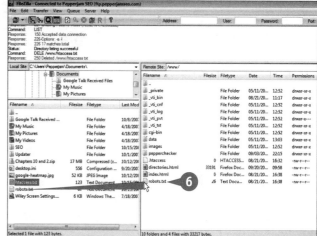

EXTRA

You can use the robots.txt file to tell the search-engine spiders where a sitemap is located with this text:
`Sitemap: http://www.example.com/yoursitemap.html`. The robots.txt standard also has the ability to
force certain crawl delay rates. You can dictate that the search-engine spiders crawl only one page per a certain
period and also specify that they may crawl only during certain hours of the day. This can aid in bandwidth
preservation because some search-engine spiders crawl pages at a very fast rate.

You can use the robots.txt generator at http://tools.seobook.com/robots-txt/generator to simplify the robots.
txt-creation task.

A canonical page is specified using an HTML attribute that declares a preferred version of a page out of a set of pages with identical or very similar content. For many websites, it is common that there are several pages for the same products. When search engines detect that multiple pages on a website have identical or very similar content, they deindex duplicates or rank only one page for a search query, depending on the search engine. Sometimes, search engines do not rank the correct pages that you would prefer to show users. A canonical attribute solves this issue. You can specify a canonical page to search engines by adding a `<link>` element with attribute `rel=canonical` to the `<HEAD>` section of individual pages.

Specify a Canonical Page

① Navigate to www.zappos.com/womens-shoes and click Women's Shoes in the side navigation.

② Select sorting features from the secondary left-hand menu.

Ⓐ Notice that when you select sorted items, the URL changes.

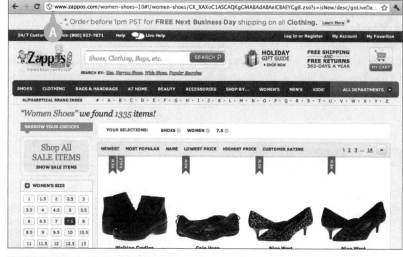

❸ View the source code for the page and notice the implementation of a rel=canonical attribute pointing to the main version of the page.

EXTRA

Keep in mind that Google treats rel=canonical more as a strong suggestion, in combination with other factors, rather than a directive. When you use rel=canonical, you can use absolute or relative links. However, using absolute links to minimize confusion and potential difficulties is recommended. Also, keep in mind that rel=canonical should only be used to specify the canonical version of identical pages of content or very similar content. It is also possible to use rel=canonical to suggest a canonical URL on a different domain.

Nofollow is an HTML attribute value applicable to hyperlinks that informs the search engines not to follow that link. Linking to another web page can influence that page's rankings in the search engines. If you want to link to a page but not influence that page's rankings, use the nofollow attribute. You can apply the nofollow attribute to any hyperlink by attaching rel=nofollow to the HTML anchor tag. It was developed to deter forms of web spamming such as comment spamming and guestbook spamming. Many blog and guestbook software applications now automatically attach this attribute to all user-posted hyperlinks.

Using the Nofollow Attribute

Build Relevancy

1. Navigate to www.krisjones.com and view the source code for the page by right clicking the content portion of the page.

2. Notice that a nofollow attribute has been added to a link to a contact page that search engines will not be able to fill out.

Prevent Blog Spam

1 Navigate to www.krisjones.com/
mark-zuckerberg-techcrunch-
san-francisco-201 and open the
source code view.

2 Notice that links to URLs within
the comments contain the
`nofollow` attribute. This link
can no longer influence the
search-engine rankings of the
linked page.

EXTRA

Chapter 8 discusses PageRank as part of Google's ranking algorithm. PageRank passes from page to page within your website. In the past, webmasters used the `nofollow` tag to try to funnel PageRank to specific pages to help improve rankings. Efforts of this nature were referred to as *PageRank sculpting.* However, the Google Search Quality team confirmed that no additional benefit came from undertaking these efforts.

One way to implement the `nofollow` attribute properly on-site is to specify page crawl prioritization. For example, you can place `nofollow` links to a member or sign-in area, that search engines cannot access, which will allow search engines to allot more link equity to other areas of your site.

STRUCTURE URLS CORRECTLY

Think of your website's information architecture as hierarchical containers full of related information. Each container should be labeled appropriately with a URL. For example, your website's baseball section should be located at www.example.com/baseball, and your website's football section should be located at www.example.com/football.

If you structure your page URLs to reflect your information architecture, you will create an easily spidered, organized, user-friendly website navigation system. The search engines can easily find each content-rich page and relate it back to its parent category. Also, it is a best practice to include the primary keyword that best describes a given page in the URL for that page.

Structure URLs Correctly

Correctly Structured URL

1 Navigate to www.google.com and search for the keyword "internet marketing."

A Notice Wikipedia.org ranks #1 with the URL http://en.wikipedia.org/wiki/Online_advertising. This is an example of a well-structured, relevant URL.

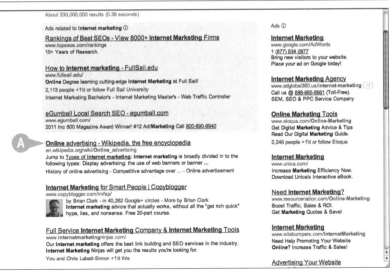

Correctly Structured Subtopic URL

1 Navigate to www.zappos.com.

2 Position your mouse pointer over the Clothing link in navigation column on the left.

B Notice the URL structure www. zappos.com/womens-clothing.

3 Navigate to www.zappos.com/ womens-shoes.

4 Position your mouse pointer over the Boots link.

C Notice the URL structure www. zappos.com/womens-boots-zj. This is another example of a well-structured, relevant URL.

EXTRA

Structuring your URLs correctly provides you with benefits beyond just improving your search-engine-optimization efforts. Well-structured URLs provide you with a blueprint for creating other advertising campaigns. One such example is a paid search, or pay-per-click (PPC), advertising campaign, which is discussed in Chapter 11. A paid search, or PPC, advertising campaign involves purchasing advertising space directly on search engines when users search for particular keywords relevant to your products or content. A properly categorized website gives you a head start in developing the keyword lists necessary to properly construct a paid search advertising campaign.

PROTECT YOURSELF WITH AN .HTACCESS FILE

An .htaccess file is the configuration file for the Apache web server. It allows you to control server functionality and has other uses, including rewriting URLs and redirecting web traffic. It enables features ranging from password-protecting directories, banning visitors from sources such as spamming crawlers, and eliminating malicious use of the Wget Linux command; and it can be used to prevent bandwidth theft from image linkers. An .htaccess file is a text file that you can create in a text editor such as Notepad. The file is uploaded to the root directory of your web server or directories underneath it. Take full advantage of .htaccess to prevent your hard work from being abused or even stolen.

Protect Yourself with an .htaccess File

Block Bad Bots

1. Open a text editor such as Notepad.

2. Type RewriteEngine On to activate the mod_rewrite module.

3. To disallow content retrieval from your website through the use of the Wget command, add RewriteCond %{HTTP_USER_AGENT} ^Wget [OR].

4. On the next line, add RewriteRule ^.* - [F,L]. This prevents the use of the Wget command to access your website.

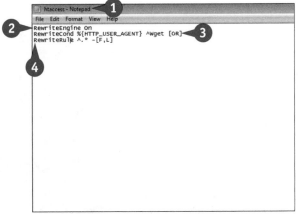

Prevent Image Theft

1. To allow visitors from your own website, add RewriteCond %{HTTP_REFERER} !^http(s)?://(www\.)?your domain.com [NC].

2. To match all image file extensions, add RewriteRule \.(jpg|jpeg|png| gif|flv|swf)$ - [NC,F,L].

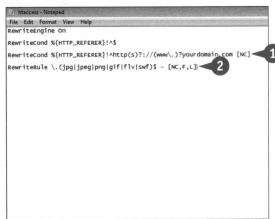

3 Save the file as htaccess.txt. This file will be renamed later to .htaccess using your FTP program. Renaming the file may be necessary because on some computers, such as Macs, files that start with a dot are invisible in the graphic user interface (GUI).

Upload to Server

1 Upload the htaccess.txt file to your web server root directory and rename it .htaccess.

The .htaccess file prevents other websites from directly linking to your images and videos.

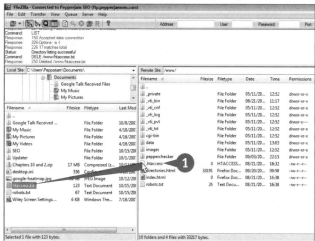

EXTRA

You can use one or more of the helpful tools located at www.htaccesstools.com to generate a variety of different .htaccess code blocks, which you can then place into a blank .htaccess file and upload to your server.

The tool automatically generates .htaccess authentication code along with an encrypted .htpasswd file to password-protect directories. If you want to protect your images, it allows you to customize .htaccess code to allow certain domains to use your images, as well as define a replacement image that appears instead of the actual image requested.

The tool also creates .htaccess code to block unwanted bot traffic or traffic from certain IP addresses.

Using Mod_Rewrite to Rewrite URLs

Mod_rewrite is an Apache web server module that enables you to redirect URL's server side without the user experiencing any indication that the redirect occurred. Mod_rewrite can be used in conjunction with proper URL structuring to generate both search-engine friendly and user-friendly URLs. This is especially relevant for websites that use content management systems that generate URLs dynamically. Dynamically generated URLs are rarely constructed with search-engine optimization in mind. Mod_rewrite can be used to create search-engine friendly URLs in these cases.

Activate mod_rewrite by adding the text RewriteEngine On to your web root directory's .htaccess file. If the file does not exist, create a blank file and upload it to your web root directory.

Using Mod_Rewrite to Rewrite URLs

1 Open a text editor such as Notepad, or open your current .htaccess file.

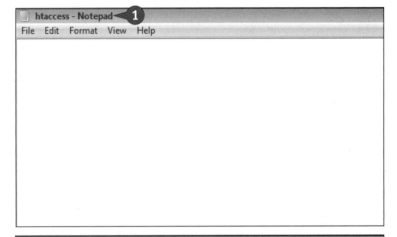

2 Type RewriteEngine On to activate the mod_rewrite module.

3 To rewrite a single static URL, add RewriteRule ^old\.html$new.html.

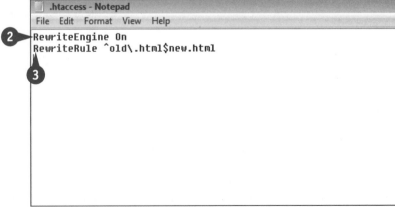

④ To rewrite a dynamic URL, add
`RewriteRule ^([^/]*)\.`
`html$ /viewproducts.`
`php?category=$1 [L].` This
redirects all traffic going to
www.example.com/viewproducts.
php?category=sports to www.
example.com/sports.html.

⑤ Upload the htaccess.txt file to
your web server root directory
and rename it .htaccess.

The `mod_rewrite` module
rewrites the URLs to make them
appear static.

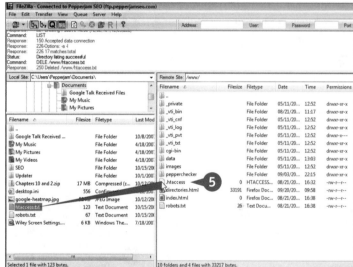

EXTRA

The Mod Rewrite Generator (www.generateit.net/mod-rewrite) is an excellent free tool that helps you rewrite
dynamic URLs into well-structured URLs that appear static.

The tool itself can seem complex at first, but with a little practice, it is an invaluable resource. First, enter an
example of the type of dynamic URL, and then choose which variables you want to remain static. You also have the
option to add any relevant keywords as a prefix or suffix. Generate individual rewrites for specific pages, or take it
a step further and generate general rules that rewrite an entire set of pages.

Many search engines, even large engines like Google, continue to index and rank both www. and non-www. versions of web pages. This can lead to problems, including duplicate content penalties and dilution of incoming link benefits. Chapter 8 discusses the search-engine-optimization benefits of building links back to your website.

You can address this problem by adding code to your web root directory's .htaccess file to set up a 301 redirect from example.com to www.example.com or vice versa. A 301 redirect is a *permanent redirect,* notifying browsers and search-engine spiders that a page has permanently moved. The new location can be a new web page or a different domain name.

Redirect Non-WWW Traffic to WWW

① To redirect non-WWW to WWW, first open a text editor such as Notepad or open your current .htaccess file.

② Add `RewriteEngine On` to activate the `mod_rewrite` module.

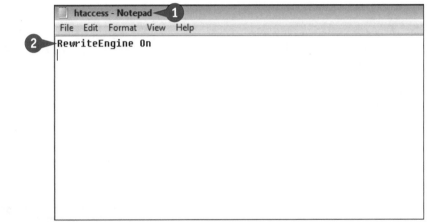

③ Add `RewriteCond %{HTTP_HOST} !^www\.example\.com$`.

④ Add `RewriteRule (.*) http://www.example.com/$1 [R=301,L]`.

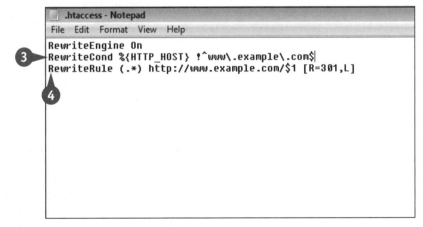

⑤ To rewrite WWW traffic to non-WWW, first add `RewriteCond %{HTTP_ HOST} !^ example\.com$`.

⑥ Add `RewriteRule (.*) http:// example.com/$1 [R=301,L]`.

⑦ Upload the htaccess.txt file to your server and make sure to rename it .htaccess.

The `mod_rewrite` module creates a search-engine-safe 301 redirect.

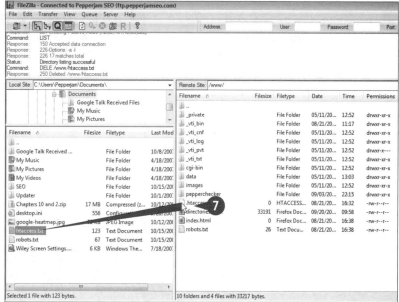

EXTRA

If you have an established website, see if you have a canonical issue with your www/non-www domain entries. To check for a canonical issue, visit www.google.com and type **site:*newdomain.com*** into the search bar. Replace *newdomain.com* with your domain name. This shows every web page Google indexed of your website. If you find both www.yourdomain.com and yourdomain.com in the list, you have an issue. Next, type **site:*www.newdomain.com*** into the search bar. If the results differ dramatically from the previous query results, you probably have a canonical issue. Note that if you purposely employ the use of other subdomains besides www., the results cannot be compared accurately.

REDIRECT WITH 301 REDIRECTS

Website redesigns often require URL changes. Unfortunately, search engines struggle with website changes. If you move a page from www.example.com/ mistydogpic1.html to a better structured URL, you should set up a 301 redirect. If the search engines indexed the original URL, you want to be sure that both visitors and the search engines know the page permanently moved during a website redesign.

If you want to move your entire website to a new domain, a 301 redirect will help preserve search-engine rankings. Once the search engine updates its web page index, it should recognize the status change and update your listings accordingly. Keep in mind that it may take some time.

Redirect with 301 Redirects

① To redirect a single page on the same server, first open a text editor such as Notepad, or open your current .htaccess file.

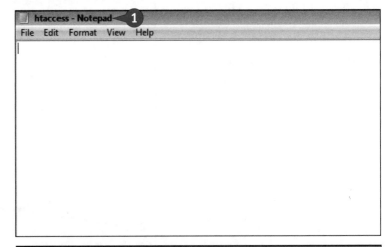

② Add `Redirect 301 /oldpage. html http://www.example. com/newpage.html`.

③ To redirect to a new domain, first add `Rewriterule (.*) http://www.newdomain.com/$1 [R=301,L]`. This redirects everything on your original domain name to your new domain name.

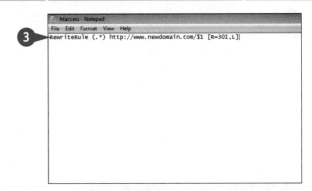

④ Upload the htaccess.txt file to your server and make sure to rename it .htaccess.

The `mod_rewrite` module creates a search-engine-safe redirect from one page to another on your website.

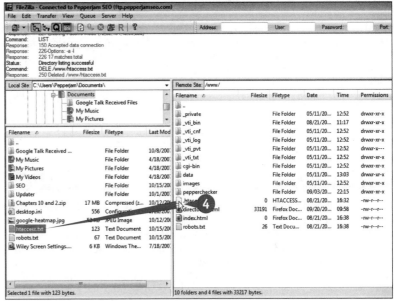

EXTRA

It is important to use 301 redirects any time you move a page on your website. You may consider moving a page to be a logical and intelligent decision, but the search engines initially see nothing but a missing page. When you remove unneeded pages from your website, consider adding a 301 redirect for those pages back to the website home page. Otherwise, if you remove the pages and the search-engine spiders continue to crawl the missing pages, they may penalize your entire site despite the deletions being intentional.

If you own the .com, .net, .org, or other extension of your domain name, you can use 301 redirects to automatically redirect to the .com extension or another extension.

An Introduction to Creating Content

Content is the lifeblood of your website — it is what visitors use to determine value and what search engines evaluate to rank your website. Well-written, original content is essential to the success of your website. The quality of your content is directly proportional to how well you are likely to rank in search engines and whether a customer will purchase something from your website. Content written for the purposes of search-engine optimization, or SEO, is designed to achieve organic rankings by appealing to the reader and to the search engine. Websites with keyword-rich, naturally flowing, original content are judged better than websites that simply stuff keywords into otherwise poorly written text. This chapter guides you through the mechanics and demonstrates proven methods for writing authentic and effectual content that not only gets visitors to take action but also significantly increases your odds of attaining desirable search-engine rankings.

Write for People, Not Search Engines

Original, naturally flowing, well-written content provides your readers with a positive, enjoyable user experience while greatly improving your chances of a top search-engine ranking. Search engines strive to keep their ranking systems as close to a meritocracy as possible: the best rankings for the best websites. The algorithms of today's popular search engines are sophisticated enough to determine whether a page is acceptable for human consumption; search engines tend to favor and reward high rankings to websites with well-written original content.

All the traffic on the Net is worthless without user click-through and conversions. The most utilized feature on the web is the Back button; the crux of this problem lies with insipid and ineffectual content creation. Keeping your content flavorful and persuasive is the best way to accomplish superlative rankings and consistent conversions.

Avoid Duplicate Content

Avoiding content that is the same as your competitors' is critical to achieving and maintaining favorable, long-standing, organic search-engine rankings. A trustworthy content writer understands the importance of writing and maintaining original content on a website. Search engines award original content and penalize identical content, making it absolutely necessary that you write unique content for your website. You also want to ensure that no plagiarists use your content on their pages. The discovery of duplicate content on your website prompts search engines to penalize you with lower rankings or omit your pages from the search results altogether. Tools exist that enable you to scan the web for instances of duplicate copy and minimize plagiarism of your work.

Using Proper Keyword Density

The goal of search-engine optimization is to make sure that your website ranks at the top of the search results when high-converting, target keywords related to your product or service are typed into popular search engines as search queries. Using proper *keyword density* is a process that includes strategically repeating select, target keywords and minimizing nontarget keywords throughout your content, so that search engines deem your website relevant to search queries that you want to rank for. Proper keyword density is a fundamental component of on-site search-engine optimization. By using tools to maximize optimal keyword density, you can incorporate a substantial number of target keywords through your content without compromising the natural flow of the writing.

Using Latent Semantic Content

Search engines use latent semantic indexing to determine a site's thematic relevance to a particular search query. Latent semantic indexing allows the content writer to establish a site's relevance through thematically linked terms. You can use latent semantic content to create relevancy while maintaining the organic flow of your content. For example, if your page is about the Washington Redskins, you can use words like "football" and "Washington, D.C." in your content to establish relevancy. You can use these connected terms to legitimize your site as relevant without inundating your copy with the keywords "Washington Redskins."

Keep Content Current

Keeping your content current is essential to maintaining favorable organic search-engine rankings. It is vitally important to your website's success that you update content fairly regularly. Search engines consider fresh content to be of greater value than outdated content, penalizing websites that remain unchanged and stagnant and rewarding websites that provide fresh content. There are many ways to keep content fresh and original. Manually changing your content routinely is time-consuming, tedious, and often results in less-authentic prose. Self-perpetuating content creation systems are preferred over the manual insertion of fresh content. User-generated content from testimonials, forums, and blogs, as well as content through content-aggregation networks are highly recommended methods of supplying your site with fresh, stimulating content.

Optimize Non-HTML Documents

Search-engine algorithms were originally capable of indexing only HTML documents. However, with advances in technology, search engines are now indexing other documents such as Microsoft Word, Microsoft Excel, Microsoft PowerPoint, Rich Text Format (RTF), and Adobe Portable Document Format (PDF). Therefore, it is acceptable to include non-HTML types of document files within the body of your website content; however, you must optimize these files to improve the results when search engines index them.

For SEO purposes, you should fill your page primarily with textual content rather than image files. A simple rule is that even if your image contains information that is viewable to humans, search engines cannot read the image unless it also appears in a basic text format. Image files might be visually stimulating and eye-catching to a reader, but they are of little value as far as search engines are concerned. Although some search engines are capable of reading some aspects of PDF files and other kinds of images, search engines cannot read text or messages within image files, and tend to regard them as empty space on your site.

It is prudent and beneficial to infuse your site with text that search-engine spiders can recognize. Include a call-to-action phrase, such as "Buy Now" or "Limited-Time Only," in a text box, or use a creative textual format, which stands out to the reader. Textual content is not as visually pleasing as images, but it garners the necessary attention from search engines. Bottom line: Text lends itself to SEO; images do not.

WRITE FOR PEOPLE, NOT SEARCH ENGINES

Search engines grant high rankings to those websites deemed most relevant and valuable to the user; therefore, writing for search engines and writing for people are not mutually exclusive concepts. By strategically weaving a few target keywords into original, well-written content, you can accomplish superior organic rankings and persuade readers to become customers.

The ultimate goal of any SEO campaign is to achieve long-standing, organic rankings with popular search engines such as Google, Bing, and Yahoo. Although content is not the only thing that search-engine algorithms take into consideration when ranking a website, content is arguably the most important. Therefore, if your goal is to obtain high organic rankings for your website, you must produce high-quality, original content that contains the keywords that you want to rank for.

Write Original, Persuasive, and Natural Content

If your content is original, persuasive, and has a natural tone, search engines tend to recognize it as worthwhile and therefore rank it positively. Conversely, if your content is overtly — or even worse, covertly — stuffed with keywords and the only purpose of the content is to manipulate search-engine results, search engines will eventually remove your content from the search results. Packing too many keywords into your content creates an awkward tone and unnatural flow. Even worse, when a search-engine spider detects superfluous keyword use, it deems a site "spammy" and devalues it accordingly.

Structure Your Content with Your Reader in Mind

For a beginner copywriter, it is beneficial to view content as the website's salesperson. It is enormously important to outline and structure your content to be as helpful and informative as possible. Your content must address the gamut of possible questions and concerns your reader may have regarding your product, service, or message. List the benefits of your product, service, or message and provide information that addresses any questions or concerns you might have as a reader. Supply genuine, thought-provoking product information rather than hollow, stale slogans. Writing distinctly helpful and user-friendly content makes your page appealing to humans and search engines alike. Before writing any content, ask yourself some questions: What are the benefits of the product, message, or service? What concerns would I have as a consumer or reader? What is truly exceptional about this product? By answering these types of questions, you alleviate any confusion or apprehensions your reader may have regarding your product, increasing your chances of conversion. People and search engines alike value comprehensive, useful information, not slogans and vague appraisals.

Avoid Poor Grammar

Search engines value the elegance and accessibility of your writing. The search-engine spiders are aware that clumsy sentences and poor grammar are displeasing to human readers; therefore, your grammar should be of the highest caliber. Search engines tend to devalue any content containing awkward sentences, clichés, erroneous grammar, or writing considered aesthetically abrasive to a reader. By keeping your prose elegant and distinctive, you increase your website's chance of attaining high search-engine rankings. It is also important to keep your content accessible to the average reader. Content that is too academic or esoteric is going to confuse the average reader, costing the website potential conversions. Do not alienate the average reader by writing in a style more befitting to a doctoral dissertation than a web page. However, content that comes across as elementary is going to generate minimal excitement and make your site look unprofessional. The key to writing accessible yet impressive content is determining the level at which your target audience reads. Besides overly academic diction, the use of colloquial language, slang, and industry jargon also detracts from the universal accessibility of content, which may lead to poor organic rankings.

Write Useful and Informative Content

It is important that your content be informative, concise, and easy to navigate. Readers on the web have an exceptionally short attention span, so avoid verbosity in your ad copy. Write concisely and use headings, subheadings, bold type, and similar formatting that illustrate the information contained in each subsequent section of your page. Start all subheads, paragraphs, and bullet points with information-carrying words or action phrases that will attract users' attention while they are scanning down your content. Keep in mind that users visit your website with a specific objective in mind. Readily accessible information increases the reader's chances of achieving an objective in a timely fashion. Readers are more likely to purchase or subscribe to your product or service if you make it easy for them.

Using Bold-Type Headings

Provide bold-type headings that inform readers on the nature of each subsection, affording them an overview of the site's benefits at a glance. Furnishing readers with easily accessible, detailed information is the best way to keep them reading. Many inexperienced copywriters make the mistake of writing their material in one large block of content without headings that grab the reader's attention. Some readers are looking for specific information, and consider the task of reading the giant blocks of content to be too time-consuming.

Using Call-to-Action Statements

Present your readers with readily accessible call-to-action options such as *Sign Up Today* or *Register Here,* prompting them to act on the information you provide. Make your call-to-action prompts eye-catching, reminding readers that they can take action whenever they feel ready. Calls-to-action make your site's user experience more engaging, allowing users to read and act at their own pace. Do not assume that average readers are inclined to read on to the bottom of your site before they make a decision.

Write with an Original Voice

With practice, copywriting becomes a learned skill. Becoming a skilled writer includes paying special attention to the originality of the writing. Originality requires you to make certain that your voice is the most powerful component of the content. Even if you are writing content that is technical, you need to understand the material well enough to explain it to the reader with your own voice. Writing with an original voice makes your content valuable to search engines and naturally compelling to readers. Writing in a manner natural to you translates as natural to your audience.

Write Interesting Content in a Friendly Tone

Use a writing tone that captures your readers' attention and keeps them interested in your work. Employing a friendly tone in your writing results in a positive response from virtually all readers. A friendly tone and humor in your copy makes your website more personal and engaging. One of your main goals is to keep readers engaged long enough for them to read all the facts; the best way to accomplish this goal is to entertain while informing. Keep your content interesting and persuasive, and you will be pleased to find that not only people but also search engines will enjoy it. The vast majority of content that is ranked on the front page of major search engines also tends to be the content that is deemed most valuable and interesting to readers. Therefore, write quality content that people like, and search engines will rank it accordingly.

AVOID DUPLICATE CONTENT

Search engines penalize website owners that publish the exact or very similar content to that already published on the web. Therefore, it is imperative to avoid duplicate content issues and to focus on building content that is original. Instances of duplicate content arise in one of two primary ways: you copy someone else's content for use on your page, or someone else copies your content for use on

his or her page. Unfortunately, Google and other search engines are not able to easily decipher content ownership, so it is important to monitor your original content often to avoid potential penalties.

Fortunately, tools exist that allow you to search for instances of duplicate content. One of the most commonly used tools is Copyscape, located at www.copyscape.com.

Avoid Duplicate Content

1 Navigate to www.copyscape.com.

2 Type the URL of your website into Copyscape's search box.

3 Click Go.

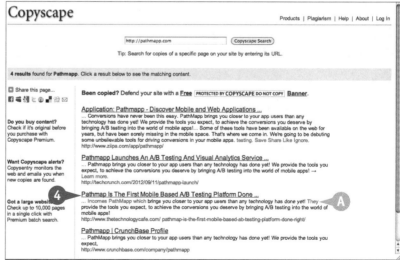

A The websites in which Copyscape found occurrences of duplicate content appear.

4 Click the identified website to view the duplicate content.

Note: *The discovery of duplicate content on your website prompts search engines to either omit your website completely from all search results, or place your content within the dreaded supplemental results. Supplemental results are not part of the main search results index and rarely, if ever, appear to a search-engine user. Getting your website kicked out of the index or placed within the supplemental results must be avoided.*

The page's content appears. Copyscape highlights certain items and/or blocks of content. The highlighted material is identical or nearly identical to content found on your page.

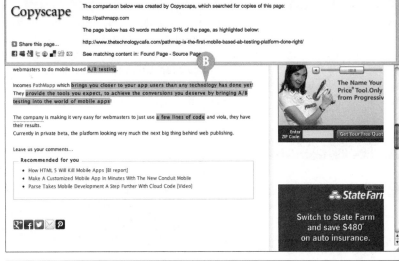

5 Navigate to www.copyscape.com/banners.php.

Copyscape allows you to generate free protected banners for your website.

Select a banner to add to your website from the available choices.

Note: *Search-engine algorithms do not have a good basis for determining who stole whose content. As a result, you may very well be the original author, but you may be penalized because Google's real concern is minimizing duplicate content, not arbitrating the rightful owner. Always be vigilant about duplicate content issues.*

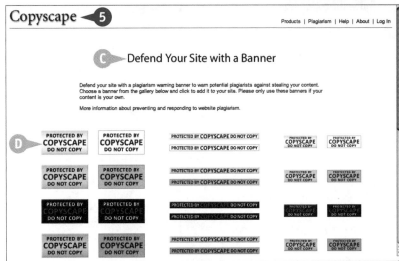

EXTRA

One of the most common forms of content theft occurs when content spammers create automated systems that steal content and simultaneously post it to so-called *Made-for-AdSense* websites. Made-for-AdSense, or MFA, websites attempt to monetize web traffic from contextual advertisements, usually from Google AdSense, by using unethical search-engine-optimization tricks, including using plagiarized content, which can temporarily result in top search-engine rankings before the perpetrator is eventually detected by search engines.

If your content was copied or is being misrepresented and you want to take action to fix it, you can submit a webspam report to Google at www.google.com/webmasters/tools/spamreport.

USING PROPER KEYWORD DENSITY

The goal of search-engine optimization is to make sure that your website ranks at the top of the search results when target keywords related to your product or service are typed into popular search engines as search queries. Using *proper keyword density* includes the strategic repetition of select, target keywords and the minimization of nontarget keywords throughout your content, so that search engines deem your website relevant to search queries that you want to rank for. By using available tools to maximize optimal keyword density, such as the Internet Marketing Ninjas' Keyword Density Analysis Tool, you can incorporate target keywords through your content without compromising the natural flow of the writing.

Using Proper Keyword Density

1. Navigate to www.internetmarket ingninjas.com/seo-tools/ keyword-density.

2. Type the URL of the website you want to analyze.

3. Click the Ninja Check button.

A. The keyword analysis of the website appears, broken down by one-keyword, two-keyword, and three-keyword phrases. This page displays up to ten of the top occurrences of the page's most dense keywords.

4. Click the Show/Hide link to see a full list of two-word phrases.

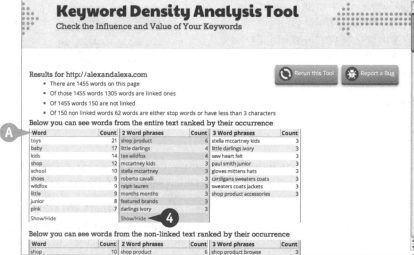

B Observe the full list of two-word phrases.

Note: *You can also expand the list of single keyword phrases.*

Below you can see words from the entire text ranked by their occurrence

Word	Count	2 Word phrases	Count	3 Word phrases	Count
toys	21	shop product	6	stella mccartney kids	3
baby	17	little darlings	4	little darlings ivory	3
kids	14	tee wildfox	4	sew heart felt	3
shop	12	mccartney kids	3	paul smith junior	3
school	10	stella mccartney	3	gloves mittens hats	3
shoes	9	roberto cavalli	3	cardigans sweaters coats	3
wildfox	9	ralph lauren	3	sweaters coats jackets	3
little	9	months months	3	shop product accessories	3
junior	8	featured brands	3		
pink	7	darlings ivory	3		
Show/Hide		heart felt	3		
		smith junior	3		
		sew heart	3		
		baby toddler	3		
		coats jackets	3		
		formal wear	3		
		sweaters coats	3		
		cardigans sweaters	3		
		product accessories	3		
		gloves mittens	3		
		mittens hats	3		
		toys gifts	3		
		pants t-shirts	3		
		sleepwear socks	3		
		outfits sets	3		
		paul smith	3		
		Show/Hide			

Below you can see words from the non-linked text ranked by their occurrence

Word	Count	2 Word phrases	Count	3 Word phrases	Count

5 To create another search, scroll down the page and locate the Run this tool again section.

6 Enter the URL of one of your competitors.

7 Click the Ninja Check button to observe a keyword density analysis of your competitor.

Note: *For more information on competitive keyword analysis, see Chapter 2.*

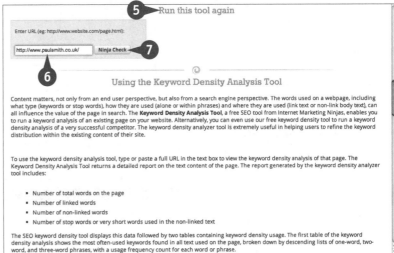

5 Run this tool again

Enter URL (eg: http://www.website.com/page.html):

[http://www.paulsmith.co.uk/] [Ninja Check] 7

6

Using the Keyword Density Analysis Tool

Content matters, not only from an end user perspective, but also from a search engine perspective. The words used on a webpage, including what type (keywords or stop words), how they are used (alone or within phrases) and where they are used (link text or non-link body text), can all influence the value of the page in search. The **Keyword Density Analysis Tool**, a free SEO tool from Internet Marketing Ninjas, enables you to run a keyword analysis of an existing page on your website. Alternatively, you can even use our free keyword density tool to run a keyword density analysis of a very successful competitor. The keyword density analyzer tool is extremely useful in helping users to refine the keyword distribution within the existing content of their site.

To use the keyword density analysis tool, type or paste a full URL in the text box to view the keyword density analysis of that page. The Keyword Density Analysis Tool returns a detailed report on the text content of the page. The report generated by the keyword density analyzer tool includes:

- Number of total words on the page
- Number of linked words
- Number of non-linked words
- Number of stop words or very short words used in the non-linked text

The SEO keyword density tool displays this data followed by two tables containing keyword density usage. The first table of the keyword density analysis shows the most often-used keywords found in all text used on the page, broken down by descending lists of one-word, two-word, and three-word phrases, with a usage frequency count for each word or phrase.

EXTRA

In the past, keyword density was a much more important aspect of search-engine optimization than it is today. Search-engine algorithms have improved tremendously and have become far more complex and much less transparent. Regardless, keyword density analysis should still be performed. If your keyword density analysis suggests that there are keywords that appear more frequently than the keywords you want the page to rank for, you should modify accordingly to focus on desired keywords.

As a rule of thumb, search algorithms apply more weight to the title of your web page than the density of the keywords on it. Therefore, your most important target keywords should be contained in your title and should also be dispersed throughout the content of your web page.

Latent semantic indexing allows the search engines to determine a page's relevance based upon its subject matter, rather than keyword density. Search engines consider a website's overall theme and then rank it based on topical relevance and authority, not on the density of its target keywords. You can construct your sentences and paragraphs using semantically linked words to help make your pages extremely relevant to your particular search terms. Covering as many thematically linked terms as possible helps establish high relevancy and a natural tone within your content.

Both Google and LSIKeywords.com offer tools to help you generate latent semantic keywords.

Using Latent Semantic Content

Google's Latent Semantic Tool

1 Navigate to www.google.com.

2 Type **~apple** as your search term.

A Note bolded terms such as *Apple, Macintosh,* and *Mac* appear.

Note: *Latent semantic content is an invaluable tool to use during the construction of your website. If a page in your website deals with Apple products, your website will benefit from covering subjects like Macs, Steve Jobs, iPads, iPhones, and iPods — terms synonymous with Apple.*

3 Type **~windows** as your search term.

B Note the bolded instances of *Windows* and *Microsoft* that appear.

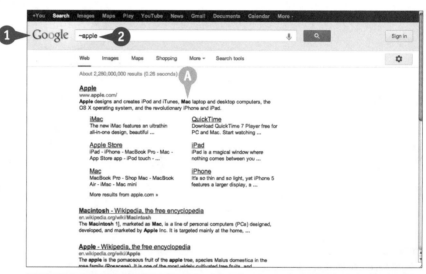

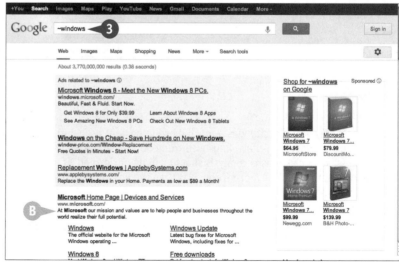

Using LSIKeywords.com

1. Navigate to http://lsikeywords.com.

2. Type **Facebook** as your search term.

3. Click Submit.

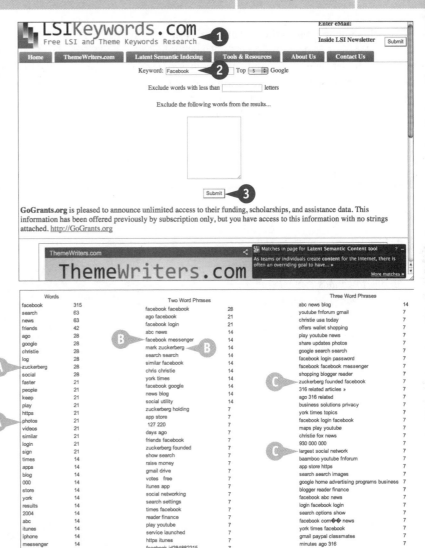

Note: *Results appear for one-word, two-word, and three-word phrases semantically related to the search term "Facebook."*

Ⓐ Note that the one-word phrases "zuckerberg" and "photos" are semantically related to the search term "Facebook."

Ⓑ Note that the two-word phrases "facebook messenger" and "mark zuckerberg" are semantically related to the search term "Facebook."

Ⓒ Note that the three-word phrases "zuckerberg founded facebook" and "largest social network" are semantically related to the search term "Facebook."

Note: *Once you identify semantically related keywords to your target keyword, you should include the identified keywords during the content-creation process.*

EXTRA

You should always mix up your anchor text when acquiring backlinks. Latent semantic indexing looks at the entire link profile of your website. If all your links are either one or two particular keywords or phrases, search engines may see this as unnatural, and your website may not rank well. For example, if your website deals with search marketing, but the only anchor text you use in backlinks is "search marketing," the search engines may detect that and penalize your website. This, along with using the same keyword over and over in your content, is often referred to as being overoptimized.

Keep Content Current

Search engines favor websites that have fresh content. Keeping your content current is fundamental and necessary to achieving and maintaining high search-engine rankings. Search engines consider fresh content to be of greater value than outdated content, penalizing websites that remain unchanged and rewarding websites that maintain fresh content.

One way to keep your content current is through Really Simple Syndication, or RSS. Integrating RSS feeds into your website requires moderate to advanced technical skills. The most common approach to integrating RSS feeds is using the programming language PHP.

Keep Content Current

① Navigate to www.freshcontent.net.

② Click Directory of Newsfeeds.

Note: *RSS technology allows you to subscribe to various content sources, such as relevant news and blog feeds, and then automatically post that content to your website. For example, you can use RSS to update your website daily with select content on subjects that deal directly with the theme of your website.*

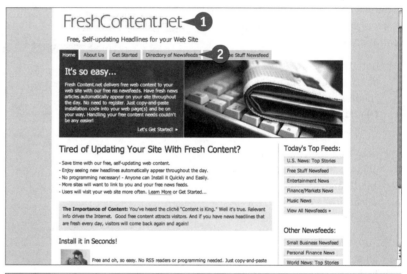

Ⓐ A variety of newsfeed categories are available for you to choose from.

③ Click a newsfeed that is relevant to the content of your website.

4 Scroll down the page, and copy the JavaScript code to the Clipboard.

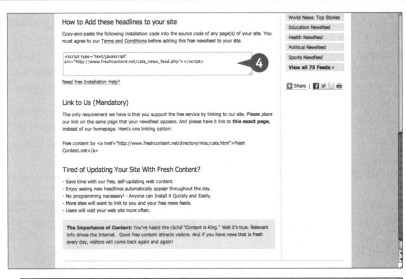

5 Paste the JavaScript code into your HTML wherever you want the FreshContent.net content to appear.

Note: *Keep in mind that although using content aggregation systems helps keep some of your website content fresh, content aggregation systems alone cannot guarantee your website a high ranking. Because RSS syndicates duplicate content, which can cause search engines to penalize your search-engine ranking, you also need to make weekly or monthly updates to the original content on each of your web pages. Another approach to keeping content fresh is to launch a company blog. A blog can serve several useful purposes, including keeping your visitors informed and educated, and allowing your website to build authority in the eyes of search engines.*

EXTRA

A plethora of free content aggregation systems is available. For example, just about every popular blog allows you to join its RSS feed, and other sources exist, such as Google News and Yahoo News. Free content aggregation provides a quick and easy approach to updating your website with fresh content, especially if the theme of your website is broad and not overly technical. If your website deals with very specific issues, such as medical services, programming, or aeronautics, you should consider a paid content aggregation service such as YellowBrix, located at www.yellowbrix.com.

OPTIMIZE NON-HTML DOCUMENTS

Beyond basic HTML files, search engines index other file formats, such as Microsoft Word, Microsoft Excel, Microsoft PowerPoint, Rich Text Format (RTF), and Adobe Portable Document Format (PDF) documents. If you choose to post non-HTML files to your website, you can optimize each document to improve the results when search engines index them.

The basic rule for whenever you attempt to optimize a non-HTML document for search-engine purposes is to make sure that it contains readable text. Images that contain text cannot be read and therefore are not properly indexed by search-engine spiders.

Sometimes you may want to convert HTML into PDF and other times PDF into HTML. HTMLDOC 1.8.27 is an easy-to-use tool that is available for download at www.htmldoc.org.

Optimize Non-HTML Documents

Convert HTML to PDF

1. Click Start → HTMLDOC.

2. In the Input tab, select Web Page.

3. To convert an HTML file located on a website, click Add URL.

   If you are converting an HTML file located on your computer, click Add Files.

4. Type the address of the website you want to convert to a PDF file.

   If you are converting an HTML file on your computer, browse to the file and click OK.

5. Click the Output tab.

6. Select an output path.

7. Select PDF as the output format.

8. Select output options and the compression level.

9. Click Generate, and HTMLDOC creates a PDF file in your selected output path.

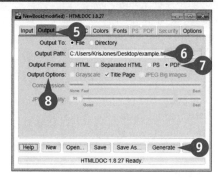

Convert PDF to HTML

1 Click Start ➜ HTMLDOC.

2 In the Input tab, select Book.

3 To convert a PDF file located on your computer, click Add Files.

If you are converting a PDF file located on a website, click Add URL.

4 To convert a PDF file on your computer, browse to the file and click OK.

If you are converting a PDF file located on a website, type the address.

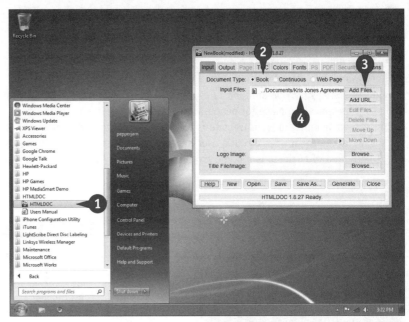

5 Click the Output tab.

6 Select an output path.

7 Select HTML as the output format.

8 Select output options.

9 Click Generate, and HTMLDOC creates an HTML file in your selected output path.

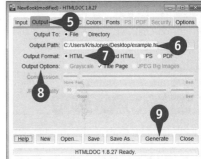

EXTRA

You can use PDF files to help your website generate leads. For example, you can set up your PDF files so that unregistered users can read only the first page or two of the file. If users want to read the remainder of the document, you can require them to submit contact information to you, such as an e-mail address, name, address, and anything else that you want to track. Also, because many search engines refuse or are unable to index very large PDF files, you can break the PDF into several separate files so that search engines will read and index them.

AN INTRODUCTION TO CREATING COMMUNITIES

Creating a community on your website is one of the most effective ways to keep your content fresh, and it also helps establish your site as an authority for your area of business. Moreover, communities help build trust and provide a venue for your visitors to become interested and educated about your products or services. Two of the primary approaches to building online communities are blogs and forums. Blogs provide an opportunity for you to position yourself as an authority, and also attract participation from your visitors by allowing them to comment and provide feedback on your blog posts. Forums provide an opportunity for multiple discussions to occur simultaneously around your area of business and stand as a meeting place for people who are interested in your products or services. Another very successful approach to building community on your website is to allow visitors to add reviews about your products. User reviews, blogs, and forums are exceptional ways to build user-generated contact on your website. Building large amounts of fresh content about your area of business is a prime strategy for building links and ranking well in the search-engine results.

This chapter explores different approaches and strategies for creating successful communities on your website.

Create a Blog with WordPress

WordPress is a popular blog software service that allows you to create weblogs quickly and easily. The product is easy to install and manage, and it is free to use. WordPress allows you to build a community by educating, entertaining, and providing useful information to the consumer through a blog. You can use your WordPress blog to educate your customers about the benefits of your products. Moreover, you can use your blog to share special offers and deals with your customers and to elicit feedback on how you can improve your business.

Create a Blog with Blogger

Similar to WordPress, Blogger is a free blog software service that allows you to quickly and easily create weblogs. There are pros and cons to using Blogger over WordPress. For example, with Blogger you can easily edit template layouts, styles, and colors, or install a third-party theme. With WordPress there is no template editing, and style sheet editing is available only as a paid upgrade. WordPress provides you with 3GB of image storage, and Blogger provides up to 1GB for free. If you intend to use a lot of high-resolution images and want to minimize your cost, WordPress may be a better option for you.

Create a Blog with Tumblr

Tumblr is an innovative blogging platform that enables users to post text, images, video, links, quotes, and audio to a short-form blog. Tumblr is similar in many respects to Twitter and Facebook because it includes the ability for users to "follow," as well as "like" or "reblog" other blogs on the site. Tumblr is often favored by social media bloggers over blog platforms such as WordPress and Blogger because of its customizability, ease of use, and social media attributes.

Write Search-Engine-Optimized Posts

If you are going to use your community as a way of generating traffic to your website, you should make sure that your blog and forum posts are search-engine optimized. The first thing you should do is use keyword research tools such as the Google AdWords Keyword Suggestion Tool to explore what your audience is searching for. You can utilize the keyword research tool to identify keywords that you want to target within your blog title, headlines, and posts. See Chapter 2 for more about keyword generation.

After you have identified your target keywords, you are ready to generate a blog post. You should highlight your target keywords in various ways, including adding them to headlines and using bold or italic font to make your keywords stand out. The benefit of search-engine-optimizing your blog posts is that when search engines index your website, you are more likely to rank for target keywords.

Make Your Blog Successful

One of the most successful approaches to getting your website to rank well in the organic search results is to create a blog. A blog allows you to continually provide fresh content on your website while building a community of readers who look to your site as an authority. Your blog does not necessarily need to be educational in nature. You may also want to entertain and reward your readers for being part of your community.

Making your blog successful requires a serious time commitment and is likely to require the resources of an expert on your particular area of business.

Create a Community with vBulletin

vBulletin is a community forum software program that lets your visitors interact, take part in discussions, ask questions, give answers, and express opinions, giving you an instant community. Unlike a blog, a community forum is more of a discussion board where members and forum moderators interact by posting questions and answers and discussing common problems. A forum encourages your visitors to return again and again by allowing interaction and information sharing.

Create a Community with phpBB

phpBB is a popular open source bulletin board software package written in the PHP programming language. Unlike vBulletin, phpBB is free. However, depending on your needs, phpBB can serve as acceptable entry-level community forum software and provide you with the ability to add user-generated content to your website.

Make Your Forum Successful

Creating a forum on your website provides an excellent opportunity for your visitors to become part of your website community. Because forums are ultimately message boards where people ask and answer questions, they can be a great place to refer a customer who has a question that may be shared by other members of the community. If a visitor has a question about the durability of a particular product or is unsure about one product over another, a forum provides a venue to get feedback and to generate interest in your products. At the same time, a forum is a great way to produce user-generated content on your area of business, which search engines tend to reward with increased rankings in the search results.

Add Reviews to Your Website

Similar to the effect of adding a blog or forum to your website, adding reviews to your website can have a positive impact on your search-engine rankings while enhancing the overall credibility and sales of your website. Reviews provide an opportunity for your website visitors to learn from previous customers while providing you with fresh user-generated content, which search engines love.

User reviews have the same selling power as testimonials. If you offer a product or service, other users' reviews can help increase sales. People find comfort knowing that others have used the product or service with good results. Although you may be concerned that users may provide negative reviews of your products, the positive effect of having user reviews on your website far outweighs the risk of an occasional negative review.

CREATE A BLOG WITH WORDPRESS

WordPress, located at http://wordpress.com, offers free blog software that allows you to quickly and easily create weblogs and manage content. A *weblog*, also known as a *blog*, is an online journal that is frequently updated by an author and typically allows readers to interact by providing comments after each blog is published. Although individuals have traditionally used blogs to entertain and share opinions and expertise, businesses also effectively

use blogs to build community through educating, entertaining, and providing useful information to the consumer. Hosting a blog through WordPress allows you to interact with your website visitors and customers. A blog creates a community on your website that you can use for various purposes to increase website traffic and improve customer relations.

Create a Blog with WordPress

1 Navigate to http://wordpress.com.

2 Click Get Started and follow the steps to set up an account.

3 Enter your e-mail address.

4 Select a username and enter a password.

5 Choose an address for your blog. You can change the wordpress.com address later.

Note: *For maximum SEO benefit, it is recommended that you host your blog on your own domain.*

A WordPress provides the option of registering a new domain as part of the sign-up process. Only select this option if you do not already have a domain name reserved for your blog.

B WordPress offers multiple paid upgrade options. Upgrading from a free account may be necessary if you intend to host your website on WordPress since there are limits on image storage and customization.

C Click the Create Blog button, which is located at the bottom of the sign-up form.

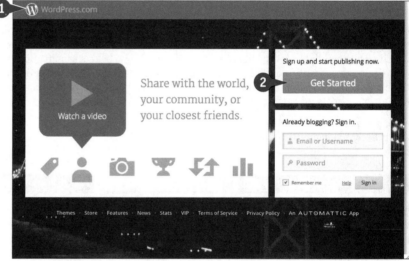

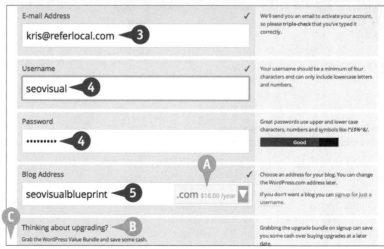

6 Log in to your WordPress account and click the Add New link under the Posts option to create your first post.

D WordPress offers a QuickPress option, which has limited functionality but allows you to quickly create and publish a post.

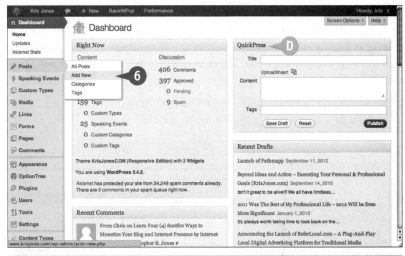

7 Write a title and the body for your post.

Note: *See Chapter 3 for more information on writing search-engine-optimized titles and content.*

E The permalink WordPress plug-in allows you to search-engine optimize your blog URL.

8 Click Publish.

Your post is now live.

9 Click Preview to see your post.

EXTRA

To host your blog, your web host must support the execution of PHP scripts. PHP is the programming language in which WordPress is written, and thus for WordPress to run at all, your web host must support it. Another technical requirement is that your web host must include a MySQL database engine because WordPress stores its data and all your blog entries in a special file, called a *database,* which allows easy and fast retrieval of content for your users.

WordPress also allows you to install numerous plug-ins that you can use to enhance your blog usability and search-engine optimization. For example, a popular usability plug-in that reduces comment spam is Spam Karma, located at http://code.google.com/p/spam-karma.

CREATE A BLOG WITH BLOGGER

Blogger, located at www.blogger.com, is completely free blog software offered by Google that allows you to quickly and easily create weblogs. Blogger is a competitor of WordPress, and there are pros and cons to using one over the other.

With Blogger you can easily edit template layouts, styles, and colors, or install a third-party theme. With WordPress,

template editing is not available, and style sheet editing is available only as a paid upgrade. Therefore, while Blogger is free, you may have to pay an additional fee with WordPress, depending on exactly what customizations you want to make.

Create a Blog with Blogger

1 Log in to your Google account and navigate to www.blogger.com.

Note: *If you do not already have a Google account, you need to create one by navigating to www.google.com/accounts.*

2 Click New Blog.

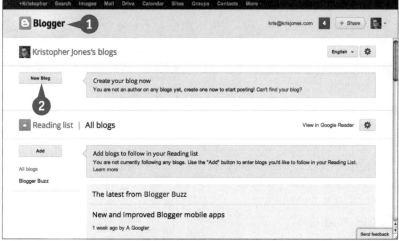

3 Write a title for your new blog.

4 Select a name to represent your blog.

Note: *Your title will also be your title tag, so make sure you write a search-engine optimized title. Your subdomain should best represent the overall theme or subject matter of your blog. See Chapter 3 for more information about writing optimized titles and domain names.*

5 Choose a template for your blog.

Note: *Keep in mind that you should host your own blog and customize it to fit the look and feel of your website.*

6 Click Create blog.

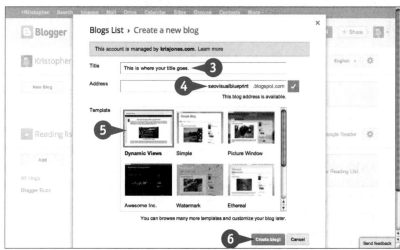

7 Click the Create New Post icon.

8 Add your post title.

9 Add your post content.

A Blogger allows you to easily embed pictures or video by clicking the associated icon.

Note: Blogger provides only 1GB for free. If storage is still a problem, you can choose a free image storage service such as Flickr, located at www.flickr.com, which allows you to upload 100MB of images a month.

10 Click Publish to publish your post.

11 Click View blog to view your post.

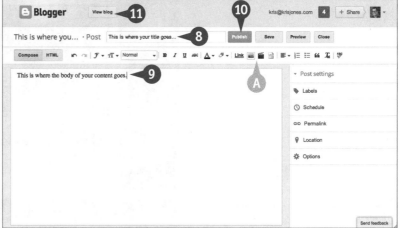

One of the biggest challenges with managing your own blog is limiting the amount of comment spam you receive. Although you can moderate and review comments prior to them being published, you may prefer a solution that automatically publishes comments but reduces or eliminates comment spam. If you want an automated solution, you can use a *CAPTCHA,* install anti-spam software, and require users who comment to log in. A CAPTCHA is typically an image showing warped or obscured letters and numbers and is used to reduce robotic comment spam by requiring the user to type a series of letters and numbers prior to submitting a comment.

CREATE A BLOG WITH TUMBLR

Tumblr, located at www.tumblr.com, is an innovative blogging platform that allows users to post text, images, video, links, quotes, and audio to a short-form blog, also called a *tumblelog*. Tumblr includes many of the attributes popular social networking sites such as Twitter and Facebook offer, including the ability for users to "follow"

other users and see their posts together on their dashboard, as well as "like" or "reblog" other blogs on the site.

Tumblr is one of the top ten most-visited sites in the United States and generates nearly 200 million monthly users. One advantage of Tumblr over other blogging platforms is that it allows you to share short-form content, such as videos and pictures, very easily.

Create a Blog with Tumblr

1 Navigate to www.tumblr.com and log in using your e-mail address and password.

Note: Unlike WordPress and Blogger, Tumblr was built to be a highly social platform. For example, inherent to the platform is the ability for you to follow other Tumblr blogs and interact with those blogs from your blog.

2 Find people you know on Tumblr and follow their blogs by clicking the Facebook or Gmail buttons.

A People who you know who use Tumblr will populate here and you will be encouraged to follow their blogs.

3 Click Next.

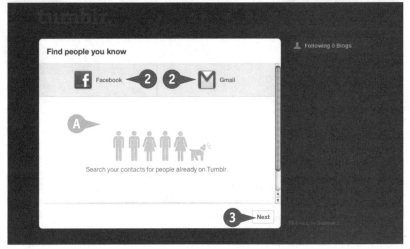

B Note the different types of posts you can create, including Text, Photo, Quote, Link, Chat, Audio, and Video posts.

C Tumblr allows you to upload an avatar, or profile picture, to your Tumblr blog.

4 Click the Photo button to create a photo post.

5 Choose an image file as part of your photo post.

D If you do not already have the photo you want to share saved to your computer, you can alternatively share the image using a URL or you can take a photo from your computer or mobile device.

6 Enter a caption. Captions show up directly under the photo and are used to describe the picture.

7 Click Create post. Your photo post is now published.

Note: *To create another post, scroll to the top of your post and select the type of blog you would like to create.*

EXTRA

Tumblr tends to be favored by social media bloggers because of its customizability, ease of use, and social media attributes. For example, Tumblr offers a Like button that allows you to tell another Tumblr user that you like her content. The Tumblr "like" functionality is similar to the popular "like" feature provided by Facebook that allows you to easily tell a Facebook friend that you like the comment that he posted on Facebook. The more "likes" that you have on a given Tumblr post, the more your post is perceived by the Tumblr blogger community as popular.

Writing search-engine-optimized blog posts is important if you want your content to rank well in search engines. You should familiarize yourself with how your blog software formats your content and make adjustments where necessary for search-engine optimization.

Use keyword research tools such as the Google AdWords Keywords Tool, located at https://adwords.google.com/select/KeywordToolExternal, to explore what your audience is searching for. The purpose of using a keyword research tool is to identify keywords that you want to target within your blog title, headlines, and posts. See Chapter 2 for more about keyword generation.

For example, if you are writing a post about a specific kind of acne treatment, you should perform keyword research around that broad topic and select five to ten keywords to include throughout the body of the post. All the keywords you select should be related to the topic of your post.

Write Search-Engine-Optimized Posts

① Navigate to http://wordpress.com and log in using your username and password.

② Select Add New under the Posts menu on the left navigation bar.

③ Enter your title in the field below the Add New Post heading.

Note: *The primary topic of your post should be included in your title tag and within any post headlines.*

④ To make a piece of text bold or italic, select the text and click the corresponding button in the toolbar.

Note: *Search engines recognize bold and italic text. For SEO purposes you should strategically bold or italicize keywords that you are trying to rank for. However, your post should ultimately appear natural to your readers and to the search engines. Do not just simply stuff keywords where they do not belong.*

⑤ To make a text a hyperlink, select the text and click the chain button.

6 Enter the URL you want to link to in the field labeled URL.

7 Enter the title of the URL. The title will show up when a user scrolls over the URL.

8 Select the Open link in a new window/tab check box if you would like a new window to open when someone clicks on your link.

9 Click Add Link.

Your link is now included in your blog post.

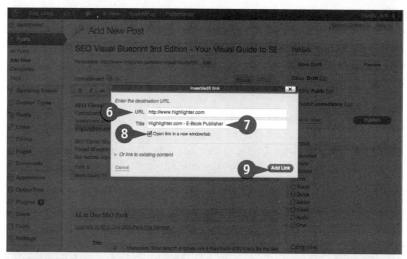

Ⓐ To insert pictures or video, click the Add Media button.

10 Drag and drop image or video files from your computer or click Select Files. Save the image.

Ⓑ You can also select media by providing a specific URL or from the WordPress Media Library.

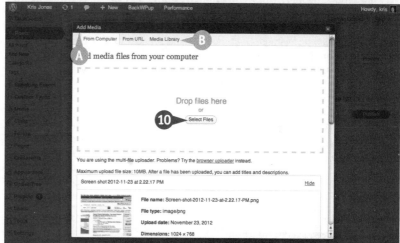

Ⓒ Your new blog post is now visible on your blog.

EXTRA

One way to generate a lot of links back to your blog is through a strategy called link baiting. *Link baiting* is when you specifically construct a post by using creative and sometimes radical hooks. A *hook* is a type of plot device typically used in screenwriting and literature to quickly capture the attention of the reader. The most common kinds of hooks include informational, news, humor, evil or malicious, and tool hooks.

115

Creating a blog is one of the most effective ways to get your website to rank well in the organic search results. A blog allows you to easily produce fresh content on your website, which will attract readers and help to establish your website as an authority for search-engine ranking purposes. Moreover, you can easily install social sharing buttons from popular social networks such as Facebook, Twitter, and Google+ to make all your content shareable by your readers. Content that entertains or answers common questions that your readers have is more likely to be shared on social media and linked to by other websites.

Keep in mind that creating a successful blog requires a serious commitment of time and resources. Although you can launch a blog for free through blog software vendors such as WordPress or Blogger, you will likely need to have a web host that can handle your traffic, server, and database demands. Expect your blog to be a significant distraction from your normal course of business. Writing interesting and useful blog posts requires a significant amount of time. In many cases, you must perform some research to back up or support your writing, and you may also need to request permission if you want to use particular images or screenshots in your work. In short, remember that launching a blog requires your absolute commitment for it to be successful.

Using Experienced Writers with Industry Knowledge

Your blog should be maintained by a high-level individual at your business who understands your products and services very well. This person does not need to be an executive-level person, but should be someone with enough experience with your products to come across as educated and knowledgeable. If your goal is to use your blog as a resource for others in your industry, make sure that all the claims that you make are factual and that you are not questioned about the authenticity of your writing.

Using an Administrator

Your blog should have an administrator. An administrator acts as a moderator by approving or declining comments and manages the overall goals of your community. For example, you may want your administrator to provide perks to those members who comment frequently. Recognizing your most active members is a great way to keep those members coming back and to build community. Expert blogger Jeremy Schoemaker of Shoemoney. com provides a great example of building community: Shoemoney.com recognizes the ten most frequent commenters by placing the members' website names with their links on the www. shoemoney.com home page. Because most of Shoemoney's readers are from the SEO community, a link on Shoemoney's home page is highly valued.

Hold Contests and Giveaways

One way of drumming up interest in your blog is to periodically hold contests or giveaways. For example, you can create a blog post in the form of a poll that asks your readers to guess what your top-selling product will be for any given week. Each guess counts as one entry in the contest. You can select the winner at random from the correct answers and give the top-selling product or some other incentive as a prize. Holding contests keeps your readers interested in your blog and provides incentive for them to talk about your business and frequently visit your website.

Offer RSS Technology

Another approach to getting people to frequently follow your blog is to offer your content through Really Simple Syndication, or RSS. RSS allows your readers to keep up with your blog automatically, which is easier than checking your blog randomly for new content. The most popular blog feed management provider is Google FeedBurner, which is a free service located at http://feedburner.google.com. Once you join Google FeedBurner and add a Google FeedBurner icon to your website, your readers can easily join your RSS feed. For example, via the Google FeedBurner blog feed management system, your readers can elect to receive an e-mail notification every time you write a new blog post. The e-mail contains either a summary of your content or the full text with a link to your website.

Break News or Piggyback News

Another way to attract new readers to your blog is by breaking news or piggybacking a news story that affects your area of expertise. For example, you can use your blog to talk about exciting news that is happening at your company. You can also provide an interpretation or a summary of a popular news story that occurs within your industry. If possible, you should spin the story by making some predictions about what the news means for your industry or why the news is good or bad. Remember that your goal is to come across as a credible authority in your field, so you should make sure that your opinions are substantive and not entirely speculative.

Interview Experts

There are several strategies that you can use to recruit new readers to your blog. One of the most effective ways to get new readers interested in your work is to interview experts and other well-known people associated with your particular industry. You should ask questions that are provocative as well as interesting, including questions about your interviewee's personal life. For example, if your business is in the manufacturing industry, a provocative question might include something about why most manufacturers have not taken proactive steps to control water and air pollution. A softer approach might be to ask the expert about the pros and cons of offshore manufacturing. Asking the expert about family and favorite pastimes is another way of making your interview personable and attractive to your readers.

Participate on Social Media Websites

A proven effective approach to marketing your blog is through participation on social media websites such as Facebook, Twitter, Google+, and others. For example, if you use images on your website, you should also upload those images to Flickr and Pinterest, which are popular photo-sharing websites. If your blog post is especially provocative, you should definitely make sure one of your readers submits it to Reddit, a popular social news website that can have a profound impact on your website traffic if the Reddit community embraces your content. Submitting your blog to Technorati is another great way to market it. Technorati is a popular blog search engine that millions of potential readers visit every day to find interesting and informative content. See Chapters 10 and 13 for more about social media websites and Technorati, respectively.

Making your blog successful is achievable if you are willing to dedicate the requisite time, energy, and creativity to making it work. In addition, a successful blog helps you to promote your products or services and increases the likelihood that other people will link to your website, which helps to improve your organic search-engine rankings.

VBulletin is community-forum software that gives you the ability to create a community that lets your visitors interact, take part in discussions, ask questions, give answers, and express opinions. Unlike a blog, a community forum is more of a discussion board where members and forum moderators interact by posting questions and answers and discussing common problems. A forum encourages your visitors to return again and again by allowing interaction and information sharing.

vBulletin is powerful, scalable, and fully customizable forum software. vBulletin is easy to install, user friendly, and easy for new members to learn to use. vBulletin has been written using the web's fastest-growing scripting language, PHP, and is complemented with a highly efficient, ultrafast back-end database engine built using MySQL.

Create a Community with vBulletin

1 Navigate to https://www. vbulletin.com/purchases and order your copy of vBulletin.

Note: *One of the clear benefits of vBulletin is that the software is search-engine friendly. Controlling the meta tags for each page of your forum is done through the easy-to-use vBulletin admin panel.*

2 Once you are logged in to your forum, select Styles & Templates.

3 Click Style Manager to customize the look of your forum or to select a template.

A The Style Manager provides you with multiple options to download or import specific stylistic templates.

Note: *You can get free skins and different forum style sheets at www. vbulletin-faq.com/skins-styles.htm. Skins are preselected template designs that allow you to change the look and feel of your forum or website. Make sure that your forum's look and feel are consistent with the look and feel of your website. You should also set up the forum on the domain of your website, such as www.example.com/ forum or forum.example.com.*

4 Select FAQ.

5 Select Add New FAQ Item.

B The FAQ Manager provides you with the ability to associate FAQs with existing parent-level categories and to define the answers to specific questions, such as rules on forum etiquette.

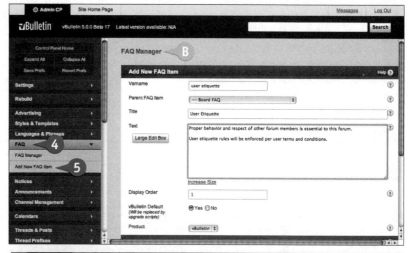

6 Select Threads & Posts.

C The Thread Manager provides you with the ability to delete or move threads or posts.

Note: *Forum structure is very important for SEO purposes. For example, it is best practice to split post topics and threads to make certain conversations are focused and are more likely to rank high on search engines. See Chapters 4 and 5 for more information and tips on proper website structure.*

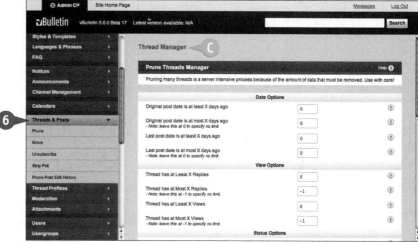

EXTRA

One of the steps that you should take to prevent search-engine spiders from visiting private areas of your forums is to create a robots.txt file. See Chapter 5 for more about robots.txt files. A private area of your website may be an area that is accessible only to paid members, or an area where you have concerns about search engines indexing duplicate content.

Here is an example of the code you can upload to your public_html directory to prevent private pages from being indexed:

```
User-agent: *
Disallow: /forums/memberlist.php
```

A complete list of code that you can upload to your public_html directory is located at www.vbulletin-faq.com/optimize-vbulletin-server.htm. If you use something other than /forums/ for your forums directory, adjust the paths accordingly.

CREATE A COMMUNITY WITH PHPBB

PhpBB is a popular open-source bulletin-board software package written in the PHP programming language. Unlike vBulletin, phpBB is free. However, depending on your needs, phpBB can serve as acceptable entry-level community forum software and provide you with the ability to add user-generated content to your website.

phpBB offers a large and highly customizable set of key features, including the ability to implement forum modifications and style changes. Because phpBB is open source, there is a large range of existing modifications that have been written by other phpBB users and programmers, which you may find useful.

Create a Community with phpBB

1. Navigate to www.phpbb.com/downloads.

2. Click Download Latest (.zip) to download the latest version of phpBB.

Note: phpBB has an easy-to-use administration panel and a user-friendly installation process, which allows you to have your basic forum set up in minutes. However, if you want to customize your forum, you can expect the process to take much longer, and it may require moderate-to-advanced expertise with PHP, CSS, HTML, and MySQL.

3. Navigate to www.diabetescommunity.dlife.com/go/forum/viewboard to view a complete phpBB forum community.

Note: This phpBB forum is highly developed and provides a good example of what is possible with phpBB.

Ⓐ dLife has used phpBB to create numerous subforums and subtopics of diabetes detection and prevention. For example, dLife community members can share photos and join groups.

4. Click Photos.

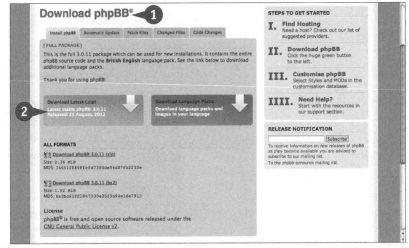

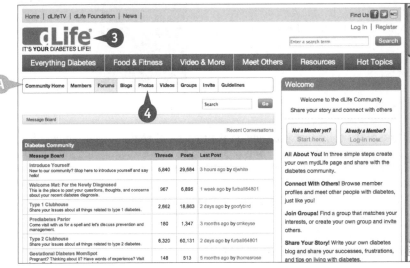

B dLife forum members are able to browse through photos of people and families affected by diabetes.

C phpBB allows you to customize your photo section so that users can search by keywords or various filters.

Note: See Chapter 13 for tips on optimizing images for SEO.

5 Click Groups.

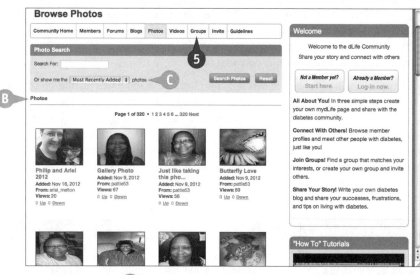

D phpBB allowed dLife to create a section of its forum dedicated to groups. Groups allow you to make content creation specific and tailored, which is a fundamental best practice of SEO.

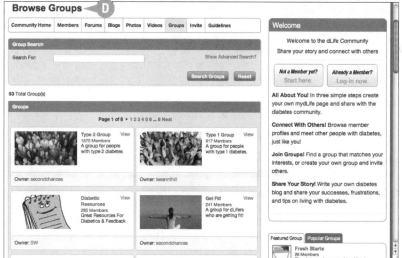

EXTRA

HotScripts, located at www.hotscripts.com, is a popular Internet directory that compiles and disseminates web programming-related resources and opinions. You can use HotScripts when you are exploring the pros and cons of different available forum and community software. Through HotScripts, you can access user reviews from a variety of current and former phpBB and vBulletin users. Moreover, HotScripts allows users to provide a rating on a one-to-five scale of user satisfaction with each forum. Ratings and reviews are broken down by date because often forum software vendors provide regular updates to improve the software based on user comments, so older reviews may not be relevant.

A community forum provides you with the ability to better communicate and interact with your website visitors, while enabling your users to generate ample amounts of relevant content. Because the content generated by your users is likely to be fresh and substantial, a community forum is a good way to rank higher in the search engines. Creating a community forum has numerous potential benefits.

Having a community forum encourages user interaction and participation on your website. You can use your forum as a tool to communicate with your visitors frequently and closely. For example, your forum is a great place to refer visitors who have specific questions about your products or services, including the benefits of selecting one product over another. In addition, if you find that your customers tend to ask the same question over and over, you can use the forum as a place to offer a comprehensive response. Your forum could also be a place where you proactively pose answers to questions you know your customers are going to have based on a policy decision. For example, if you must increase shipping charges, you can use your forum to provide details on why you made that decision.

Allow Users to Post Questions

Most community forums allow users to post customer-service-related questions to be answered by a forum moderator or by other members. This is a great way to reduce the demand typically placed on your customer service team because one customer's questions or concerns are likely to be shared by others. Moreover, if you have a moderator control the forum, you will be made aware of a problem and can deal with it quickly before it becomes more widespread and difficult to manage.

Evaluate Consumer Feedback

When you have a forum, you can understand more about your visitors by reading the conversations and discussions between them. Your visitors are likely to talk about your products, services, and website, which is hopefully a good thing. Regardless of whether it is good or bad, consumer feedback can be invaluable and can help you market your products or services more effectively. Keep in mind that the idea of having a forum on your website does not solely have to be about promoting your products and services. Equally valuable is the information that you can get from your customers to improve your overall website initiatives.

Optimize for Search Engines

One of the clearest benefits to having a community forum is that the content created on the forum helps you rank higher in the search engines. The primary reason that forums rank well within search engines is that they tend to contain fresh, concentrated content. Content on forums is typically focused on a very specific niche. By allowing your members to express opinions and share expertise on your particular area of business, you are communicating to Google and other search engines that you are an information hub. In this way, existing members keep coming back to participate on your forum and hopefully buy your products, and you also create content that ranks well in the search engines, thereby generating new users for your website.

Dedicate Requisite Time and Resources

Making your forum successful requires a substantial dedication of time. However, you can have your existing customer service team or a key employee or two help moderate the forum. In addition, once your forum is established and a few key members emerge based on frequency of participation, you can ask them to help moderate the forum. In general, you need not spend more than 10 to 15 hours per week managing the forum, especially if you have active members looking after the board and providing responses to other members. However, if you want to be proactive and post questions before a member asks them, you may need to dedicate more time to managing the board.

Conduct Contests or Giveaways

One way of generating participation on your forum is to periodically hold contests or giveaways. For example, you can give away a $100 iTunes gift card to the person who submits the most compelling testimonial about your products or services. Another idea might be to provide a giveaway like a logo T-shirt or mug whenever someone on your forum exceeds a certain number of posts. Many successful forums offer active members milestone awards. As mentioned earlier, one way of rewarding your most active members is by giving them moderator status. Moderator status is usually designated by an icon or some other symbol that notes the status of the member.

Set Rules

To create a successful forum, you need to have very specific rules about what is and is not allowed. You may decide that the forum is a place where you allow members to promote their own services. For example, you should have a policy that disallows or minimizes members from posting self-serving links to their websites for SEO purposes. Moreover, you may want to have a policy that forbids competitors from coming to your board and posting advertising messages or maliciously stirring rumors or posting false information. Finally, a forum is supposed to be a place where the community helps to set rules and standards. Therefore, you should consider asking your most active members what rules and policies they think should be implemented on your forum in order for it to attract new members and provide existing members with valuable information.

Ask Friends and Colleagues to Post Questions and Comments

When you first launch your forum, ask your friends and employees to post on it. Your employees can start by posting common questions and concerns shared frequently by your customers. For example, you can start a forum post around what products have sold best during the holiday season. Your friends and employees can simply respond with their opinions and you can step in with the answer based on your experiences. You can also use your first few forum posts to ask members what they want to know more about and how you can best use the forum to help them. Finally, your first few forum posts could be on topics about which you are interested in requesting feedback from customers. For example, you can pose questions about desired shipping methods or experiences with packaging.

Share Information about New Products

Probably the most effective use of a forum if you have an e-commerce website is to share information about new products as well as to inform members about promotions and special incentives. For example, you may provide an exclusive percentage-off offer to all your members or a special free-shipping coupon to active members of your forum.

Regardless of your approach, a forum is a great place to keep your customers interested in your products and informed about special deals and offers.

ADD REVIEWS TO YOUR WEBSITE

Adding reviews on your e-commerce website can have a positive impact on your search-engine rankings while enhancing the overall credibility and sales of your website. Reviews provide an opportunity for your website visitors to learn from previous customers, while providing you with fresh user-generated content, which search engines love.

Adding the ability for users to review products on your website is an effective approach to keeping your content fresh. Each user review adds original content about your product or service to your website that is often keyword-rich. User-generated content is free and tends to be favored by search engines because it is considered authentic.

Add Reviews to Your Website

Add Reviews to Your Website

1 Navigate to www.review-script.com/purchase/browse_products.php.

Note: *User reviews have the same selling power as testimonials. Although you may be concerned that users may provide negative reviews of your products, the positive effect of having user reviews on your website far outweighs the risk of an occasional negative review.*

2 Select a review script from the available paid download options and install the script.

3 Observe reviews from the installed review script.

A Visitors are able to rate products from one to five stars.

B Visitors are able to write reviews at the product level.

Note: *A user who may be considering purchasing a product on your site may check back frequently to read new reviews to help in the decision-making process. The more active your users are on your website, the more likely they are to find your site credible and useful, and the more likely the user is to become a customer.*

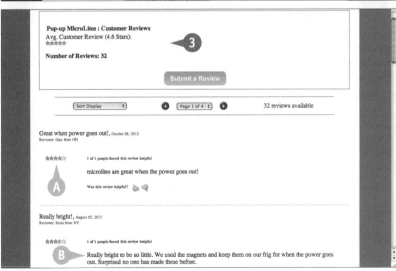

Download EasyReviewScript

1 Navigate to www.easyreviewscript.com/features.asp and download EasyReviewScript.

Ⓐ EasyReviewScript comes with a sample database and MySQL table create files. The entire script is fully customizable so you can change the look and layout as much as you want to match your site.

Ⓑ EasyReviewScript is easy to install and requires very little configuration and support. You can customize EasyReviewScript to the look and feel of your site using HTML or CSS, which is essential if you intend to add your forum community to an existing website.

2 View the EasyReviewScript product page example.

Ⓒ Users click the Rate/Review It button to go to a product review page.

Note: *EasyReviewScript allows your visitors to rate and review products, pictures, articles, and more. EasyReviewScript also allows you to log the IP address of each reviewer so you know where the reviews are coming from.*

EXTRA

Review-Script.com uses a PHP script with a MySQL database back end. If you prefer working with ASP instead of PHP, you can use EasyReviewScript v1.0, located at www.easyreviewscript.com. Both Review-Script and EasyReviewScript require only a basic understanding of ASP or PHP and MySQL. In addition, a basic level of HTML is required during installation and is necessary if you want to make significant alterations to the appearance of the script. You can customize EasyReviewScript to the look and feel of your site using HTML or CSS, which is essential if you intend to add your forum community to an existing website.

AN INTRODUCTION TO BUILDING LINKS

In a fraction of a second, Google's search algorithm computes how many websites link to your website and the value of each individual link. Google automatically performs this process millions of times every day: Google believes that calculating links and taking into consideration such things as what those links say, along with the quality of the websites they come from, is an effective method of determining a website's authority. Google partly ranks websites based on how authoritative they are in their respective markets. Delivering relevant results and determining authority is the foundation of the Google search engine.

In short, if a lot of quality websites link to your website, you are probably doing well in Google's organic, or nonpaid, results. However, if you have just a few links, you are probably scouring resources to figure out what you can do to improve your search-engine rankings. This chapter presents a step-by-step guide on how to effectively build links to your website so that Google and other search engines will determine that your website is an authority and thereby give it a good ranking in the organic search results.

Evaluate Competition

The first step to effectively building links is to evaluate your competition. What works for your strongest competitors can also work for you. At this early stage of the link-building process, your goal should be to build the foundation for an effective search-engine-optimization business plan. You should take evaluating competition seriously and spend the requisite time necessary to rank your competition and take advantage of their success.

Evaluate Potential Linking Partners

Not all links are created equally, so you should evaluate each potential linking partner for quality. You can do this by analyzing numerous link-quality factors such as the age of the domain. By focusing on quality links, the major search engines are more likely to recognize you as a quality contributor to your website's subject matter.

Gather Link Intelligence with Open Site Explorer

Open Site Explorer is a link analysis tool that provides basic or advanced intelligence of the links pointing to a particular website. When you visit a website home page URL, Open Site Explorer allows you to view your link data in greater detail, including the number of links pointing to a particular website. Open Site Explorer offers a wide variety of settings that you can use to view your link data for greater insight.

Acquire Quality Links

You can save yourself a measurable amount of time by approaching link building from the standpoint of building quality links versus building a large quantity of links. Too often, website owners believe that they need thousands of links to rank well in the search engines. That is simply not true, regardless of which vertical, or industry, your website is in. For optimal success, your approach should be dictated by quality over quantity.

Developing the skill set required to quickly evaluate potential link partners includes learning how to identify the age of a domain, the uniqueness of content, and the potential for incoming traffic. Evaluating potential link partners for quality and focusing on those quality links is a key part of link building, and gives you an opportunity to focus on some of the important factors that search engines take into consideration when determining the quality of the websites that link to your website.

Using Effective Anchor Text

Once you have identified potential link partners, determine the anchor text to use for each link. This part of the Google algorithm focuses not on how many links you have pointing back to your website, but on what those links say. Approaching the rest of the link-building process with a list of keywords that you want to use as anchor text is essential to your link-building success. You should use a variety of anchor text throughout your link building to ensure that the search engines can determine the overall theme of your site.

Content Marketing with Guest Blogging

Content marketing with guest blogging is publishing content on other websites to build your brand and build links to your site. To use this brand building and link-building method, you need to create guest blogging content and publish it on the host's website.

Content Marketing with Infographics

When you do content marketing using infographics, you are brand building and link building with graphically represented information. The infographic acts as a linkable asset that you can promote to attract mentions and build links to your website.

Encourage Community Participation

Participating in communities such as blogs and forums that allow you to post a link back to your website is a fun and effective strategy for generating website traffic and building links. However, keep in mind that your participation on blogs and forums should be substantive and relevant. Although commenting on relevant blogs and forums seems tedious, it is one of the quickest approaches to building links and also gives you the opportunity to learn more about what people in your industry are talking about. Participating in these conversations not only allows you the opportunity to increase your own website traffic and search-engine rankings, but also it can help you learn how to grow your business in other ways.

Request One-Way Links

Another method for building links is to request one-way links directly from websites. This involves screening potential website linking partners for quality and then sending a link request through e-mail. These recipients may not have ever considered linking to your website, and contacting them could potentially give you the opportunity to acquire high-quality links for a very low price.

EVALUATE COMPETITION

One of the most effective ways to find quality potential link partners is to mimic the efforts of successful competitors. What works for competitors can also work for you. Any web page that links to a competitor is a candidate to link to your web page as well.

Because high-quality inbound links play a large role in Google's organic ranking algorithm, you should create

a list of web pages that link to your top competitors. First, identify your top competitors. Focus on pages that target the same audience you target. Then, find out where competitor links come from. Bing Webmaster Tools offers a free link source you can leverage for this research. Lastly, attempt to acquire high-quality competitor links.

Evaluate Competition

Note: This task uses the website ReferLocal.com as an example.

1. Navigate to www.bing.com/toolbox/webmaster.

2. Sign up for a free Bing Webmaster Tools account.

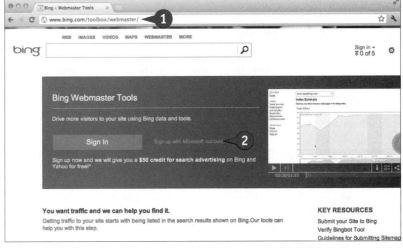

3. In the sidebar menu, click Diagnostics & Tools.

4. When the sidebar menu expands, click Link Explorer.

128

5 Enter the URL you would like to see backlink data for.

6 Click Explore.

Ⓐ Filter by site allows you to see backlinks from only a specific site.

Ⓑ Anchor text allows you to filter backlink data to show only the backlinks with requested anchor text.

Ⓒ Scope allows you to specify if you want to see backlink data for a domain or URL.

Ⓓ Additional query only shows pages that link to the specified URL that also rank for the entered search term.

Ⓔ Click the Source drop-down list to choose backlink data for the URL or domain.

7 Click Export to export the results into a spreadsheet.

Ⓕ Click the icon next to title instances in the title column to navigate to the URL page in your browser.

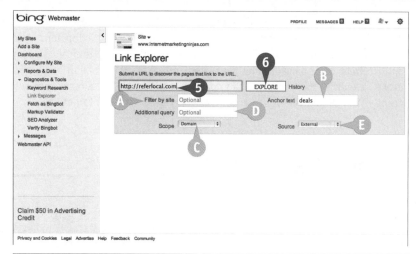

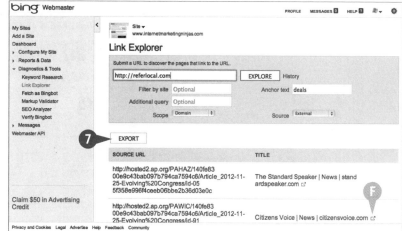

EXTRA

Bing shows you only a small sampling of the total number of incoming links, but you can utilize the sorting options to identify high-quality candidates for competitor-based link prospecting research. You can deepen your backlink prospecting by examining the backlinks to pages that link to your competitor's backlinks.

Keep in mind that not all links are created equally. After generating this list of prospective linking partners, evaluate each web page individually before spending time trying to make the acquisition. The next task explains more about evaluating links. After narrowing down your list, you should contact the web page owners directly to discover what the owner might require to obtain a link, as discussed in the task "Request One-Way Links."

EVALUATE POTENTIAL LINKING PARTNERS

You can determine what is considered a quality link by analyzing a number of factors. Consider the age of the domain you are trying to acquire a link from — Google tends to treat older domains that have been around for several years with more respect than domains registered recently. You should also try to acquire as many links as possible from domains with .edu and .gov top-level domain extensions. Also, prospect for links that have unique and topically relevant content to your website's subject matter. Additionally, focus on acquiring links from pages that already rank well for the keywords and terms that you are targeting.

Evaluate Potential Linking Partners

Find the Age of a Domain

1. Navigate to www.domaintools.com.

2. Enter a domain name in the Search Domain Ownership Records box.

3. Click Search for Domain.

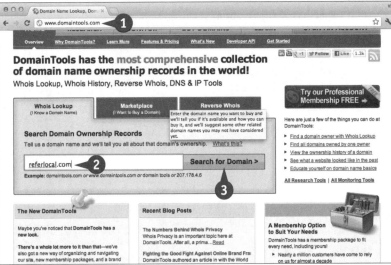

4. In top navigation tabs, click the Registration tab.

Ⓐ You can determine the age of the domain from the Created date.

Using the SEO Book Toolbar

1 Navigate to http://tools.seobook.com/seo-toolbar in your browser.

2 Click Download Now.

A Sign up for free SEO Book account to gain access to download the SEO Toolbar.

Note: *You must use the Firefox browser for this add-on.*

3 Click the "I" icon in the toolbar that appears next to the SEO Book logo.

4 An overlay on your browser screen will appear, filled with backlink data.

Note: *Utilize this data to analyze the potential value of a prospective linking partner.*

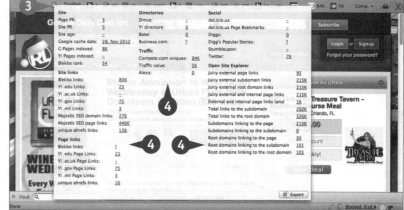

EXTRA

You may want to consider examining other factors when analyzing potential linking partners. Make sure that sites you are trying to acquire links from have incoming links that are relevant to their own content. If so, those sites are likely to be authoritative and trusted resources for that subject matter. You should also take into consideration the number of and quality of outbound links from a particular site. An outbound link is a link from a page of one site to another site. If you acquire a link from a site that is linking to hundreds of other unrelated sites, search engines are likely to discount the link.

GATHER LINK INTELLIGENCE WITH OPEN SITE EXPLORER

Open Site Explorer, located at www.opensiteexplorer.org, is a link analysis tool that provides basic or advanced intelligence of the links pointing to a particular website for $99 per month. Using a paid link index of the web, such as Open Site Explorer, provides more data and more sorting features than free sources such as Bing Webmaster Tools.

When you enter your URL, you can view website link intelligence in Open Site Explorer by internal or inbound links, and external links pointing to the website or web page selected. You can also view content sorted by the number of backlinks and view the anchor text to the pages among other data.

Gather Link Intelligence with Open Site Explorer

Run a Basic Report

① Navigate to www.opensite explorer.org.

② Register for a free trial.

③ Enter the URL for webpage or domain that you would like to analyze.

Ⓐ Use the Show drop-down list to specify whether you would like to see followed, no followed, or redirected links, or all inbound links.

Ⓑ Use the From drop-down list to select whether you want to see internal, external, or all links.

Ⓒ Use the To drop-down list to select whether you want to view links for a page, subdomain, or root domain.

Ⓓ Use the And drop-down list to view links grouped or ungrouped.

④ Click Filter.

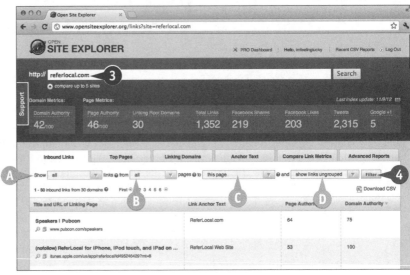

Compare Link Metrics

1 Click the Compare Link Metrics tab at the top of the page.

2 Click + Add URL.

3 Enter the URL.

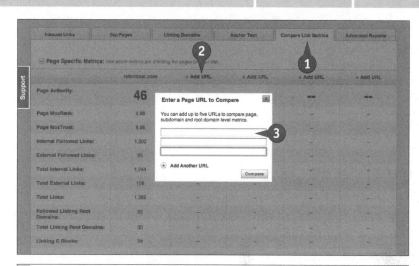

4 Add additional URLs by clicking other + Add URL links.

Note: *This report is useful for comparing metrics between a page on your site and a competitor's page.*

EXTRA

Open Site Explorer is just one of many useful SEO tools available as part of SEOmoz PRO membership. Other tools included in the PRO membership that are useful for SEO include Rank Tracker, a tool for tracking your organic keyword rankings in major search engines; On Page Report Card, which grades how well a page is optimized for a specific keyword; and the Keyword Difficulty Tool, which provides a useful analysis of how difficult it is to rank for a particular keyword.

Other features included with a SEOmoz PRO membership include a Q & A forum, webinars, and a beginners guide to SEO, which makes SEOmoz a good tool for those new to SEO.

133

ACQUIRE QUALITY LINKS

Just a couple high-quality links can provide the same if not a greater search-engine-optimization benefit than hundreds of low-quality links. All the major search engines embrace this approach to link building.

Google uses a numerical system called *PageRank* (PR) to help express the relative authority of a web page. Google assigns every web page on the Internet a PageRank value of 0–10 based on a calculation of the quantity and quality of backlinks. Tools such as prchecker.info and SEO Book Toolbar show a toolbar PR metric. Although PageRank is not as accurate a metric as it used to be, it is a point of reference. Link index vendors provide their own calculations, such as the SEOmoz MozRank and MozTrust.

Acquire Quality Links

1 Navigate to www.prchecker.info/ check_page_rank.php.

2 To check the PageRank of the domain ReferLocal.com, type **http://referlocal.com** into the text box.

3 Click Check PR.

4 Enter the word verification.

5 Click Verify Now.

A The PageRank for the domain in question appears.

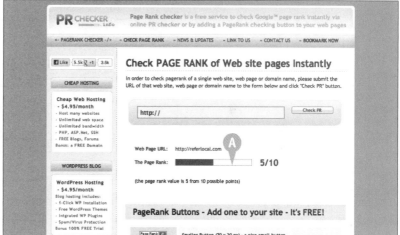

EXTRA

Aaron Wall of SEOBook.com offers a fantastic free Firefox extension called SEO for Firefox at http://tools. seobook.com/firefox/seo-for-firefox.html. After you install this plug-in, your Google search results will contain information about each result, including PageRank, age, incoming links, and more, which saves you time from having to gather this information manually.

Industry insiders believe that search engines partially rank websites based on how *trusted* they are in their markets. In fact, Yahoo published a paper in 2004, located at www.vldb.org/conf/2004/RS15P3.PDF, about a technique called *TrustRank* for calculating web page quality. This TrustRank score is not public; however, you can assume that sites ranked in search engines for competitive keywords likely possess a high trust score.

USING EFFECTIVE ANCHOR TEXT

Choosing appropriate anchor text for both your incoming and outgoing links can play a large role in increasing your search-engine rankings for the terms and keywords your site is targeting. *Anchor text* is the clickable text attached to a hyperlink.

When building links to your web page, you should always attempt to acquire links with highly descriptive anchor text. Search engines use anchor text to determine the theme of the page being linked to, and anchor text is an important factor in search engines' ranking algorithms.

Using Effective Anchor Text

Anchor Text in Search Results

1 Navigate to www.google.com.

2 Search for "seo software."

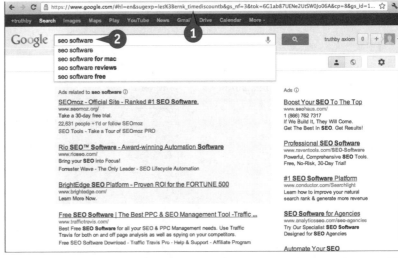

A Note that www.seomoz.org is ranked as the fifth organic listing.

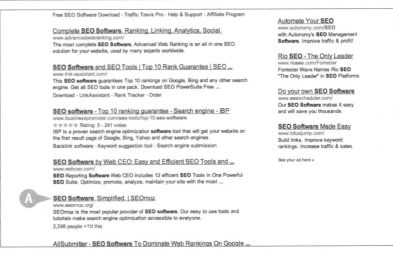

Anchor Text on Seomoz.org

1 Navigate to www.seo.com/blog/utah-seos-pack-mozcation-tour-stop.

A Notice the link with anchor text *SEO software* pointing to seomoz.org. This helps seomoz.org rank well for a search for the term "SEO software".

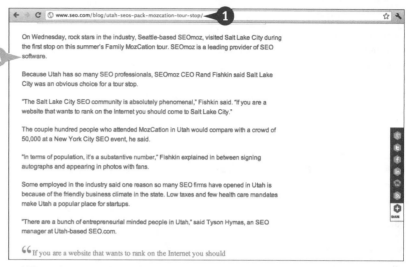

2 Navigate to www.salesforce.com/uk/socialsuccess/social-media-how-to-guides/expert-interview-social-media-measurement.jsp.

B Notice the link with anchor text *SEO Software* pointing to seomoz.org. This helps seomoz.org rank well for a search for the term "SEO software."

EXTRA

If you already have incoming links to your website, you may want to analyze and potentially alter the anchor text of these links using Open Site Explorer. Enter your website URL into Open Site Explorer and click the Anchor Text Distribution tab in the top navigation panel and click the anchor text selections to view links that point to your site with the selected anchor text.

If you find many inbound links to your site that do not have descriptive anchor text, contact those website owners and request they consider changing the anchor text to something more relevant to your site content. Suggest alternate anchor text for the link. Many webmasters agree to this request because a link with descriptive anchor text provides a better experience for their visitors.

CONTENT MARKETING WITH GUEST BLOGGING

Guest blogging is a relationship-building and link-building method where you collaborate with bloggers by providing them with content for their blog that references you with a citation, usually in an About the Author section. When guest blogging, you can make certain that your posts are not only valuable to the reader but also optimized for maximum search-engine ranking. Building

contacts and relationships with publishers in your space is key and several tools can help you do this. One of these tools is MyBlogGuest.com, which is a community for guest bloggers that connects publishers with free content and guest writers with an opportunity for brand building and link development.

Content Marketing with Guest Blogging

1 Navigate to www.myblogguest.com.

2 Fill out the form on the home page.

Note: *Filling out your profile entirely and including past blog posts you have written will give publishers an idea of your expertise, your experience, and whether your writing style fits their overall brand messaging.*

3 Click Forum at the top of page.

4 Scroll down and click Looking for a guest author.

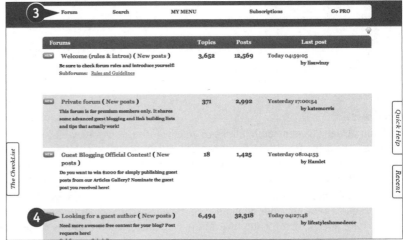

5 Select the category relevant to your website and browse the selections.

6 Click on a selection based on your writing expertise and the topical relevance.

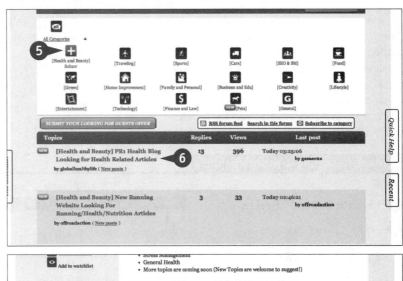

7 Send private message to express interest in writing and explain why you are well qualified to write the article.

Note: Sometimes it helps to leave a comment to alert the poster that you sent a private message.

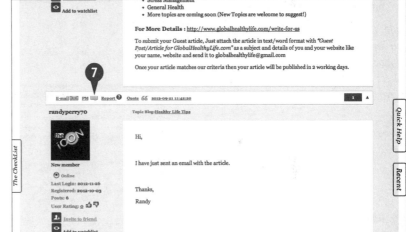

EXTRA

One great tactic you can use to strengthen your guest blogging promotional efforts is to link to past guest posts that you wrote with other publishers when relevant. This helps strengthen your relationship with the other publishers, since you are helping their brands. Additionally linking to your prior guest posts also helps your link-building efforts because it can make the prior guest post a more powerful link source to your website.

Focus on building relationships with publishers who not only allow guest blogging but also are highly authoritative in your particular area of business. Influential publishers are likely to have large social media followings and will often agree to promote your posts through social media and other marketing channels.

CONTENT MARKETING WITH INFOGRAPHICS

Content marketing with infographics is another opportunity to develop relationships and build authoritative links to your website. An *infographic* is a graphical representation of information or data. Complex concepts can become easy to understand when graphics visualize trends and patterns of data. The key to successfully using an infographic as part of your online marketing efforts is presenting careful topical research that will be interesting to potential social sharing and blog audiences in a way that is intuitive and graphically interesting.

Once you have created your infographic, you can use a variation of the competitor-based link-building approach discussed in the evaluating competition task in this chapter to promote your infographic to relevant audiences.

Content Marketing with Infographics

1 Navigate to http://visual.ly.

2 Select a category that is relevant to your website and browse the infographics.

Note: *Once you see an infographic you like, add the source URL to the Clipboard and browse visual.ly to collect a list of infographic URLs relevant to your own.*

3 Navigate to www.technorati.com and search for blog posts topically relevant to the infographic you have created.

Note: *Make sure that the blog post links you add to your list are recent and that blogs you add to your list are frequently updated and have active users.*

4 Search backlinks of infographics links and blogs you have collected in Open Site Explorer.

Note: You can also use Bing Webmaster Tools for this research.

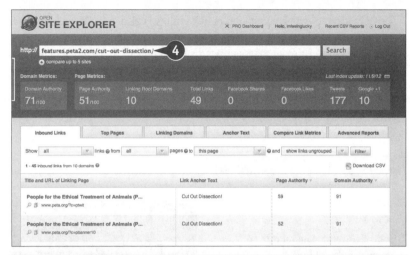

5 Click the Download CSV link to export results.

Note: Reach out to webmasters at destination domains sourced from your combined list of infographic backlinks and relevant blogs.

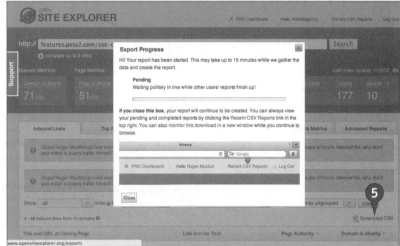

EXTRA

Just as with guest blogging, use a multichannel approach to promoting your infographic. Leverage your social media profiles and relationships with publishers to spread the word about your infographic. Once you have concluded your cross-channel promotion, another way to identify relevant prospects is to leverage Google Reverse Image Search. Search your infographic in Google Reverse Image Search and identify anyone who is using your infographic on his or her site without citing you as a reference. Request a citation back to your website from publishers who used your infographic without citing you as the original content source. In fact, you can leverage this tactic with any linkable asset on your website by querying a link index such as Open Site Explorer.

Participating in online communities like forums is also an effective strategy for building links and generating traffic. Forums are Internet message boards that enable you to participate in ongoing discussions about a variety of topics. Most forums allow you to participate by simply signing up for a free account with your e-mail address and very little personal information.

Forums are moderated, but unlike blogs, your forum posts are often posted for public viewing without prior review. You should still provide useful and constructive responses to avoid having your posts labeled as spam. Adding value to the community increases the likelihood that your link and comment stay posted and that the other forum participants will visit your site.

Encourage Community Participation

Register to Participate in a Web Forum

1 Visit a web forum related to your site's content.

Note: *Join and participate in forums that are topically related to your website. You can find topically relevant forums by using search engines to look up keywords related to your website.*

2 Register as a user.

Note: *Although forums are powered by different software, most have a link for you to register as a user.*

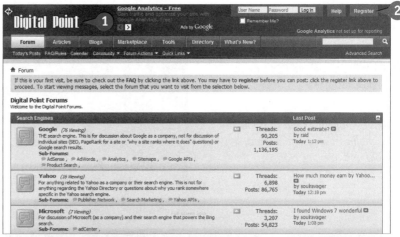

3 Enter the necessary information, such as your name and username, to create an account.

You will receive an e-mail with a link to verify your account.

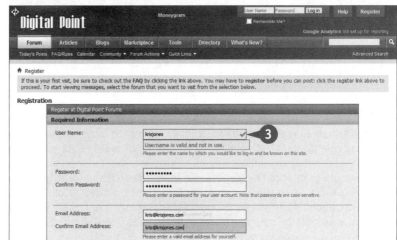

Make a Post

1 Search for a thread relevant to your website's content.

2 Participate in the conversation and include your link in the post if it is relevant and useful to the topic at hand.

EXTRA

Unlike blog comment links, forum post links do not contain a `nofollow` attribute, making them useful for increasing your search-engine rankings. Some forums allow you to place a link directly into your forum *signature,* which is a personalized line of text that follows each post. This method of acquiring links on a forum is less obvious than placing a link directly into forum posts, and it is sometimes encouraged by forum moderators.

You can use search engines to find forums relevant to the content of your site by creatively constructing search queries. Try a query like **inurl:forum pets.** Because many forums are located on a URL such as www.mydomain. com/forum, this type of query should provide mostly forum results.

A one-way link request involves sending an e-mail to a website owner expressing interest in obtaining a link to your website from a page on his or her website. It is the most difficult method of obtaining quality links, but it is likely to produce the best results because the links are coming from handpicked sites that meet your quality criteria.

Most of the sites you should be targeting when doing one-way link requests should come from your competition-evaluation efforts. Target only links that meet quality link criteria. Also, try to request descriptive anchor text with your link.

Request One-Way Links

1 Navigate to www.dmoz.org.

Note: DMOZ lists many old and established websites whose owners normally do not sell links. Often, these owners are unaware of the value of such a link, and they may not require compensation of any kind, making DMOZ a primary place to find high-quality one-way links.

2 Search for sites related to your content. As an example, search for "spinach lasagna."

The search results appear.

Browse through the websites and look for ones that appear relevant to your content. Look for sites that meet the link quality criteria discussed earlier in this chapter.

3 Click a site. In this example, click the www.igourmet.com link to Spinach Lasagna Val d'Aosta.

4 Look for a method to contact the website owner to request a link. In this example, click Customer Service and look for an e-mail address or contact form.

5 Click Contact Us and a form will appear.

Note: *Write a thoughtful e-mail to the owner of the website requesting a link back to your own website. Be sure to include the link as you want it to be added, including the proper anchor text.*

EXTRA

When you contact webmasters for a link request, remember that you are asking them to take time out to review your site and add the link to their sites. Be sure to go out of your way to show sincere interest in the site you are requesting a link from. Perhaps you can comment on an article on the site, or alert the webmaster if you can find a typo or some other error on the site that can easily be fixed. A good link request appears genuine and authentic. A bad link request comes across as spam.

Some site owners may be inclined to add the link without any sort of compensation because they feel the content of your page can provide their visitors value. Most website owners look for something in return.

AN INTRODUCTION TO GOOGLE ANALYTICS

Google Analytics is a free analytics solution designed to give you a complete view of every aspect of activity on your website. Understanding how to properly analyze and implement the numerous types of data that Google Analytics provides gives you a considerable edge over your competition in the quest for top search-engine rankings. A robust analytics program is an often overlooked but entirely vital part of a successful search-engine-optimization, or SEO, campaign. After all, without knowing what is currently working for your website, you have no idea which areas need to be improved, or which successes can be expanded upon. Google Analytics presents you with multiple advantages as a site owner, from the ability to track goals and sales to the knowledge of where your visitors exit your website. The first step is to ensure you properly install the tracking code on your website. The second is to learn how to use Google Analytics as a tool to improve your website performance.

Install Google Analytics

To use Google Analytics with your website you must create an account and install tracking code on your website. Installing tracking code is what allows Google Analytics to capture, collect, and analyze the information about the way users reach and interact with your website. The most important detail in the installation process is making sure that your tracking code is correctly placed on every single page of your website. This ensures that all your Google Analytics reports are as accurate as possible. Without proper installation, you cannot make accurate judgments about the performance of your website, which can severely damage the success of your SEO campaigns.

Set and Track Goals

If your website includes some sort of lead generation such as a newsletter subscription, catalog request, or even something as simple as a contact page, goal tracking can make gauging the success of your online marketing campaigns simple. Any goal action can be traced back to the original source of the visitor, which allows you to determine which traffic sources are working for your site, which search keywords are performing the best, and which methods are ineffective. The Google Analytics goal-setting feature is especially useful when targeting keywords in your SEO efforts. Knowing ahead of time which keywords are already converting for your site and targeting those keywords until you reach the top organic positions is a very effective SEO strategy.

Apply Filters

The tracking code for Google Analytics tracks the user behavior for each visit to your site. At times, you may want to track certain parts of your site separately, or exclude certain traffic from reports. For these reasons, Google Analytics has made it simple to apply filters to your website profile to ensure your data is as accurate and useful as possible. Adding filters to exclude your own IP address prevents your own internal traffic from skewing the data about your true website performance. This ensures certain statistics such as time on site, pages per visit, and visitor loyalty are derived from actual site performance.

You can also use Google Analytics filters to track specific directories located on your website. This filter is best utilized in a separate website profile, and it is very useful for quickly analyzing a section of your website. It is most helpful for larger sites that have multiple areas, such as a forum, a blog, a resource directory, or an e-commerce section.

Track External Clicks

If you are setting up any traffic trades, or promoting any affiliate offers on your website, keep track of how many clicks you are sending to external sites. For traffic trades, this information can help you negotiate better link placement if you are sending a substantial amount of traffic. For affiliates, this information is invaluable if you monitor the accuracy of the affiliate program statistic reporting. Another added benefit of

tracking your external clicks is explaining bounce rates. A *bounce* occurs when a website visitor leaves your website without visiting any other pages. If your home page has numerous external links and a high bounce rate, you can research exactly how many of the recorded bounces came from a user clicking an external link.

Automate Reporting

If you want to keep a separate archive of your website's progression, setting up automatic e-mail reporting can be extremely useful. This feature of Google Analytics allows you to specify which information you want to have reported, and the time interval between reports. The reports can be e-mailed to you, or anyone else you choose, in a variety of formats,

including PDF and CSV. This makes sharing information and tracking your website growth extremely easy, and the PDF option allows you to keep separate hard copies of your website data. Having past data available for quick and easy reference can prove extremely useful when you are making decisions about future campaigns.

Find Keywords

An extremely efficient strategy for deciding what keywords to target in your SEO efforts involves looking at what is already working for your website. Terms for which your website is already ranking in the top 50 results are typically easier to dominate than terms where your website is not ranked at all. Looking through your traffic sources in Google Analytics is a very simple way of finding out which keywords are sending you traffic. When analyzing your list, if you come across a keyword

that is sending a considerable amount of traffic despite a ranking on the bottom of the first, or on the second page of results, you have found a fantastic target for SEO. Finding these keywords ensures that you target only keywords that send sufficient traffic. Also, when using this method in combination with goal tracking, you can focus your SEO efforts toward keywords that you know convert well.

Track E-Commerce

If your website lists products for sale, using Google Analytics to track your orders can be an invaluable tool to your SEO, pay-per-click (PPC), and media campaigns. If properly installed, Google Analytics can track a purchase at your website to the original source of the visitor who made the purchase. This allows you to track exactly how much revenue was generated

from each keyword that is currently driving traffic to your website. When you have accurate data about which traffic sources are sending sales, you can push to extract more traffic from those sources to ensure high profits from your search-engine marketing efforts.

Google Analytics provides detailed statistics about your website and allows you to efficiently monitor important aspects of your site from one centralized location. It provides detailed reporting features, including graphs and charts, to give you a visual look at your website statistics.

The data provided by Google Analytics allows you to make accurate, informed decisions about everything from SEO and PPC advertising success to your website design, linking partners, and marketing campaigns. Google Analytics is an extremely cost-effective and robust tracking- and website-analytics software that allows you to effectively analyze and monitor your website statistics in near real time.

Create an Account

Create a Google Account

1 Navigate to www.google.com/accounts.

2 Click Sign Up.

Note: *Fill in the required information and follow the instructions to complete the sign up.*

You have successfully created a Google account.

Sign Up for Google Analytics

Note: *To complete these steps, navigate to www.google.com/analytics and click Create an account. The Analytics sign in page appears.*

1 Enter the e-mail and password you just created to sign in to Google Analytics.

2 Click Sign in.

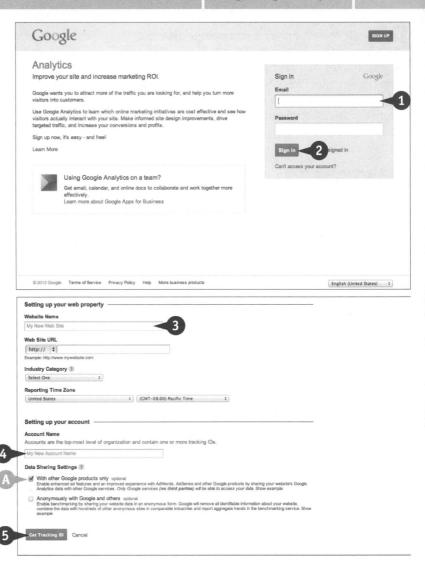

The Google Analytics Account Creation page appears.

3 Enter the website name, website URL, industry category, and reporting time zone of the website you want to track.

4 Enter the account name.

Note: *The account name is the name you assign to your website within Google Analytics.*

Ⓐ Notice the Data Sharing Settings. Confirm that With other Google products only is selected.

5 Click Get Tracking ID and accept the Terms of Service.

You have successfully created your Google Analytics account.

EXTRA

Google Analytics gives you the option to grant additional users the ability to view your website profiles. You do this by clicking on the relevant account name, entering the Admin section of the profile, clicking the Users tab, and clicking + New User. You must then enter the e-mail address of the person to whom you want to grant access. Note that the e-mail address you enter must already be a valid Google account. If the user does not have a Google account, he or she can sign up for free at www.google.com/accounts.

Next, select the account type, which either limits the additional user to a view-reports-only setting, or grants that person full administrative abilities. Google Analytics allows you to restrict or grant user access to reporting features of your choosing.

INSTALL TRACKING CODE

For Google Analytics to track your website data, the tracking code must be correctly installed on each page you want tracked. You can find this code at any time inside the Analytics Profile Settings section of your Google Analytics account. After you install this code, you can capture a wide variety of data about your website visitors. Among other statistics, Google Analytics tracks and reports the number of visitors, the average time users spend on your website, the paths users take to navigate your content, and the points at which visitors completely exit your site.

After you paste the tracking code into your pages, double-check that you have inserted everything correctly.

Install Tracking Code

① Sign in to your Google Analytics account and click the relevant account name and profile. The Reporting tool appears.

② Click Admin to access the settings.

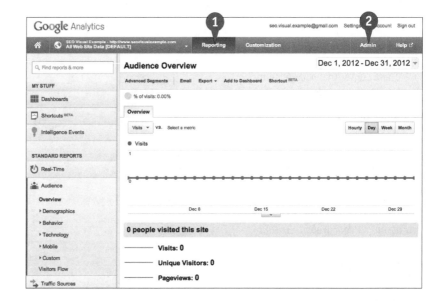

③ Click the Tracking Info tab.

The Google Analytics Tracking Code page appears.

④ Copy your tracking code from the Tracking Code page.

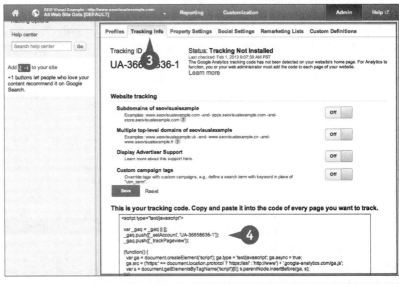

⑤ Paste the code into each page of your website, directly before the `</head>` tag.

Note: To avoid receiving inaccurate data, you should install the tracking code on every page of your site. This ensures that your reports are not skewed by visitors navigating to a page on your site that is not tracked.

EXTRA

Google Analytics provides a simple tool to check the proper installation of tracking code. On your Google Analytics home page, click Admin to enter the Account Administration page and click the account and then the property that you would like to check. You are then taken to that property's Profiles page. Click the Tracking Info tab and you are then taken to a page that displays whether your Google Analytics tracking code has been correctly installed. The status "Receiving Data" means your code has been installed successfully.

The statistics that Google Analytics reports are not real time, but you are able to view updated statistics throughout the day.

SET CONVERSION GOALS

Google Analytics gives you the option of defining specific conversion goals to help gauge the success of your marketing efforts. Conversion goals can consist of things like newsletter sign-ups, catalog requests, product purchases, or contact form submissions. Creating conversion goals, and the conversion funnels that may accompany them, is as simple as entering the URLs of the pages in your goal settings.

Setting conversion goals is a very important part of the analytics process and is especially useful because specific events can be tracked to the source of the visitor. Tracking the source of your visitor enables you to see where your highest quality traffic is originating from, and then target that source more aggressively.

Set Conversion Goals

1. Sign in to your Google Analytics account and click the relevant account name and profile. The Reporting tool appears.

2. Click Admin to access the settings.

3. Click the name of the profile to which you are adding a goal.

4. Click the Goals tab.

5. Click + Goal.

The Google Analytics Goal page appears.

6 Give the goal a relevant name: Contact Page, for example.

7 Select the goal type: for example, URL Destination. The URL Destination goal lets you specify a page with its own URL as a goal. This allows you track how many visitors viewed the page and how they arrived.

8 Enter your goal URL. This URL can be your home page or another page that acts as the beginning of your conversion goal cycle.

9 Select your match type based on your individual goals.

10 If you want your goals to be case sensitive, select that check box.

A You can choose a goal value and set up a goal funnel during this stage of the setup process.

11 Click Save.

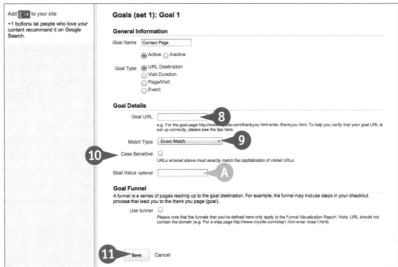

EXTRA

The three available goal match types are *head, exact,* and *regular expression.* A head match matches identical characters starting from the beginning of the string up to and including the last character in the string you specify. Use this option when your page URLs are generally unvarying but when they include additional parameters at the end that you want to exclude. An exact match is a match on every exact character in your URL without exception from beginning to end. Use this when your URLs for your site are easy to read and do not vary. A regular expression uses special characters to enable wildcard and flexible matching. This is useful when the stem and trailing parameters can vary in the URLs for the same website page.

Exclude Your IP Address with Filters

You can use the filter settings in Google Analytics to prevent your own internal or network traffic from appearing in your reports. This feature is useful because you likely will browse your own website regularly to check for broken links, broken images, typos, and so on. Also, you likely will set your website as your default home page. All

these browsing habits can lead to inaccurate data in your analytics reports.

When looking at your reports in Google Analytics, be sure to have your information as accurate as possible because you will use this information to make informed decisions about many aspects of your website, including design, content, and conversion goal funnels.

Exclude Your IP Address with Filters

1 Sign in to your Google Analytics account and click the relevant account name and profile. The Reporting tool appears.

2 Click Admin to access the settings.

3 Click the name of the profile to which you are adding a filter.

4 Click the Filters tab.

5 Click + New Filter.

The Add Filter to Profile page appears.

6 Give the filter an appropriate name: for example, Internal Traffic.

7 Leave the Predefined filter option selected.

8 Select Exclude traffic from the IP addresses that are equal to from the Filter Type menus.

9 Enter your IP address in the corresponding field.

10 Click Save.

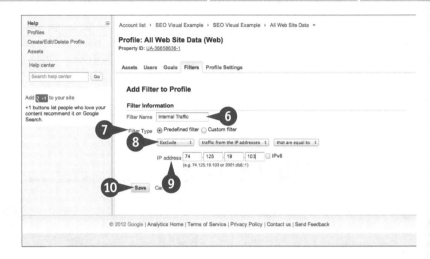

EXTRA

When adding an IP address, or an IP range to your filters, use *regular expressions*. Regular expressions are commonly used when performing textual data manipulation tasks. When using an exclude filter, which you use when excluding an IP address or range, Google Analytics excludes the visitor data only if the information from the regular expression matches the data in the corresponding field. Fields may include IP address, visitor location, screen resolution, and language settings, among others. For basic filters, use of regular expressions is fairly limited. Note that Google Analytics also offers good examples to work from when you are going through the basic filter addition process.

If one filter is going to be common to several website profiles, you do not need to remake each filter. You can simply create the filter once, and then add the additional websites through the Filter Manager. This can be accessed through the initial Analytics Settings page, through the Filter Manager link in the bottom-right section of the page. Simply click Edit next to the appropriate filter, add the desired domains, and save your changes.

EXCLUDE TRAFFIC FROM A PARTICULAR DOMAIN

You can use the Google Analytics domain filter to remove a company network from your reporting. For example, if you are the administrator of Google Analytics on your company's blog, you may not want the traffic from your coworkers to show up in your reports because the number of people in your office visiting the company blog is not an accurate reflection of the actual growth of the blog. Including this type of data may skew important reporting data such as the average time on your site and visitor loyalty. Therefore, you may choose to filter out traffic coming from any network to which you may be connected.

Exclude Traffic from a Particular Domain

1 Sign in to your Google Analytics account and click the relevant account name and profile. The Reporting tool appears.

2 Click Admin to access the settings.

3 Click the name of the profile from which you would like to exclude a particular domain.

4 Click the Filters tab.

5 Click + New Filter.

6 Give the filter an appropriate name.

7 Leave the Predefined filter option selected.

8 Select Exclude traffic from the ISP domain that are equal to from the Filter Type menus.

9 Enter the name of the domain you want to exclude.

Note: *This example excludes google.com.*

10 Leave Case Sensitive option No selected.

11 Click Save.

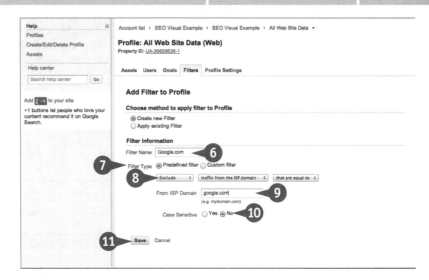

EXTRA

Excluding an ISP is especially useful if your city is serviced by a small, local Internet service provider. Excluding your local ISP effectively removes all traffic from your family and friends who live in your area. This ensures that your data is as reliable as possible. In this situation, having multiple profiles displays the amount of local traffic you are receiving. Simply compare the data from the account with the local ISP filtered out to the account without the filter. The difference between these two equals the total amount of traffic you are receiving from your local ISP.

If you are going to exclude an ISP from your reports, you should create an additional profile before adding this filter. This ensures your ability to view statistics of your website with and without the domain exclusion filter in place. Keep in mind that filtering out an entire ISP can remove a valuable amount of data from your reports, and it may lead to inaccurate analytics. Having separate accounts allows you to still retain that critical data.

INCLUDE ONLY CERTAIN DIRECTORIES

Google Analytics gives you the ability to specify and include or exclude tracking to any location of your website. This procedure is useful if you want to analyze only specific landing pages, or any other specific area of your website. Also, if your website is broken up into

multiple categories or themes, you may want to track each of these separately. To do this, simply make a new profile for the existing domain, and then apply the filter to track only a certain directory. This information is very useful when negotiating rates with potential advertisers.

Include Only Certain Directories

1 Sign in to your Google Analytics account and click the relevant account name and profile. The Reporting tool appears.

2 Click Admin to access the settings.

3 Click the name of the profile from which you would like to exclude a particular directory.

4 Click the Filters tab.

5 Click + New Filter.

6 Give the filter an appropriate name.

Note: *Try to avoid picking a name for your new profile that leaves room for confusion as to which profile is tracking the full domain and which profile is tracking an individual directory of the site. This becomes important when you want to share reports with someone else.*

7 Leave the Predefined filter option selected.

8 Select Include only traffic to the subdirectories that are equal to from the Filter Type menus.

9 Enter the name of the subdirectory you want to include.

10 Leave Case Sensitive option No selected.

11 Click Save.

EXTRA

Although you will likely find tracking a certain directory of your website separately useful, you may also find having reports available for your entire domain a good idea. For this reason, you should make a new website profile whenever you want to track an individual directory. To set up an additional profile, click + New Profile from the account's Profiles page. After selecting a relevant name and saving the profile, you can then go ahead and apply the appropriate filter to this new copy of your website profile.

Try to avoid picking a name for your new profile that leaves room for confusion as to which profile is tracking the full domain and which profile is tracking an individual directory of the site. This becomes important if and when you want to share reports with someone else. Following these rules has the added benefit of minimizing the possibility that someone with restricted analytics access accidentally receives data from restricted sources.

TRACK EXTERNAL LINKS

When constructing your website, you are likely to have both internal and external links. Internal links refer to the links that send the visitor to other pages within your site, and external links refer a visitor to a website other than your own. Google Analytics can show you how your visitors navigate your internal links, but what if they leave your site by clicking an external link? By tweaking the way you construct your external links, Google Analytics can keep track of how many visitors you are sending out, despite the absence of your tracking code on these outside pages.

Track External Links

1 Open the source file for the page that contains the external link you want to track and locate the link.

2 Insert the following at the end of the link: onClick="recordOut boundLink(this, 'Outbound Links', 'example.com'); return false;".

Note: *The best practice for separating sites is to use the URL of the site you are linking to. Using the name of the website may get confusing and does not allow you to distinguish where you sent the visitor if you have multiple external links to various pages on another domain. Some examples of good names include "example_com" or "example_com_pagename."*

Repeat this process for each link you want to track.

3 After 24 to 48 hours, view your website statistics by clicking Content on the sidebar and selecting the Events Overview page.

A Clicks on the tracked outbound links are then logged as Event Actions with their respective labels.

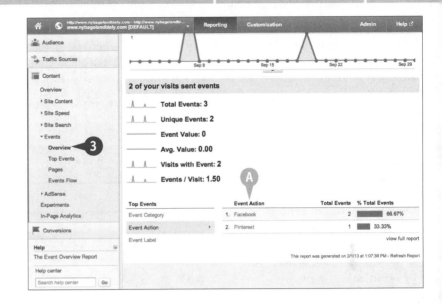

EXTRA

Designing and using a relevant, easy-to-remember structure for tracking your outbound links is very important. The first step is to decide on a folder name that is not being used in your actual website. Some examples may include "outgoing," "external," or "clicks." This keeps all the pages for external clicks organized.

Logging clicks on your outbound links can also supplement your bounce rate. If a page has a high bounce rate, you may be wondering where all that traffic is going. However, if you log your outbound clicks, you can determine how many of your visitors clicked external links and went elsewhere instead of to other pages on your site.

Automate Reporting

Google Analytics automated reporting is extremely useful because it allows you to automatically e-mail reports to other people who are involved with your company or website without giving them access to view all the collected data in your analytics reports. For example, you may want to show a consultant ongoing reports on your page views, but not on your revenue or traffic sources.

Be cautious when deciding the frequency of your automated Google Analytics reports. If you have a limited amount of storage space in your e-mail inbox, you may quickly reach your limit if you have several PDF files being mailed to you daily.

Automate Reporting

Schedule Automated Reports

1 Sign in to your Google Analytics account and click the relevant account name and profile. The Reporting tool appears.

2 Click Email.

3 Fill in the e-mail address to which the report should be sent. Separate multiple e-mail addresses with commas.

4 Fill in a relevant subject.

5 Select the file format you want to receive.

6 Select the frequency with which you would like the report to be sent.

Note: *Google Analytics does not include any data from the current day when your report is sent. Your reports show the collected data up to the last fully completed day.*

7 Enter a relevant message body.

8 Click Send.

Your reports are now scheduled.

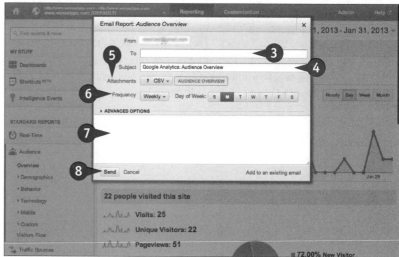

Delete Automated Reports

1 Go to the Admin settings for the Analytics Profile and the Assets tab should be selected.

2 Click Scheduled Emails.

A list of Scheduled Emails will be available to edit.

EXTRA

Adding additional e-mail recipients to existing Google Analytics e-mail reports is easy. At any time, you can include additional e-mail addresses to your pre-existing schedules by simply navigating to the Scheduled Emails settings page, selecting the schedule you want to edit, and adding the new e-mail address. Similarly, this method can be used to remove an e-mail address from receiving any additional reports.

You are able to delete any scheduled e-mail report by clicking Admin, navigating to the profile the report is attached to, clicking the Scheduled Emails link, and then clicking the Actions menu from the schedule you want to remove and choosing Delete. Be aware that the removal of these schedules is effective immediately.

The reports can be sent in a variety of formats, including PDF, XML, CSV, and TSV. The PDF option is ideal if you want to print your reports for your own records or for sharing with others. The XML, CSV, and TSV files are ideal for building long-term databases of your website statistics.

Using Analytics to Find New Keywords

You can use the Traffic Sources report in Google Analytics to locate new keywords to add to your PPC campaigns and SEO efforts. Selecting a traffic source like Google or Yahoo presents you with a list of keywords. These are the words your viewers are searching for and using to eventually land at your website. You can also view the number of hits, goal conversions, and the e-commerce value of each individual keyword.

Many of the top searched keywords in your report will also be the keywords you have already been targeting in your marketing efforts. However, if you take the time to mine the data contained in the report, you are likely to find keywords that will significantly improve your overall business efforts.

Using Analytics to Find New Keywords

1 Sign in to your Google Analytics account and click the relevant account name and profile. The Reporting tool appears.

2 Click Traffic Sources in the menu on the left.

The Google Analytics Traffic Sources menu expands.

3 Click Overview.

A A report appears that shows the top ten keywords based on visits.

4 Click View full report.

Scan and filter the list to find words or phrases that you have not actively targeted but that are sending in traffic.

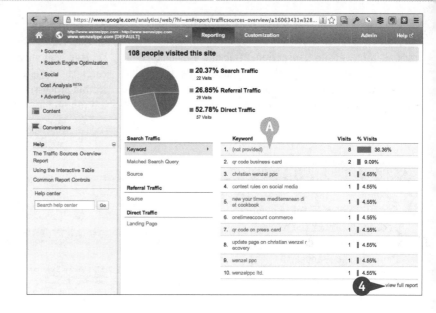

EXTRA

Searching through your keyword reports may also help you identify common words or phrases that your target audience is using when looking for your products or services. By tapping into commonly used phrases about your topic, you can develop a successful campaign that targets low-volume but high-converting keywords.

When looking through your keyword reports, limit yourself to analyzing at least 30 days of historical data or more. Looking at these large time ranges gives you a more accurate view of the potential in your referring keywords. For example, just because a particular keyword may have sent you one visitor and one conversion in the same day does not mean that that pattern will continue over time. On occasion, an isolated conversion slips in without being an indication of any sort of pattern. Similarly, a keyword may send you 20 visitors one day, but only 3 visitors the next day. Looking at larger time frames gives you a much more accurate estimate of actual traffic volume and value.

To properly gauge what traffic sources are the most successful for an e-commerce website, you must track all your website transactions. Tracking e-commerce transactions allows you to attach a solid dollar value to each keyword that brings visitors to your site, as well as an average value per visit from each of your traffic sources.

Before you can track any of your website transactions or view reports that attach dollar values to your traffic sources, you must first correctly set Google Analytics to catch the order data from your shopping cart. The first step in this process is letting Google Analytics know that you are running an e-commerce website.

Set Up E-Commerce Tracking

1 Sign in to your Google Analytics account and click the relevant account name and profile. The Reporting tool appears.

2 Click Admin to access the settings.

3 Click the name of the profile for which you will track e-commerce.

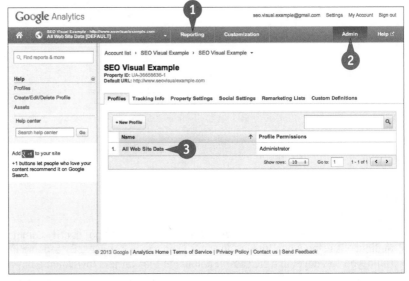

The Google Analytics Profile Management page appears.

4 Click the Profile Settings tab.

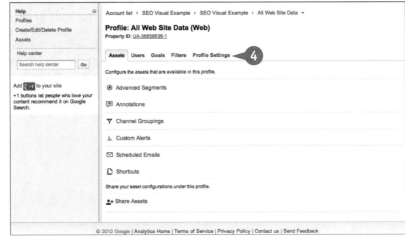

The Google Analytics Edit Profile Information page appears.

5 Under the E-Commerce Settings heading, choose Yes, an E-Commerce Site.

6 Click Apply.

Google Analytics now recognizes your website as an e-commerce store.

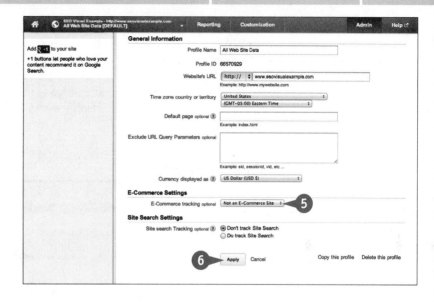

EXTRA

After e-commerce tracking is successfully installed, allow time to pass so that enough meaningful data is collected to make accurate decisions. Depending on your sales volume, a month or less should be sufficient time to collect meaningful data. View the e-commerce report for your website profile. In the bottom-right corner, your sales sources are listed. Click any of these links that are search engines. For example, use Google Organic. Clicking Google Organic opens the list of your top keywords for the month. Click the Revenue column to sort your keywords by the amount of revenue each earned. You now have a list of your most valuable keywords.

You can track your e-commerce transactions by inserting the tracking code on your Thank You or receipt page. This is the page customers see after their orders have been processed, and it typically includes which products were purchased, their price, and the total amount.

The variables that are included in the code you place on your receipt page will vary depending on the shopping

cart software that you use. If your webmaster is unsure of the actual variables, check the documentation for your shopping cart software. Alternatively, if you have a shopping cart that is hosted by a third party, contact the company that hosts your cart and ask the company to identify each variable for you.

Insert Tracking Code on Your Thank You Page

1 Ensure that the regular Google Analytics tracking code is correctly installed on your Thank You or receipt page.

```
<html>
<head>
<title>Receipt for your clothing purchase from KJ Clothing</title>
<script type="text/javascript">

var _gaq = _gaq || [];
_gaq.push(['_setAccount', 'UA-36658636-1']);
_gaq.push(['_trackPageview']);

(function() {
    var ga = document.createElement('script'); ga.type = 'text/javascript'; ga.async = true;
    ga.src = ('https:' == document.location.protocol ? 'https://ssl' : 'http://www') + '.google-analytics.com/ga.js';
    var s = document.getElementsByTagName('script')[0]; s.parentNode.insertBefore(ga, s);
})();

</script>
</head>

<body>
    <p>Page Content</p>

    <script src="some_random_script.js"></script>

    <p>Page Content</p>

</body>
</html>
```

2 Below the regular tracking code, paste the portion of code that catches the variables from your shopping cart.

Note: *You must replace the placeholders inside the brackets with the actual variables for whichever shopping cart your site is using. Do not include the brackets in your final code. While not all arguments are required, you should supply an empty placeholder for unspecified arguments to avoid errors. For example, you would add an item containing only order ID, SKU, price, and quantity like this:*
`_addItem("54321", "12345", "", "", "55.95", "1");`.

```
<html>
<head>
<title>Receipt for your clothing purchase from KJ Clothing</title>
<script type="text/javascript">

var _gaq = _gaq || [];
_gaq.push(['_setAccount', 'UA-XXXXX-X']);
_gaq.push(['_addTrans',
    '1234',           // order ID - required
    'KJ Clothing',    // affiliation or store name
    '11.99',          // total - required
    '1.29',           // tax
    '5',              // shipping
    'San Jose',       // city
    'California',     // state or province
    'USA'             // country
]);

    // add item might be called for every item in the shopping cart
    // where your ecommerce engine loops through each item in the cart and
    // prints out _addItem for each
_gaq.push(['_addItem',
    '1234',           // order ID - required
    'DD44',           // SKU/code - required
    'T-Shirt',        // product name
    'Green Medium',   // category or variation
    '11.99',          // unit price - required
    '1'               // quantity - required
]);
_gaq.push(['_trackTrans']); //submits transaction to the Analytics servers

(function() {
    var ga = document.createElement('script'); ga.type = 'text/javascript'; ga.async = true;
    ga.src = ('https:' == document.location.protocol ? 'https://ssl' : 'http://www') + '.google-analytics.com/ga.js';
    var s = document.getElementsByTagName('script')[0]; s.parentNode.insertBefore(ga, s);
})();
```

3 While not strictly required, it is a good idea to call _trackPageview() on your receipt page if you want to associate that particular page with the transaction data.

```
                                    Shopping Cart.html
1   ▼  <html>
2   ▼  <head>
3      <title>Receipt for your clothing purchase from KJ Clothing</title>
4   ▼  <script type="text/javascript">
5
6        var _gaq = _gaq || [];
7        _gaq.push(['_setAccount', 'UA-XXXXX-X']);
8        _gaq.push(['_trackPageview']);
9   ▼    _gaq.push(['_addTrans',
10         '1234',              // order ID - required
11         'KJ Clothing',   // affiliation or store name
12         '11.99',           // total - required
13         '1.29',             // tax
14         '5',                 // shipping
15         'San Jose',       // city
16         'California',     // state or province
17         'USA'              // country
18  ᴸ   ]);
19
20       // add item might be called for every item in the shopping cart
21       // where your ecommerce engine loops through each item in the cart and
22       // prints out _addItem for each
23  ▼    _gaq.push(['_addItem',
24         '1234',              // order ID - required
25         'DD44',             // SKU/code - required
26         'T-Shirt',         // product name
27         'Green Medium',  // category or variation
28         '11.99',           // unit price - required
29         '1'                 // quantity - required
30  ᴸ   ]);
31       _gaq.push(['_trackTrans']); //submits transaction to the Analytics servers
32
33  ▼    (function() {
34         var ga = document.createElement('script'); ga.type = 'text/javascript'; ga.async = true;
35         ga.src = ('https:' == document.location.protocol ? 'https://ssl' : 'http://www') + '.google-analytics.com/ga.js';
36         var s = document.getElementsByTagName('script')[0]; s.parentNode.insertBefore(ga, s);
37  ᴸ   })();
38
```

APPLY IT

Here are the variables that you must edit, along with a brief explanation.

Transaction line variables

[order-id]	Order ID number
[affiliation]	Store affiliation optional
[total]	Total amount
[tax]	Tax amount
[shipping]	The shipping cost
[city]	City
[state/region]	State/Province
[country]	Country

Item line variables

[order-id]	Order ID number same as transaction line
[sku/code]	The product's SKU code
[product name]	Name of the product
[category]	Product category
[price]	Price of the product per unit
[quantity]	Quantity of the product ordered

USING THIRD-PARTY SHOPPING CARTS

Third-party shopping carts allow e-commerce merchants to accept credit cards as a payment option and have the added benefit of being hosted by a third party. It can be a lot easier during the initial setup, but when you want to track third-party shopping cart transactions with Google Analytics, you must take some extra steps.

The basic idea behind tracking while using third-party shopping carts is to get the information about the sale transferred from the remote cart back to your website, which may not seem like a problem at first because you can include your tracking code on the remote page. However, you must pass along some information about your customer to the secure site that hosts your cart.

Using Third-Party Shopping Carts

1 If you use a third-party shopping cart on a domain other than your website, adjust your Google Analytics tracking code to fit the format shown here. Note that you need to insert your actual Google Analytics user ID:

```
<script>
var _gaq = _gaq || [];
_gaq.push(['_setAccount',
'UA-12345-1']);
_gaq.push(['_setDomainName',
'example-store.com']);
_gaq.push(['_setAllowLinker',
true]);
_gaq.push(['_trackPageview']);
</script>
```

```
1  <html>
2  <head>
3  <title>Receipt for your clothing purchase from KJ Clothing</title>
4    <script>
5      var _gaq = _gaq || [];
6      _gaq.push(['_setAccount', 'UA-12345-1']);
7      _gaq.push(['_setDomainName', 'example-store.com']);
8      _gaq.push(['_setAllowLinker', true]);
9      _gaq.push(['_trackPageview']);
10   </script>
11 </head>
12
13 <body>
14   <p>Page Content</p>
15
16   <script src="some_random_script.js"></script>
17
18   <p>Page Content</p>
19
20 </body>
21 </html>
```

2 Edit the links from your domain to the shopping cart domain to fit the following format: `<a href= "http://www.my-example-site.com/shopping-cart" onclick="_gaq.push(['_ link', 'http://www.my-example-site.com/shopping-cart.html']); return false;"> Purchase Now</a>`

```
1  <html>
2  <head>
3  <title>Receipt for your clothing purchase from KJ Clothing</title>
4    <script>
5      var _gaq = _gaq || [];
6      _gaq.push(['_setAccount', 'UA-12345-1']);
7      _gaq.push(['_setDomainName', 'example-store.com']);
8      _gaq.push(['_setAllowLinker', true]);
9      _gaq.push(['_trackPageview']);
10   </script>
11 </head>
12
13 <body>
14   <p>Page Content</p>
15
16   <a href="http://www.my-example-site.com/shopping-cart"
17     onclick="_gaq.push(['_link', 'http://www.my-example-site.com/shopping-cart.html']); return false;">
18     Purchase Now</a>
19
20   <script src="some_random_script.js"></script>
21
22   <p>Page Content</p>
23
24 </body>
25 </html>
```

3 If you use forms to submit the data to the third-party shopping cart, use the form shown in the example. This passes the information along correctly to the shopping cart domain:

```
<form name="f"
method="post"
onsubmit="_gaq.push(['_
linkByPost', this]);">
```

```
                                                    Thank You Page.html
1    <html>
2    <head>
3    <title>Receipt for your clothing purchase from KJ Clothing</title>
4        <script>
5            var _gaq = _gaq || [];
6            _gaq.push(['_setAccount', 'UA-12345-1']);
7            _gaq.push(['_setDomainName', 'example-store.com']);
8            _gaq.push(['_setAllowLinker', true]);
9            _gaq.push(['_trackPageview']);
10       </script>
11   </head>
12
13   <body>
14       <p>Page Content</p>
15
16       <a href="http://www.my-example-site.com/shopping-cart"
17       onclick="_gaq.push(['_link', 'http://www.my-example-site.com/shopping-cart.html']); return false;">
18       Purchase Now</a>
19
20
21       <form name="f" method="post" onsubmit="_gaq.push(['_linkByPost', this]);">   ◀━ 3
22
23
24       <script src="some_random_script.js"></script>
25
26
27       <p>Page Content</p>
28
29   </body>
30   </html>
```

EXTRA

If you run into a situation where the company that hosts your third-party shopping cart claims it is unable to allow you to set up Google Analytics to track your sales, you should strongly consider selecting another e-commerce shopping cart provider. Some of the issues you may want to consider include, first, what kind of service you are paying for when you are unable to use the largest and most encompassing free analytics tool. Second, would it be worth it to host your own shopping cart?

Hosting your own shopping cart can be a bit of work, but it makes tracking your transactions much easier. As previously mentioned in the task "Set Up E-Commerce Tracking," using the e-commerce feature of Google Analytics provides access to the absolute metric for success: the total revenue generated for any given period. Not having this information means you could be missing the opportunity to discover some real gems in the form of overlooked keywords that convert at a high rate.

AN INTRODUCTION TO SOCIAL MEDIA OPTIMIZATION

Social media optimization, or *SMO,* is a form of marketing that focuses on generating traffic and buzz through various social media websites, including Facebook, Twitter, and Google+. Social networks allow you to build large lists of contacts and supporters that can help spread the word about your business and website. Social news services such as Reddit provide a platform for others to vote on your content and share your story with others. Finally, video-sharing websites such as YouTube allow you to upload, view, and share video clips with millions of potential visitors.

This chapter outlines how you can use social media websites to generate traffic and buzz, and to build links to your website. SMO is an extension of your search-engine optimization (SEO) efforts, and emphasizes using social media websites to build links that can get your website ranked well organically in search engines.

Network with Facebook

Facebook is a popular social networking website that allows you to build lists of friends and interact with people all over the world through profile pages, pictures, videos, message boards, and various technology applications. Facebook is one of the top ten most trafficked websites in the United States, boasting more than 1 billion active members and growing

quickly. You can use Facebook to interact with current and prospective business associates while generating considerable traffic to your website and buzz about your business. Facebook is a service used by businesses of all sizes and people of all ages to network and communicate in real time.

Create a Facebook Business Page

Facebook allows you to create dedicated pages to promote your business. With more than 1 billion active users, it is imperative that you create a dedicated Business Page on Facebook. A dedicated Business Page allows you to easily connect with Facebook members and provide them with important information about your company, including your website(s), contact info, press releases, videos, blog RSS, Twitter updates, company news, and more. Facebook pages are a great way to grow your audience and interact with current and prospective customers.

Generate Leads with Facebook Ads

Facebook Ads allows you to amplify messages you post to your Business Page, as well as build your audience on Facebook or on any specific external website. Facebook allows you to target its entire network of more than 1 billion active users, but the real value in Facebook Ads is the ability to precisely target specific Facebook users based on demographics, social context, and location data.

Maximize Exposure with StumbleUpon

StumbleUpon is a peer and social networking technology that includes a toolbar that you install in your web browser. The StumbleUpon toolbar allows you to discover and rate web pages, videos, photos, and news articles. Getting your web pages, videos, photos, and news articles submitted to StumbleUpon is an effective way to generate buzz and traffic, and to build backlinks to your website.

StumbleUpon is a great resource for locating interesting websites and videos. Using StumbleUpon regularly provides countless examples of the kind of content that most users find interesting — this kind of content is what you want to produce to maximize your exposure on StumbleUpon and other social networks.

Microblog with Twitter

Twitter is a free social networking service that allows you to microblog by sending short updates of 140 characters or less to others by texting a message from your mobile phone, typing a message from the Twitter site, using instant messaging from Jabber or Google Talk, or using the Twitter app on your mobile device or tablet computer. Twitter is the most widely used

microblogging network in the world. Microblogging is a very powerful and increasingly popular way to communicate with friends and clients, build buzz, and generate prospective business leads. Many celebrities, as well as popular bloggers and writers, use Twitter to network with friends in real time.

Build Followers with Twitter Search

Twitter Search is Twitter's powerful and increasingly popular real-time search engine. Unlike major search engines, such as Google, Bing, and Yahoo, that update their search indexes every few days or weeks, Twitter Search updates its entire database of tweets as they occur. The most powerful way to use Twitter

Search and build the number of people who follow you on Twitter is to type keywords into Twitter Search that relate to your specific product or service. When Twitter delivers search results, you should follow those users who mention the target keyword.

Network with Google+

Google+ is a fast-growing Google-owned social networking platform that allows you to introduce yourself to others; connect with friends and family; follow interesting people; share images, videos, and interesting content with small groups of people; and easily vote on and share other people's content. Launched as a primary competitor to Facebook in June 2011,

Google+ has more than 500 million registered users and is growing in popularity very quickly.

Google+ is an important product to leverage for SEO purposes because it provides the Google search engine with extensive social data, which in turn is used as a primary indicator for search-engine ranking.

Grow Your Professional Network with LinkedIn

LinkedIn is a popular business-oriented social networking site that allows you to network with business professionals and build a list of contacts. By building a database of contacts with people you know and trust in business, you have access to a large network of friends with whom you can conduct business,

offer jobs, and promote your business. The people in your LinkedIn contact list are referred to as *connections*. You can invite anyone, regardless of whether that person is a LinkedIn user, to become one of your connections.

Share Videos with YouTube

YouTube is a video-sharing website that allows users to upload, view, and share video clips. Posting videos on YouTube is easy and requires minimal time and investment on your part.

Successful videos on YouTube can generate thousands or even millions of unique views, which can result in significant

exposure for your business. Videos that make it to the coveted YouTube home page are often covered by the national news media. Posting interesting videos on YouTube can help generate buzz and get people and news websites talking about your website or business.

Generate Traffic with Pinterest

Pinterest is a social-networking and photo-sharing website that allows users to create and manage theme-based image collections, such as events, interests, hobbies, and more. Users can browse other collections of images called pinboards, "repin" images to their own collections, or "like" photos. Pinterest is one of the top 50 websites in the world with nearly 50 million users and growing quickly, and it is especially popular with the female demographic.

Network with WebmasterWorld

WebmasterWorld is the oldest and most authoritative Internet marketing and webmaster forum community on the web. WebmasterWorld features thousands of discussions on a range of topics, including SEO, social media, and affiliate marketing. Specific forum threads exist on Google, Facebook, and Twitter and often include breaking news and analysis from experienced webmasters.

NETWORK WITH FACEBOOK

Facebook is a popular social networking website that enables you to build lists of contacts and interact with people all over the world through profile pages, pictures, videos, groups, and various technology applications. Facebook is one of the top three most trafficked websites in the United States and boasts more than 1 billion active members. Facebook allows you to build unique pages for personal or business use. Your personal page, commonly referred to as your profile page, is a great way to connect with old friends, classmates, coworkers, and others who you have a personal relationship with.

Network with Facebook

Create a Facebook Profile

Note: *Although you can share information about your business on your profile page, it is best practice to launch a separate, unique Business Page if your primary purpose on Facebook is to promote your business.*

1 Navigate to www.facebook.com and log in to your personal account.

A The Facebook Timeline is a space on your profile page that allows you and your contacts, also known as *friends,* to post messages for you and your friends to see. Your Facebook Timeline is a good place to share pictures and update your friends on your life.

2 To edit information on your page, click Update Info.

3 Add relevant information about your work and education.

4 Click the Edit link to update existing work and education information.

Note: *Facebook is a great resource for sharing relevant work experience and education with your friends. It is common to receive job prospects and business connections based on your profile information, so make sure it is accurate and up to date at all times. Include your website URL and Twitter handle.*

5 Click the Edit link to update information about yourself.

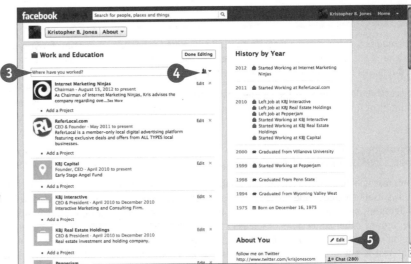

Find and Join Facebook Groups

Note: *Facebook groups are great places to network and prospect for business leads. You should join the groups that best reflect your area of expertise.*

① From your personal Facebook page, search for the topic you are interested in.

② Select a relevant group from the list.

Ⓐ Relevant Facebook pages are displayed below Groups based on your search query. Liking specific Facebook pages allows you to receive updates and information that you would not receive otherwise.

③ Click Join Group.

You can now participate in the group discussions.

Ⓑ Use the search tool to find new Facebook groups to join.

Note: *You should join as many groups related to your business as possible. Groups provide an opportunity to network with others in your area of expertise or interest and may lead to new business contacts and leads.*

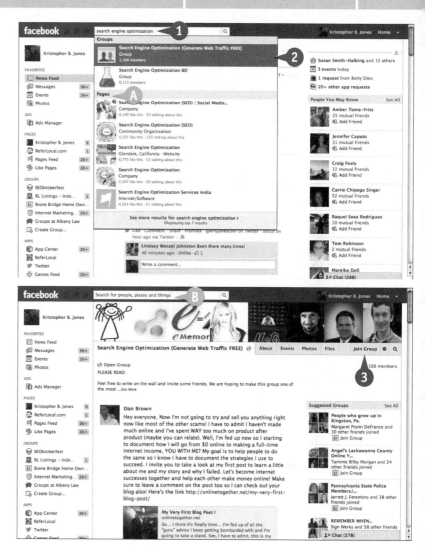

EXTRA

Your personal Facebook page is limited to a maximum of 5,000 friends. If you reach the limit and still want to add more friends, you need to delete connections by going to your personal page and clicking the Friends link. Facebook displays a list of all your existing friend connections. To delete a friend, simply scroll over the Friends icon associated with the friend you would like to delete and select Unfriend from the drop-down list.

Note that another option for promoting your business on Facebook is to create a dedicated Business Page, which is covered in the next section. There is no limit on the amount of connections you can have on a Business Page.

CREATE A FACEBOOK BUSINESS PAGE

Facebook offers a dedicated tool for businesses called Facebook Business Pages to help you grow your business, build your brand, and develop relationships with your customers. Unlike personal Facebook pages, Facebook Business Pages have increased functionality such as analytics and unlimited connections. With more than 1 billion active users on Facebook, it is essential that you create a dedicated page and use it as a promotional tool for your business.

A dedicated Facebook Business Page allows you to provide connections with your company overview, website(s), contact info, press releases, videos, blog RSS, Twitter updates, company news, and status. Moreover, you can interact with your fans by responding to comments and easily display promotions or Facebook-only offers.

Create a Facebook Business Page

1. Log in to your Facebook account and navigate to www.facebook.com/pages/create.php.

2. Select the most relevant business or entity classification. Note that most businesses fall under the Local Business or Place classification.

Note: *Facebook Business Pages are free. However, there are several paid options, such as Facebook Ads or promoted posts, that allow you to significantly increase your business's exposure.*

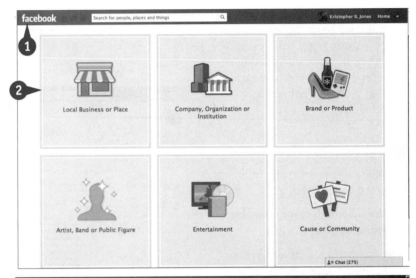

3. Choose a relevant category for your business.

4. Add accurate profile information for your business.

5. Agree to Facebook's terms and conditions.

6. Click Get Started.

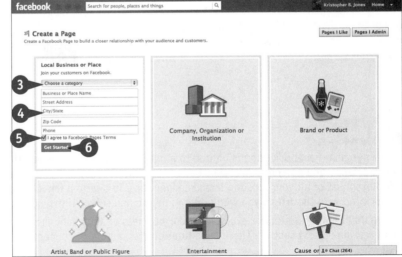

A You can easily post a message to your Facebook Timeline that becomes visible to everyone who has liked your page. The Facebook Timeline allows you to grow your business, build your brand, and develop relationships with your customers by posting relevant content about your business.

B You can add pictures and videos to your Facebook Timeline.

Note: *The key to a successful Facebook Business Page is to engage your connections and grow your base over time. Keep in mind that you need to update the page regularly with fresh content, images, and videos, and work proactively to build connections.*

7 Click the Offer, Event link to create and post an offer to your connections.

Follow all the steps to post an offer on your Facebook Timeline.

C The offer is now visible on your Facebook Timeline.

EXTRA

Facebook offers a paid advertising tool called promoted posts, which allows you to promote specific posts that you make to your Facebook Timeline. Promoted posts appear higher in your News Feed, so there is a better chance your audience will see them. Promoted posts are especially useful for maximizing the distribution of special, limited-time offers and other posts that are intended to drive business transactions or leads.

The cost to promote a post depends on several factors, including your geographic location and how many people you would like to reach. Promoted posts are limited to the reach of your existing connections. However, Facebook offers a product called Facebook Ads, which allows you to promote your business and Business Page to a larger audience.

GENERATE LEADS WITH FACEBOOK ADS

Facebook Ads are paid messages coming from businesses, and they can include social context about friends. People who like your Facebook Business Page spend about twice as much on your service or products than people who are not connected to you on Facebook. Facebook allows you to target its entire network of more than 1 billion active users, but the real value in Facebook Ads is the ability to precisely target specific Facebook users based on demographics and location data.

For example, with Facebook Ads you can target your ads specifically to only show up when they are triggered by location, gender, age, likes and interests, relationship status, or workplace and education data from your target audience.

Generate Leads with Facebook Ads

Create a Facebook Ad to Generate More Facebook Likes

1. Navigate to www.facebook.com/ads/create and choose a Facebook destination or enter a URL.

2. Click the Get More Page Likes option.

Note: *When Facebook users like your page, they will receive updates from you in their News Feed.*

3. Enter text for your ad.

Note: *You should use promotional language or call-to-action text to drive user response to your ad.*

4. Select the part of your Facebook Business Page you want traffic to be directed to. Options include your Timeline, map, photos, or videos.

5. Upload an image to be shown as part of your ad.

Note: *Your image should add value to your ad and increase the likelihood of driving response. Select images that stand out and are likely to elicit a response.*

Ⓐ Your ad appears as it will be seen by Facebook members.

6. Scroll to the bottom of the form and complete the remaining steps, including setting your budget and selecting targeting options.

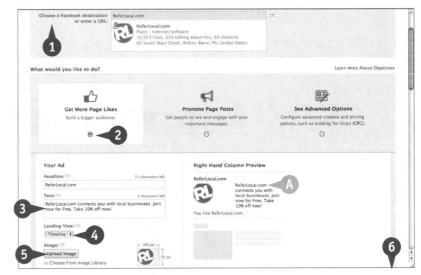

Create a Facebook Ad to Promote Page Posts

1 Navigate to www.facebook.com/ ads/create and select the Facebook destination you would like to promote.

Note: *A Facebook page post refers to when you post a URL on your Facebook Timeline. This type of post occurs when you direct your connections specifically to a page on your website. If you would like to drive more traffic to a page you have shared on your Facebook Timeline, this is the best ad type.*

2 Select the Promote Page Posts option.

3 Select the page post you want to promote.

4 Select the check box if you would like to have an ad updated automatically every time you post.

Note: *Only select the check box if all the posts you make to your Facebook Timeline are commercial. If it is your first time using the Promote Page Posts ad, do not select the check box.*

A Your ad appears as it will be seen by Facebook members.

5 Scroll to the bottom of the form and complete the remaining steps, including setting your budget and selecting targeting options.

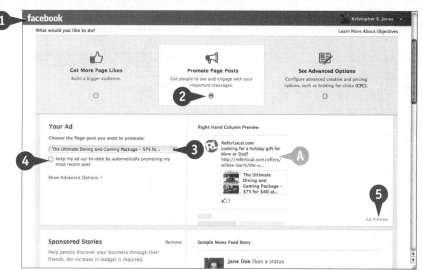

continued

Generate Leads with Facebook Ads (continued)

Select Facebook Ad Targeting Options

1 Scroll to the bottom of your Facebook Ad.

2 Select the location where you would like your ad to display.

A Broadening or narrowing the location increases or decreases the overall reach of your ad.

B As you broaden or narrow your ad based on targeting options, Facebook displays the approximate size of your prospective audience.

3 Select the age of the audience for which you would like your ad to display.

4 Select the gender of the audience for which would like your ad to display.

C Enter a precise interest if you want to further restrict the prospective audience viewing your ad.

D Enter a broad or specific category if you want to further restrict the prospective audience viewing your ad.

E Facebook provides further advanced targeting options that will narrow your audience based on your marketing objectives.

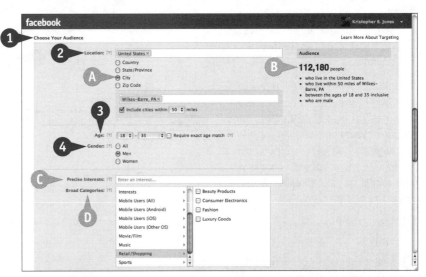

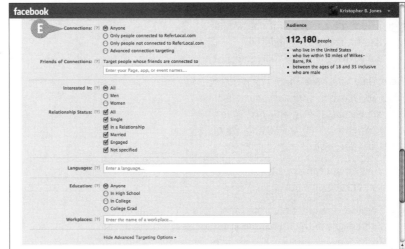

Select Facebook Ads Pricing and Review Your Ads

Ⓐ Once you finish targeting your ad, you need to select your Facebook Ads pricing and review your ads.

① Enter a New Campaign Name.

② Select a Campaign Budget.

③ Select a Campaign Schedule.

④ Select an Optimization option for your ads.

⑤ Click Review Ad.

Ⓑ Review your ads for accuracy.

⑥ Scroll to the bottom of the page and place your order or edit your ads.

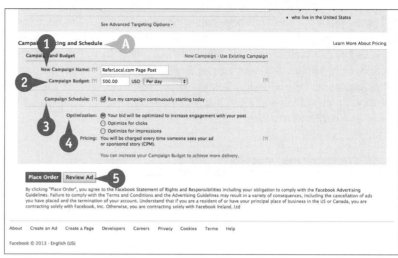

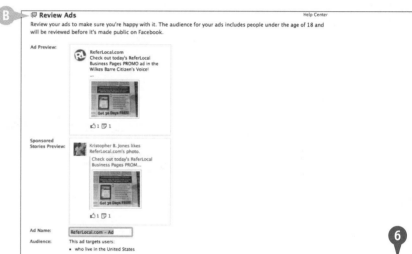

EXTRA

In addition to having the ability to target your advertisements to very specific groups of people as described in the previous task, Facebook advertising also allows you to leverage the power of friend-to-friend marketing through an advertising product called *Sponsored Stories*. Sponsored Stories are messages coming from friends about them engaging with your page, app, or event on Facebook. Friends of friends are more likely to respond to an advertisement if someone they trust, such as an existing friend, has already engaged with the ad. Sponsored Stories are part of the Facebook Ads product, and there is no additional charge to leverage the product.

Maximize Exposure with StumbleUpon

StumbleUpon is a peer and social networking technology that includes a toolbar that you install on your web browser; you can use this toolbar to discover and rate web pages, videos, photos, and news articles. StumbleUpon also allows you to submit your own web pages, videos, photos, and news articles, all of which can help you generate buzz, traffic, and backlinks to your website.

The key to generating buzz, traffic, and links from StumbleUpon is to make sure that your content is submitted and available to other StumbleUpon users. You may want to have other people submit your content so that you can vote positively on it and not appear partial to other StumbleUpon users.

Maximize Exposure with StumbleUpon

① Navigate to www.stumbleupon.com/downloads.

② Click the download link that corresponds to your preferred browser.

③ When prompted, follow the instructions to install the StumbleUpon plug-in to your browser.

Note: As an Internet user, you surf the web and encounter countless websites throughout the day that you like and dislike. By installing and using the StumbleUpon toolbar, you can vote for websites you like and dislike simply by clicking the Thumbs Up button on the toolbar when you are on a website you like, and clicking the Thumbs Down button when you see a website you dislike.

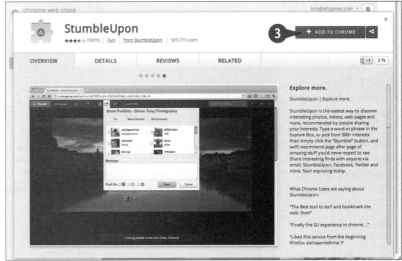

4 After installing the add-on and becoming a StumbleUpon member, visit your website — in this example, www.referlocal.com.

5 Click I Like it.

6 Click Stumble. When you stumble, you will see only pages that friends and like-minded StumbleUpon users have recommended.

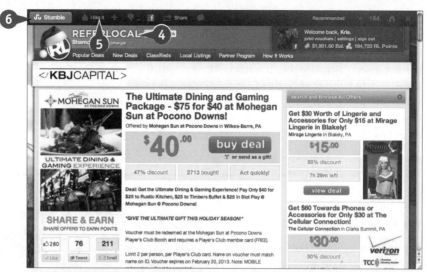

A This is an example of a recommended site for the author's StumbleUpon account.

Note: In addition to voting on websites you come across on your own, the StumbleUpon toolbar allows you to randomly visit other websites by clicking the Stumble button. When you click the Stumble button, the StumbleUpon algorithm displays websites that you may find interesting based upon your personal interests and previous voting behavior. The Stumble button allows you to find cool websites and vote on whether you like them.

EXTRA

StumbleUpon has an online video service called StumbleVideo that can provide a large amount of traffic to your videos. StumbleVideo shows users online videos based upon user preferences along with popularity as determined by votes from other members of the StumbleUpon community.

Unlike StumbleUpon, StumbleVideo does not require registration, and you are not required to download the StumbleUpon toolbar to watch videos. Instead, you simply go to the video.stumbleupon.com website, select a video, and then click the Stumble button whenever you want to watch another video. StumbleVideo offers users several useful features, including the ability to search for other popular videos and to share videos with friends via e-mail.

MICROBLOG WITH TWITTER

A very powerful and increasingly popular way to communicate with friends and clients, build buzz, and generate prospective business leads is through *microblogging*. Microblogging is a form of blogging that allows you to write brief text updates, usually less than 200 characters, and publish them, either to be viewed by anyone or by a restricted group you select. Microblogging is a form of social networking that enables you to keep your

followers up to date with what you are doing at any given time of the day.

The most widely used microblogging network is Twitter. With more than 200 million active members, Twitter is a free social networking service that allows you to microblog by sending short "tweets" of 140 characters or less to others.

Microblog with Twitter

Sign Up for Twitter

1 Navigate to www.twitter.com.

2 Log in to your account or sign up for a new account.

Note: *When you sign up for Twitter, your communication settings are automatically set to public. This means your updates automatically go to both your friends and to the public timeline.*

Follow People on Twitter

Twitter allows you to build a list of friends and associates who view your microblogs.

1 Navigate to www.twitter.com/who_to_follow/interests and browse popular people to follow by category.

2 Search for people to follow based on topic, full name, or @username.

A Twitter automatically makes Follow recommendations based on your user profile and interests.

B The Find friends feature allows you to easily build Twitter followers by sending them e-mail invitations from popular e-mail programs, such as Gmail, Hotmail, Yahoo, and AOL.

3 Click Me to navigate to your personal Twitter start page.

4 Click the Write a Message icon.

5 Fill in the What's happening field with your marketing message.

Note: *One of the ways you can use Twitter to generate website traffic and buzz is by sharing daily deals, special offers, or exciting product news with your readers. If you have an e-commerce website, you may want to send out a message each morning announcing your top-selling products.*

6 Click Tweet.

C Note that your post is now live and part of the main Twitter stream.

Note: *Twitter allows you to quickly communicate and share news. For example, if you manage a music website, you can use Twitter to break news about concerts and entertainment gossip. To promote yourself or your website, you can simply include a tag at the end of each message, such as "Brought to you by X.com."*

D Twitter allows you to send private messages to anyone who follows you.

EXTRA

Another useful feature of Twitter is the *retweet*. A retweet is when you share a tweet posted by another Twitter user with your own Twitter followers. The typical format of a retweet is RT followed by the message. For example, RT @krisjonescom: Internet Marketing Ninjas Chairman Kris Jones to Speak at Upcoming SES NY Conference. Similarly, Twitter offers a Retweet button that automates the retweet. Keep in mind that others may also retweet your posts, which can result in exponential exposure for your tweet.

Build Followers with Twitter Search

Twitter Search, located at https://twitter.com/search, is Twitter's powerful and increasingly popular real-time search engine. Unlike major search engines such as Google and Bing, which update their search indexes every few days or weeks, Twitter Search updates its entire database of tweets as they occur.

The immense popularity of Twitter has resulted in a trend in search-engine marketing called "real-time" search. In fact, Twitter has become a primary resource for breaking news and information on everything from celebrity gossip to politics and world affairs. For instance, Twitter broke multiple real-time stories on everything from the 2012 US Presidential election to the 2013 school shootings in Newtown, Connecticut before the information was available through other media resources, which highlights the importance of incorporating Twitter into your search marketing and web promotion strategy.

Build Followers with Twitter Search

Note: One of the most powerful ways to use Twitter Search and build the number of people who follow you on Twitter is to type keywords into Twitter Search that relate to your specific product or service. When Twitter delivers search results, you should follow those users who mention the target keyword.

① Navigate to https://twitter.com/search.

② Type a keyword related to your business into the Twitter search bar.

③ Click Search.

ⓐ Observe real-time results for affiliate marketing.

ⓑ Note that Twitter recommends people to follow based on your search query.

④ Click any profile picture.

⑤ Click Follow to begin following the user — in this case, the author of this book, @krisjonescom.

ⓒ Twitter shows the most recent tweets for @krisjonescom.

ⓓ Twitter shows the most recent images posted by @krisjonescom.

You can return to the search results to follow more users interested in your original search.

⑥ For another search, navigate back to https://twitter.com/search.

⑦ Type a keyword related to your business into the Twitter search bar.

⑧ Click Search.

Note: *Twitter makes it easy to publicly thank a person complimenting you, or address a person criticizing you, by responding to the original tweet with an @ symbol followed by the username of the person you want to respond to. For example, "@krisjonescom — thanks for saying you enjoy our widgets! We strive to constantly improve, so if you have any additional feedback, positive or negative, please share."*

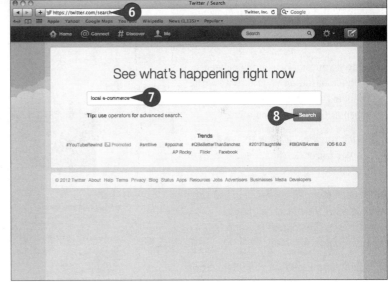

EXTRA

One of the most effective uses of Twitter Search is to monitor what people are saying about your brand. By simply typing your brand name into Twitter Search, you can access all the instances where your brand was mentioned on Twitter. Accessing Twitter search results allows you to see what people are saying about your brand, which can be especially useful if someone is happy or unhappy with some aspect of your product or service. If someone is unhappy, you can immediately reach out to that person and work to address the problem publically or through Twitter's private messaging system.

NETWORK WITH GOOGLE+

Google+, located at https://plus.google.com, is a powerful Google-owned social networking platform that allows you to introduce yourself to others; connect with friends and family; follow interesting people; share images, videos, and interesting content with small groups of people in circles; and easily vote on and share other peoples' content. Launched as a primary competitor to Facebook in June 2011, Google+ has more than 500 million registered users.

Google+ is an important product to leverage for SEO purposes because it provides the Google search engine with extensive social data. In fact, Google has already begun to incorporate Google+ data into search engine results and over time Google+ will play an increasingly important role in influencing Google search results.

Network with Google+

Add Friends to Your Google+ Account

1 Navigate to https://plus.google.com and log in to your Google+ account.

Follow directions to complete your profile and set up your Google+ account.

A Google automatically recommends friends based on your activity with people through other Google products, such as Gmail and Google Talk.

2 Click the View all link to see a larger list of Google's friend recommendations.

Note: *Once you add friends, you will see content from them and be able to interact with the content by sharing it, commenting on it, or +ing it.*

B Similar to Facebook, Google+ allows you to post content, including images, videos, and links, that is made available to your followers.

3 Click the Add all button to add all of Google's friend recommendations.

C You can add friends individually.

D Scroll down the page for additional friend recommendations.

4 Click Finish.

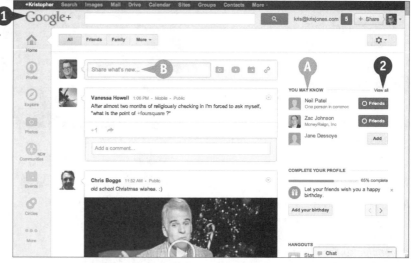

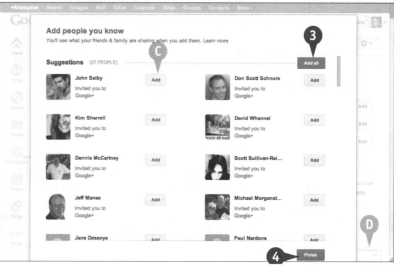

Join and Interact with Google Communities

1 Navigate to www.plus.google.com/communities.

Note: Google Communities presents an opportunity for you to network with like-minded people and allows you to build your authority on Google+.

A Search and join communities based on your interests or profession.

B Google allows you to create your own community. Building your own public community is an effective way to build your reputation and authority on Google+.

2 Discover and join a community by clicking the corresponding community icon.

3 Click the Ask to join button.

Note: Once you are accepted into the group, you can post content to the group and interact with other members' content by commenting, sharing, or +ing things you really like.

C Scroll over the profile images of any member to add that member as a friend.

D You can easily search for content by category.

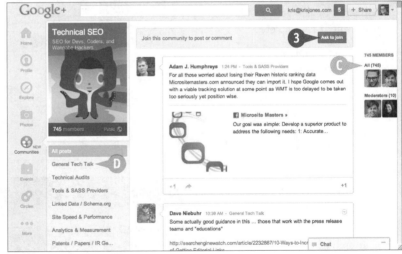

EXTRA

You can leverage Google+ a number of ways to help improve your SEO. When setting up your profile, be sure to embed links to each of your websites and social media profiles. Once your account has been set up, you should share links to each of your websites and any content that is associated with your business. Moreover, you should share links that are valuable in your area of expertise as it will increase the likelihood that others will +1 the content and links you share.

Make sure to follow influencers and actively engage with them and the larger Google+ community, particularly those with interests similar to your areas of expertise and influence.

LinkedIn is a popular business-oriented social networking site that enables you to build a professional network of contacts. The primary purpose of this social network site is to allow you to maintain a list of contact details of people you know and trust in business. The people in your LinkedIn contact list are referred to as *connections*. You can invite anyone, regardless of whether the person is a LinkedIn user, to become one of your connections.

Every time you create new connections, you are, in turn, tapping into a potentially large network of business leads that you can use to help grow your business.

Grow Your Professional Network with LinkedIn

Optimize Your LinkedIn Profile

1. Navigate to www.linkedin.com and log in to your LinkedIn account.

2. Click the Profile link.

3. Click the Improve your profile button to update your profile and make sure it is complete.

Note: *Make certain that all the information on your profile is current and includes all your past educational and professional activities. Your LinkedIn profile serves as a very powerful source for search engines to use to determine your authority for SEO.*

Ⓐ Click the Contact Info link to make certain your contact information is accurate and complete.

4. Follow the prompt to complete your profile.

Note: *Your prompt to complete profile information may be different than what you see in this figure.*

5. Click Next to complete additional profile information and further optimize your LinkedIn profile.

Ⓑ LinkedIn provides information on the areas of your profile that will be enhanced as part of profile optimization.

6. Click Add Connections.

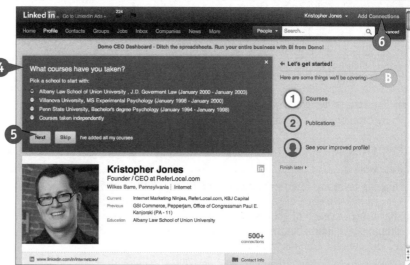

Add Connections and Grow Your Professional Network

1 Select your e-mail provider.

2 Click Continue and follow the steps to send LinkedIn Connection invitations.

Note: *Each time you add a new connection to your LinkedIn network, you gain access to that person's connections. For example, by adding a new connection, you gain indirect access to that person's direct connections (your second-degree connections) and also the connections of your second-degree connections (called third-degree connections).*

Join Groups to Grow Your Professional Network

1 Click the Groups link and select Groups You May Like from the drop-down list.

Ⓐ LinkedIn suggests groups to join based on your activity and engagement with the LinkedIn site.

2 Join relevant groups.

Note: *You can use your network of business connections to recruit employees by sending an internal message through LinkedIn outlining your needs to your contacts. In addition, you can use your connections to explore various business opportunities and to attract people to your website.*

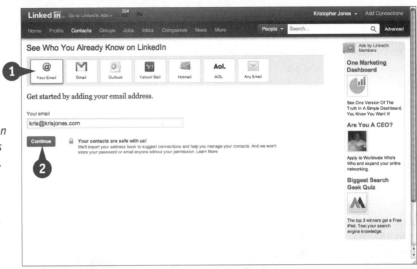

EXTRA

The basic LinkedIn service is free, but there are limits on the amount of InMail you can send and how many *open introductions* you can have at any given time. Open introductions refer to the number of contact requests your contacts can make on your behalf to other LinkedIn members that are neither accepted nor declined. InMail is LinkedIn's internal e-mail system, and introductions let you contact or be contacted by LinkedIn users in your network through the people you know. In this way, your connections can introduce you to anyone in your network (or introduce anyone to you) by forwarding messages through a chain of trusted professionals.

Video websites such as YouTube provide one of the most powerful forms of communication you can use to attract potential visitors and pique their interest in your products, services, and website. YouTube is a video-sharing website that allows users to upload, view, and share video

clips. Posting videos on YouTube is easy and requires minimal time and investment on your part.

You should leverage YouTube as part of your overall marketing strategy to improve your SEO, while also generating website traffic, word-of-mouth referrals, and business leads.

Share Videos with YouTube

Share Videos with YouTube

Note: *Your goal in creating a YouTube video may be to inform or entertain your audience. Entertaining videos tend to create more buzz and result in more viewers than informational videos, so you might choose to create videos that do both. Regardless, try to make your videos interesting so that people will want to share them with friends.*

1 Navigate to www.youtube.com.

2 Sign in to your YouTube account.

Note: *If you already have an account with Google, you can simply log in using your Google username and password.*

3 Click Upload.

4 Click Select files to upload.

5 Locate the video that you would like to upload and click Choose.

Ⓐ Note that YouTube offers you the ability to create videos in real time using your web camera, a video slide show of images, or a Google+ product called Hangout.

Optimize Your YouTube Video for Search

① Write a title that includes target keywords that you would like to rank for in search. For example, the title of this video is optimized for Cute Kid Video.

② Write a description that includes target keywords, such as cute kid video, Northeastern Pennsylvania, krisjones.com, and kbjcapital.com.

③ Add tags that include your target keywords and other words to describe the content of your video.

Ⓐ Note that YouTube offers suggested tags based on your title and description.

Ⓑ Share your video on Facebook, Twitter, and Google+.

④ Set your Privacy Settings to Public. This setting allows the greatest number of people to find your video.

⑤ Select a category that best represents the content of your video.

⑥ Scroll to the bottom of the page to save your video.

⑦ Click the YouTube link to see your video.

Ⓒ Your video now appears live on YouTube.

EXTRA

Videos that receive widespread acceptance and attention, usually resulting in millions of video views, are said to be *viral*. Viral videos are original works that are so unique, funny, or sensational that viewers share them with friends and strangers through blogs, e-mail, and other forms of communication.

Make sure you get credit for your videos. For example, you can wear a promotional T-shirt featuring your business during the video, or simply add your website URL to the credits at the end of each of your videos. Phrases like "Sponsored by Business A" or "Learn more at Business.com" are typical. Another approach is to include a trailer about your business at the beginning or end of each video.

GENERATE TRAFFIC WITH PINTEREST

Pinterest is a social-networking and photo-sharing website that allows users to create and manage theme-based image collections, such as events, interests, hobbies, and more. Users can browse other collections of images called pinboards, "repin" images to their own collections, or "like" photos. Pinterest is one of the top 50 websites

in the world with nearly 50 million users, and is especially popular with the female demographic.

Uploading images from your website and creating pinboards allows you to generate traffic to your website and may improve your SEO. Pinterest is of particular benefit to websites that are rich with colorful and interesting images.

Generate Traffic with Pinterest

1 Navigate to http://pinterest.com/about/goodies.

2 Click the Pin It button to install a Pin It button to your bookmarks.

A Note that the Pin It button has been added to your bookmarks. Simply click the Pin It button from your Bookmarks bar whenever you would like to share an image from a specific web page on Pinterest.

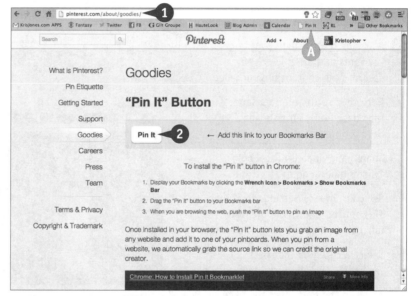

3 Navigate to your website to share an image on Pinterest; for example, go to www.referlocal.com.

4 Click the Pin It button in your Bookmarks bar.

Note: The page displays all the available images on your page that are sharable on Pinterest.

5 Select the image that you would like to post to Pinterest and click Pin It.

Note: To maximize traffic to your website, share images that are colorful, interesting, and most likely to be repinned by other members of Pinterest.

B Verify that the desired image has been captured to share on Pinterest.

6 Create a pinboard. A *pinboard* is a location on Pinterest that is associated with your user account and contains collections of images. If you have already created a pinboard for this image, select it from the drop-down list.

Note: *If you want to create a new pinboard, select Create New Board from the drop-down list.*

7 Describe your picture. Be descriptive and include keywords that people might search to find the image.

8 Select the check box next to the Twitter icon so that Pinterest automatically posts the image share on your Twitter wall.

9 Click Pin It to publish your image to Pinterest.

C Your image pin now appears on your pinboard.

Note: *Your image is now searchable on Pinterest and can be discovered by others who follow your Pinterest account. Search engines may also index your image.*

D Share your pinboard on Facebook.

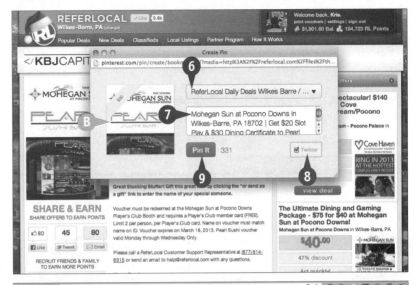

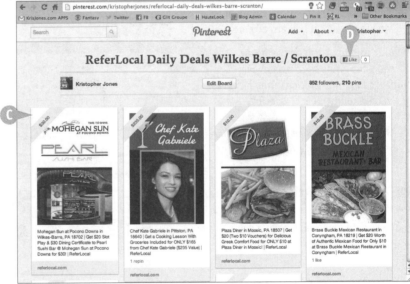

EXTRA

Pinterest can have a positive impact on your website traffic and search-engine rankings. By sharing images on Pinterest, you are making those images and descriptions available to the fast-growing Pinterest community as well as search engines. You can add Pin It buttons next to each image on your blog or website to make it very easy for others to easily share those images on Pinterest. You can work keyword targeting into Pinterest posts as well. Simply use the same target keywords in the Pinterest description as your page that includes the image, along with a link back to your website.

WebmasterWorld is the oldest and most authoritative Internet marketing and webmaster forum community in the world. WebmasterWorld features thousands of discussions on a range of topics, including SEO, social media, and affiliate marketing. Specific forum threads exist on Google, Facebook, and Twitter and often include breaking news and analysis from experienced webmasters.

WebmasterWorld is a great resource for learning more about online marketing and networking with web users with similar interests. WebmasterWorld is also a great place to establish yourself as a web expert by offering insights on your particular discipline. Basic membership is free.

Network with WebmasterWorld

Join the WebmasterWorld Community

① Navigate to www.webmasterworld.com.

② Click the register link if you are not yet a WebmasterWorld member or the login link if you already are.

Note: *If you are registering as a new member, make sure to complete your profile to build trust with existing members of the community. This is especially important if you intend to interact with the WebmasterWorld community, including posting comments and new topics.*

Interact with the WebmasterWorld Community

① Navigate to www.webmasterworld.com/home.htm and log in to your account.

② Locate a topic that interests you and click the subject header; for example, General Search Engine Marketing Issues.

Ⓐ Scroll up or down to locate more topics. Note that most topics are free to access, but some topics are reserved for paid subscribers.

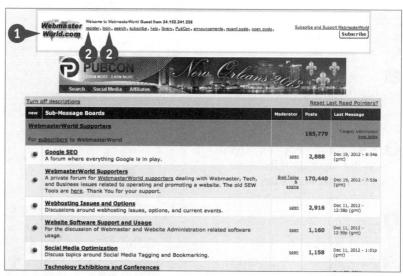

B Your selected topic appears with a list of subtopics.

C You have the option of creating a new subtopic within this category.

3 Locate and select a subtopic; for example, Redirects and backlinks.

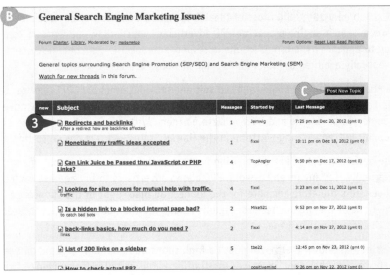

D Your selected subtopic appears.

E Click the Post Reply button to respond to the post.

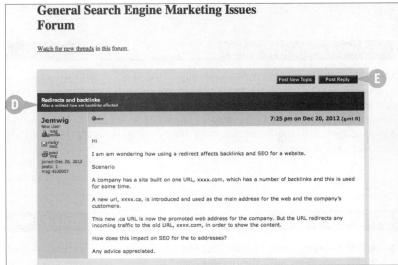

EXTRA

The key to building respect and authority on WebmasterWorld and other similar forums is to respond to posts where your expertise or experience adds value. If you read a post and feel that you have special insight that can add value, you should respond. In addition, if you have a question that can benefit from responses from the community, you should post a new topic. Whenever you add a new topic, make sure you post it in the most relevant part of the forum.

Interacting on forums is an excellent way to build your reputation in your specific profession. Forums are abundant with helpful information and are generally considered highly authoritative by search engines like Google.

AN INTRODUCTION TO PAY-PER-CLICK CAMPAIGNS

In February 1998, Bill Gross of Idealab launched the first pay-per-click, or PPC, search engine, GoTo.com. The GoTo.com search engine pioneered PPC advertising, which allows advertisers to bid on how much they would be willing to pay to appear at the top of results in response to specific searches. GoTo.com later became known as Overture, and was eventually acquired by Yahoo and renamed Yahoo Search Marketing.

In the fall of 2000, Google followed suit and introduced its own PPC service, Google AdWords. Similar to Yahoo Search Marketing, Google AdWords lets prospective advertisers sign up and show advertisements triggered by keywords on the Google search engine and its syndicate partners. Within a few years, Google AdWords quickly became the largest and most popular PPC advertising platform in the United States and remains so to this day.

The basic concept of PPC advertising is very simple. Although the goal of search-engine optimization, or SEO, is to rank "naturally" for any given keyword, PPC allows advertisers to bid against each other for a particular keyword or phrase. Advertisers therefore compete for the highest ad placement in the sponsored results, which typically appear above and to the right of the organic results. Organic results are the nonpaid results located below the sponsored listings on the center of the search results page.

Testing has shown that having both a high sponsored and high organic ranking greatly increases the credibility of your website and, therefore, increases the traffic to your website. If you think of the search results page as a piece of real estate, a powerful strategy is to get your company's name onto that piece of property as many times as you can.

Learn About AdWords Accounts

The Google AdWords platform is constantly evolving so it is important to keep an eye on the latest AdWords news and releases. You can find many sources for this information online; however, the best information comes directly from Google. Joining AdWords communities and following AdWords blogs is essential to PPC success.

Create an AdWords Campaign

When you open a Google AdWords account, you should be prepared to create your first campaign, ad group, text ad, and keywords. If you have not already created a website for your product, you must do so before you can create a PPC campaign. Be prepared to fill in the required information, including a name for your campaign and the text ad that will be shown on the search results. You should have a pretty good idea of what you want to accomplish before you begin.

Target Your Campaign

You can use targeting when you want your text ads shown only to a specific geographic area. You can also target specific languages. Google lets you implement advanced targeting strategies, which is one of the major reasons advertisers have embraced the AdWords online advertising platform. Google enables you to target your PPC ads to virtually any geographic location you want, including local, regional, state, national, and international location targeting.

Write Effective Ad Copy

Text ads are the link between your website and the search results pages. The more targeted and effective your ad copy is, the greater the number of quality customers directed to your website. There are many approaches to writing ad text. Come up with a few variations and test them against one another. PPC advertising platforms such as Google AdWords simplify creating and testing ad copy.

Using Keyword Matching Options

An important aspect of optimizing your PPC account is selecting the correct matching option for each keyword. There are three main options: broad, phrase, and exact. These matching options determine how much and what kind of traffic your text ads receive. Negative keywords help you eliminate unwanted clicks from users who will not benefit from your site. Whether you are trying to get rank organically or with paid search, the keywords you choose are a large factor in your online marketing strategy.

Set Bidding Strategies

When you set a bid within the Google AdWords platform, you are indicating what you are willing to pay for a click. Setting the right bids helps your PPC campaign succeed. There are various bidding strategies that you can choose from; you can explore different options while you experiment with your account. Do not be afraid to spend a little more if the return is worth it.

Export PPC Reports

One of the major benefits of advertising online is robust, real-time, keyword-level PPC reporting. Google AdWords is no exception to this — it lets you run PPC reports on an account, campaign, ad group, and even keyword level. All the information you will ever need to make intelligent decisions is at your fingertips. To master PPC advertising, you first have to master the art of reporting.

Track Conversions

To run the most valuable reports for your PPC account, you must be able to track what customers are doing when they visit your site. The installation of conversion tracking code on your website allows you to track visitor behavior and website conversions, including e-commerce transactions, e-mail submissions, lead form completions, or any other conversion that you choose. You can track whichever information is important to you and your online efforts and make decisions based upon this data.

Using Google AdWords Editor

As your AdWords account expands, it also becomes more difficult to manage. AdWords Editor is an offline tool that allows you to bulk edit and seamlessly manage your campaign so that you can make the most of the time you spend working on your PPC account. The program is offered by Google for free and can help you bulk edit Google AdWords keywords and ad copy. Google Editor is the tool that professionals use, and it is very easy to use, even for a beginner.

Optimize Your Account

Do not forget that once you have your account up and running, you still have a lot of work to do to get things moving in the right direction. You must maintain your PPC account daily if it is going to grow and succeed. Try a lot of different approaches to see what works best based on your particular needs.

When you combine all the available options of PPC advertising, you possess a powerful marketing tool that can hardly be matched. Your text ads can reach the widest audience you choose, or the narrowest; the range is up to you. Remember, however, that these accounts spend money in real time. If you make a change, you need to watch that change and how it affects your account. A careless mistake that slips through the cracks can accrue a lot of fees before anyone notices.

PPC advertising can be a valuable tool in your toolbox if you take your time and build a high-quality account. Combined with your organic traffic, PPC traffic can help you capture all the clicks available for your particular list of keywords. If there is a term you just cannot seem to get your site ranked for naturally, PPC is the answer.

The more important thing to remember is to be creative. Find the keywords that nobody else is bidding on. Write the ad copy that sets you apart from the competition. Drive your traffic to the most relevant destination page on your website. What you take away from your PPC campaign depends on what you put into it.

You can use a Google AdWords account to purchase PPC advertisements on Google and the Google Search Network. The Google Search Network consists of Google partner websites, including highly trafficked websites such as AOL.com, About.com, and Ask.com. There are three major levels within a Google AdWords PPC account:

Account, Campaign, and Ad Group. An account is a unique e-mail address and password with unique billing information. Your account is targeted to the time zone and currency you select. An advertiser can have multiple accounts linked together within a Client Center.

Learn About AdWords Accounts

① Navigate to http://support. google.com/adwords.

Ⓐ You can learn the basics about AdWords by navigating the tabbed sections at the top of the page.

② Click the link to the AdWords blog to read the latest AdWords news.

Note: *Because Google updates its pages often, you may not see this link. Navigate to http://adwords. blogspot.com if the link does not appear.*

③ Subscribe to the RSS feed to stay up to date.

④ Click AdWords Community.

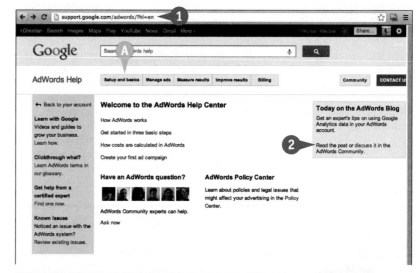

B View the latest tips from AdWords experts.

C Ask the AdWords community for help and advice.

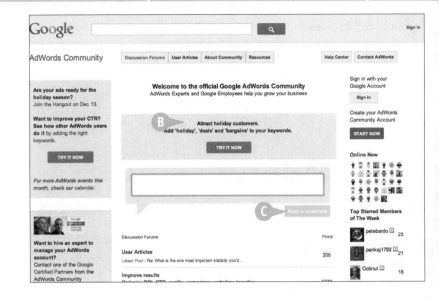

EXTRA

Microsoft's Bing Ads is Google's closest competitor and offers many of the same features as AdWords. Many web searchers use Microsoft's Internet Explorer web browser, which defaults to Bing. This group may not ever see your ads on Google or any of Google's distribution partners and are therefore worth targeting with Microsoft's PPC platform.

In October 2010, Microsoft took over the Yahoo algorithmic and paid search results. This was called the Yahoo and Microsoft Search Alliance and was an attempt by the two companies to better compete with Google and provide more value for web publishers. For search marketers, it was one less platform and one less account to optimize each day.

You should be prepared to create your first campaign, ad group, text ad, and keywords when you open an AdWords account for the first time. The system requires new advertisers to not only enter basic website information but also complete the steps required to display an actual PPC advertisement before account creation can be completed. There is a one-time charge of $5, which you should be prepared to pay with a major credit card prior to account activation.

When you first begin to create your account, you can create a Starter Edition or a Standard Edition AdWords account. The examples in this book use a Standard Edition account; choose a Standard Edition account to ensure that your screen matches those depicted in the step-by-step instructions.

Create an AdWords Campaign

1 Sign in to your AdWords account and click New campaign.

Note: *You will be given three choices. You can target Search, Display, or both. Despite having the option, you should never target both Search and Display with the same campaign. Keeping this data separate will help you make better decisions later on.*

2 For this example, click Search Network Only.

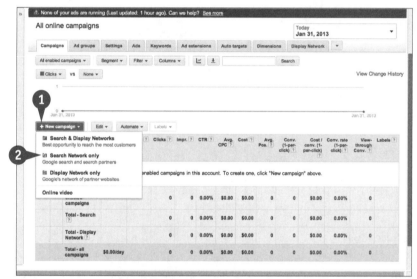

The campaign settings screen appears.

3 Give your campaign a descriptive name that will allow you and others to easily determine the campaign's focus and targeting options; for example, "Brand Terms – USA Targeted – Search."

Ⓐ If you are a beginner, you can leave the default campaign settings alone. You can always come back and adjust things later.

4 Select the location your campaign is going to target.

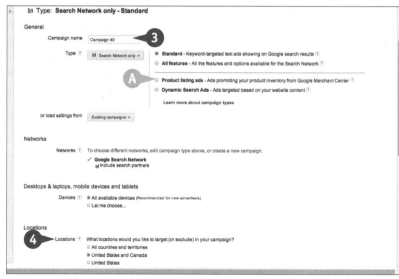

5 Enter the default maximum bid for each keyword.

6 Enter the maximum daily budget.

Note: *These options will vary greatly depending on your product/service, geographic area, and budget available.*

B You can skip Ad extensions for now.

7 Click Save and continue.

The Create ad group screen appears.

8 Name your ad group. Remember to be descriptive. Ad groups should focus on a particular product or service. A good rule of thumb is that each page on your website should have at least one dedicated ad group.

9 Create your headline. The headline should compliment your ad group name. If your ad group is "Blue Widgets," your headline should be "Blue Widgets for Sale."

10 Create your descriptions. Try to include a value proposition and a call to action.

11 Enter your display URL. This should simply be the main URL for your website.

12 Enter the destination URL. Use the most specific URL available for each ad group.

13 Scroll down to Keywords.

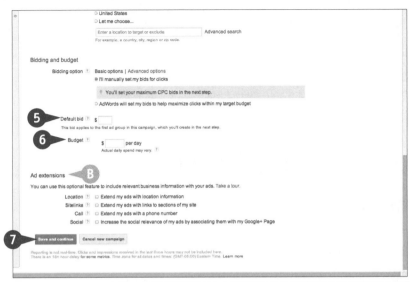

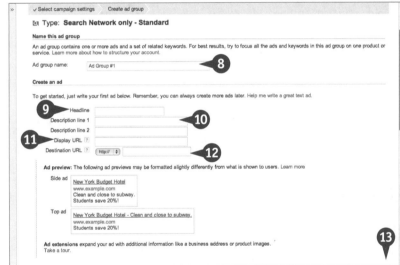

EXTRA

If you already have a Google account, you should use it as your AdWords login. Otherwise, choose a secure e-mail address that you use often and create a password with at least seven characters, both letters and numbers.

You can edit your information, with the exception of currency and time zone, at any time after you verify your account. Google provides numerous tools that allow you to make quick edits or mass edits to any of your advertisements. Moreover, with Google you can easily locate ads that are not appearing and quickly determine what needs to be done for the ad to appear live on the Google search engine.

continued ➤

You can make many adjustments to your campaign settings to take advantage of the advanced functionality Google AdWords offers.

Be sure to accurately set a campaign daily budget and select whether you want your budget spent on a "standard" or "accelerated" basis. Choose the Standard setting to

allow Google to spread your clicks throughout the day while hitting your daily budget. Choose the Accelerated setting to spend your daily budget as quickly as possible. If you spend your entire daily budget in the first hour of the day, your ads cannot run for the remaining 23 hours. Try starting with an accelerated ad display to determine how long it takes to spend your daily budget.

Create an AdWords Campaign (continued)

14 Select your keywords. You do not need hundreds. Typically 10–20 keywords per ad group is sufficient.

15 Scroll down the page to the Ad group bids section.

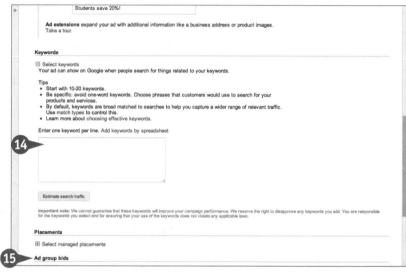

16 Set your default bid. Starting at $1.00 is safe.

17 Click Save ad group.

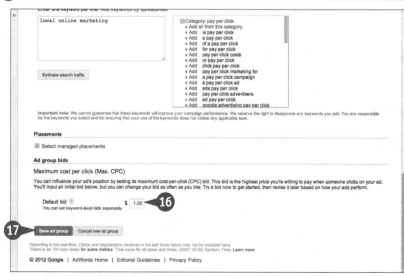

C Your ad is now enabled.

18 You can now see whether your ads are showing or whether you need to make adjustments to your bids.

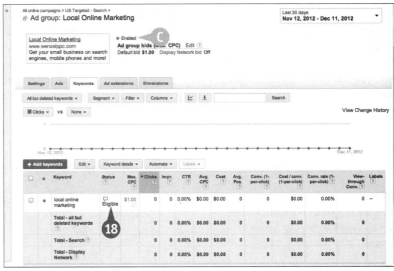

D AdWords will immediately tell you whether your ads are showing, why they might not be showing, and your Quality Score.

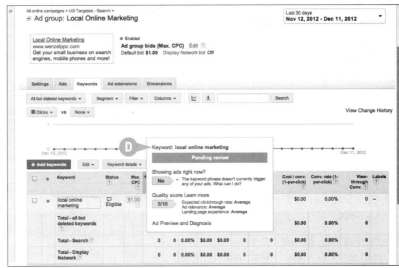

EXTRA

Another valuable tool AdWords offers is the Ad Preview and Diagnosis mode. To access it, click the Ad Preview and Diagnosis link when you are investigating the status of your keywords. A new browser window opens, where you can type in a keyword and search by clicking Preview. The preview tool strips out any data that Google has collected based on your search history and shows you the search results that an average person searching for your product or services would see. This is the best way to preview your ads, test your keywords, and compare your ads with the competition.

Sometimes you may want to create a new campaign rather than add a new ad group. Language and geographical targeting are established on a campaign level. If you want to isolate different regions with different ad text, you can create a new campaign with specific location and language settings to be sure that your ads are relevant to the users who are searching for them. You can also

set separate daily budgets at the campaign level. Many advertisers create a separate campaign for trademarked terms. Trademarked terms tend to lead to a much higher conversion rate than nontrademarked keywords and therefore should be shown at the highest position in the sponsored results.

Target Your Campaign

Note: *To complete this task, first navigate to https://adwords.google. com and sign in to your AdWords account.*

1 Click the Settings tab.

2 Click the name of the campaign with the settings you would like to adjust.

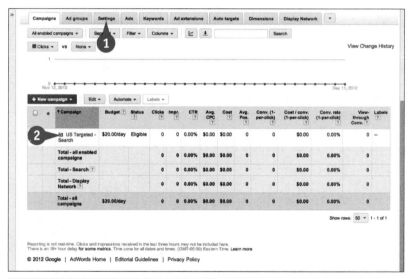

3 Click Edit next to the Networks settings.

4 Deselect the Include search partners check box to limit your ads from showing anywhere other than Google.

5 Save your changes.

Ⓐ Note that you can target ads to appear only on specific devices.

❻ Select the Let me choose option and choose the devices you would like to target. It is a good idea to create separate campaigns to target mobile devices since they tend to perform differently.

❼ Click Save to save your device targeting options.

Ⓑ Note that you can also adjust your campaign's bidding and budget options on this screen at any time.

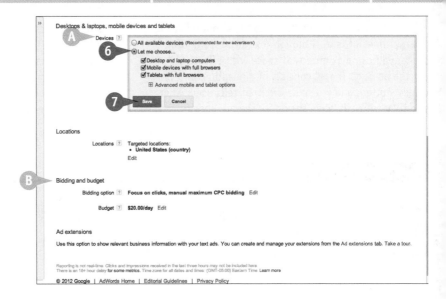

EXTRA

Google's targeting features work in a number of different ways to ensure that your location and language-targeted campaigns are delivering ads to the correct user demographic. The first thing Google verifies is the user's *IP address.* An IP address is a unique number assigned to each computer connected to the Internet and usually denotes a general physical location.

Another Google AdWords targeting option is query parsing. For example, if a user searches for the keyword "Philadelphia bookstores" and you have the keyword "bookstores" targeted to the Philadelphia geographic region, your ad appears to that user.

Keep in mind when targeting various locations and languages that the landing pages on your website should coincide with these settings. In other words, if you are creating a campaign that is targeted to people who speak Spanish, your website should also include information in Spanish. If your campaign is targeted to a specific location, try adding a map of that area to your landing page.

WRITE EFFECTIVE AD COPY

Each of your Google AdWords text ads contains exactly four lines of text. Although text ads have limited space, you can maximize that space with effectively written ad text. The ad consists of a headline, two lines of description, and a display URL that tells users what site they will visit when they click the ad. Specific character limits exist for each line of text. A headline can be up to 25 characters long, and the description lines may contain up to 35 characters. For a complete list of requirements, consult the AdWords Policy Center at http://adwords.google.com/support/aw/bin/static/py?hl=en&page=guidelines.cs.

Write Effective Ad Copy

Analyze a Competitor's Ads

1 Navigate to www.google.com.

2 Type a keyword that you are creating an ad for.

A Analyze your competitors' ads to see what types of ads are currently being run. Notice whether they list prices, shipping deals, and so on.

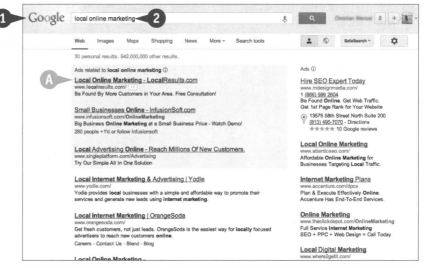

Create a New Text Ad

1 Log in to your AdWords account and click a campaign.

2 Click New ad group.

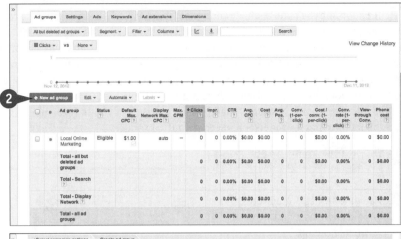

3 Name your new ad group.

4 Write a headline for your new ad using keywords that directly relate to the keywords you want the ad to appear for.

5 Write a description that is likely to entice someone to click your ad. For example, keywords such as "official website" add credibility and "timeless elegance and distinction" communicate value.

Scroll to the bottom of the page to complete the required information and then click Save ad group.

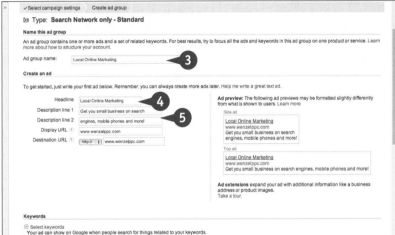

EXTRA

Google AdWords includes a useful feature called dynamic keyword insertion, which inserts text automatically into your ad based on the specific keyword a user types into the search engine.

To use Google's dynamic keyword insertion, you have to add the following phrase into your ad text: {keyword:}. Here is an example of dynamic keyword insertion being used in the headline of a text ad.

> {KeyWord:Shop for Books Here}
> Used and rare books available.
> Best-sellers available too!
> www.example.com

In this example, if the user were to search for the term "NYC Bookstores," the ad would automatically show the keyword as the headline.

> NYC Bookstores
> Used and rare books available.
> Best-sellers available too!
> www.example.com

If the user searched for a keyword that was too long to appear in its entirety, Google would default to the backup phrase entered and the headline would appear as "Shop for Books Here."

USING KEYWORD MATCHING OPTIONS

An important component of keyword generation on Google AdWords is selecting the correct matching option for each keyword. You can use keyword match options to improve your PPC efforts by making sure that your text ads appear when you want them to based on various keyword matching options. There are three main options: broad, phrase, and exact match. Each matching type limits or increases the likelihood that your ad triggers for a given keyword. Broad match is the default setting for every keyword. Therefore, all your keywords will display on broad match unless you specify otherwise by adding quotes around the keyword for phrase match or brackets around the keyword for exact match. For example, the syntax for phrase match is "example" and the syntax for exact match is [example].

Using Keyword Matching Options

1. Navigate to https://adwords.google.com and sign in to your AdWords account.

2. Click a campaign.

3. Click the ad group you want to add keywords to.

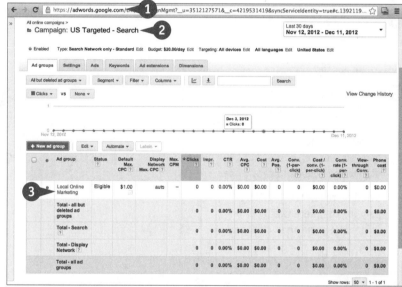

4. Click Add keywords.

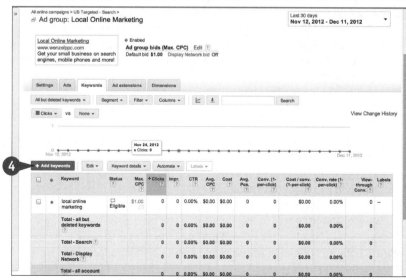

5 Review the various advanced match type options.

6 Apply advanced match types to your new keywords.

7 Click Save.

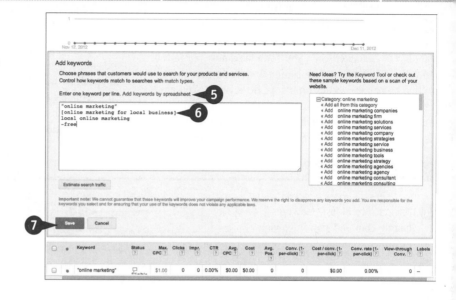

EXTRA

There is a fourth type of keyword that you can add to your account that is not really a keyword at all. *Negative match keywords* do not trigger ads; rather, they prevent your ads from showing when a certain term is part of the search query. One of the most common negative keywords used is "free." If you sell a product like books, you most likely do not want your ad to appear when a user searches for "free books online" or "free books." Using the negative keyword "free" prevents your ad from showing when "free books online" or "free books" is entered into a search engine.

Negative keywords can also be used with phrase and exact type keywords to prevent ads from showing for more specific terms. Google calls this *embedded match* and it is a more advanced form of keyword matching. If an advertiser sells Harry Potter books but does not want to show for the term "Harry Potter," it can be added as an embedded match. If an advertiser does this, the ads trigger for the term "Harry Potter books" but not the term "Harry Potter."

SET BIDDING STRATEGIES

Setting bid strategies enables you to maximize your exposure on PPC search engines such as Google and Yahoo. For example, when you set a maximum bid in the AdWords platform, you are telling Google how much you are willing to pay for a click on a specific keyword. You are not setting the amount you automatically pay for each click. Based on what other advertisers are bidding for the same keyword, you may be charged less for each click; the only

guarantee is that you will never be charged more than the limit you set.

Bids are something you must monitor daily. Your competitors will try to edge your ads out of positioning on a regular basis, and you need to be aware of what is happening on the results pages in order to maintain your desired position.

Set Bidding Strategies

1 Navigate to https://adwords. google.com and sign in to your AdWords account.

2 Click a campaign.

3 Click the ad group within which you want to edit bids.

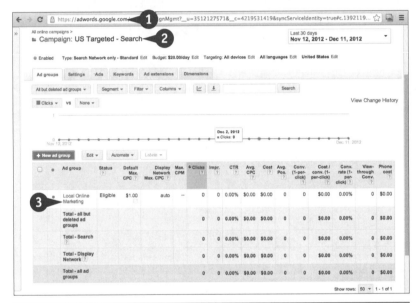

4 Select the keywords you want to edit.

5 Click Edit and from the drop-down list choose Spreadsheet edit.

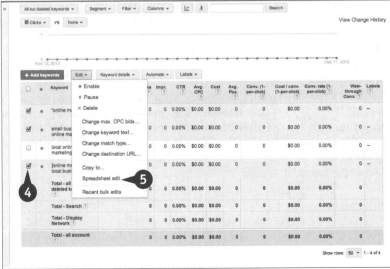

6 Edit one or more of your keyword bids.

Note: *You can edit multiple bids by selecting a cell and dragging the corner down the page, just like you would when working in a spreadsheet application such as Excel or Numbers.*

7 Click Save.

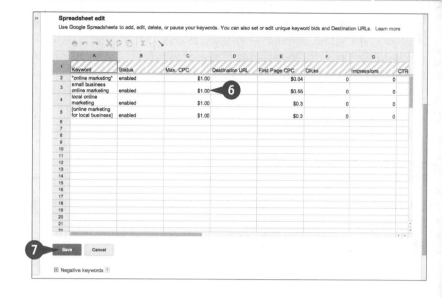

EXTRA

When determining your bidding strategy, ask yourself the following question: How much is this keyword worth to my overall campaign? If you expect a keyword to drive a lot of sales, you want that particular keyword to have a large budget and to be positioned where it will be visible to most users. A high maximum bid with a position strategy of one to three would be a good idea for such a keyword.

On the other hand, if you have a keyword that you suspect may perform poorly but you still want it to appear on Google, you want to set a low max bid. This way, the ad shows lower in the results but still has a chance of being clicked. This could result in an occasional low-cost conversion that you may not have otherwise gotten if you chose not to run the keyword at all.

It takes time to figure out what works for your particular product. Do not be impatient with your bidding strategies. Once you optimize your keyword bids, your account will perform to its full potential, but you will have to actively manage the account to maintain your success.

EXPORT PPC REPORTS

The Google AdWords report exporter is a powerful feature of your AdWords account that enables you to create fully customized reports. The reporting feature allows you to run reports on the account, campaign, ad group, and keyword levels. Important data about the performance of your Google AdWords account is available to you through the reporting feature.

The Google AdWords reporting feature allows you to pinpoint what is and is not working within your AdWords account. You can run reports daily at the keyword level to maximize your return on investment at a very granular level, and also run detailed historical reports to discover which keywords have performed well in the past.

Export PPC Reports

Note: To complete this task, first sign in to your AdWords account.

1 Click the Keywords tab.

A Consider applying a filter before exporting your report. For example, you may want to filter out all keywords that have not had an impression in the last 30 days.

2 Click the Download report button.

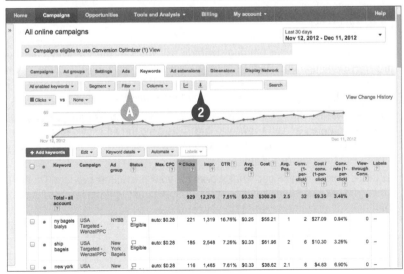

③ Name your report.

④ Choose the report's format.

⑤ You can apply a segment to your report such as Day or Week.

⑥ If you wish to e-mail and/or schedule reports, choose who will receive the e-mails.

⑦ Select a frequency for e-mailed reports.

⑧ Click Create.

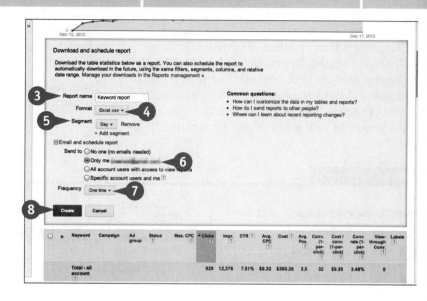

EXTRA

Report scheduling is a great way to stay up to date with your account. Too many automated reports, however, can fill up your inbox and overwhelm you and your colleagues with too much data.

You can cancel an automated report any time by going into the Report management screen and deleting the report. Navigate to the Report management screen by expanding the navigation sidebar on the left side of the AdWords interface. When you click Reports, you are presented with a listing of your scheduled reports if you have any. You can also make any changes to the report if you decide later to include or exclude any information.

If you are trying to cancel e-mails for scheduled reports, you can simply change the report's e-mail frequency without deleting the report. Click the selection in the Frequency column for the report and select One time in the menu that appears.

A key factor in the setup of your Google AdWords account is the installation of conversion tracking code on your website. Conversion tracking allows Google to monitor what occurs on your website after a potential customer clicks an AdWords advertisement. When you enable conversion tracking, Google installs a cookie on the user's browser as soon as one of your ads is clicked. If the

click results in a conversion, the Google cookie passes that information back to the AdWords interface and reports the transaction.

Once Google's conversion tracking registers a conversion, the transaction is defined as a *cost-per-action*. Cost-per-action is the total amount spent divided by the number of conversions.

Track Conversions

Note: *To complete this task, first sign in to your AdWords account.*

1 Click Tools and Analysis.

2 From the drop-down list, click Conversions.

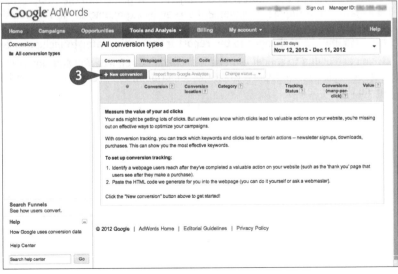

3 Click New conversion.

④ Name your conversion.

⑤ Choose a Conversion location. In this example, conversions will be tracked on a web page.

⑥ Click Save and continue.

⑦ Choose a Conversion category. This step is only for your own account organization.

⑧ Provide details about the page where your conversion will be tracked.

🅐 You can optionally add a value to your conversions. If you have already determined that a newsletter sign-up is worth $5 to your business, you can add that value here and your reports will automatically calculate your return on investment.

🅑 It is good practice to alert your website visitors if you are tracking their actions. Here you can customize the notification to match your website.

⑨ Click Save and continue. Place the code on your site as instructed to begin tracking conversions.

EXTRA

For advanced conversion tracking, Google offers four primary types of unique conversions you can define. The Purchase/Sale label is used by online commerce sites to track individual customer orders, including the revenue that the sale generated. The Lead label allows you to track how many users visited a certain page and entered their contact information. The Lead label may be useful for a website whose primary purpose is to drive leads for a business or an e-commerce site that sends catalogs. The Sign-Ups label tracks how many users may have subscribed to a newsletter, downloaded a document, or requested e-mail updates from the site. Finally, the Page Views label can tell you when a visitor browses a valuable page on the site. If your phone number is on the site, you may want to compare how many times it was viewed to how many times it was called.

USING GOOGLE ADWORDS EDITOR

AdWords Editor allows you to download your account, make additions and changes at any level of your account, and then post those changes directly to Google when you are done. You can work on your AdWords accounts from any location and then simply post those changes when you are able to connect to the Internet.

However, AdWords Editor is best used for making bulk changes to your account. You can copy and paste directly from a Microsoft Excel worksheet to create multiple campaigns, ad groups, text ads, and keywords quickly and easily. There is also a search capability within Editor that allows you to search throughout multiple campaigns and make changes to the individual ads and keywords that meet your criteria.

Using Google AdWords Editor

1 Navigate to www.google.com/intl/en/adwordseditor to download Google AdWords Editor.

2 Choose your operating system.

3 Click Download AdWords Editor.

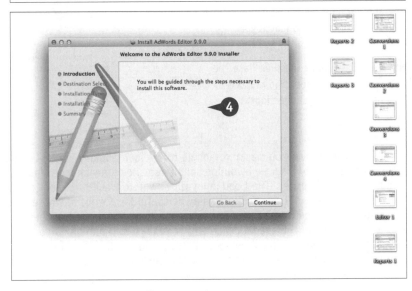

4 When the download completes, launch the installer and follow the steps to install Google AdWords Editor to your computer.

5 Open AdWords Editor and import your AdWords account by clicking Add account then Add/manage accounts.

6 Click Add account, and enter your AdWords e-mail and password.

You can now manage your campaigns, ad groups, ads, keywords, and more within AdWords Editor.

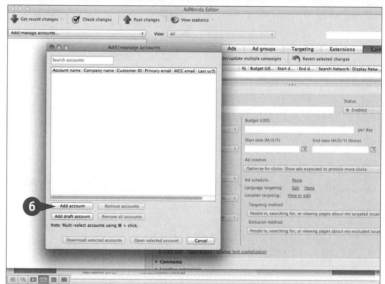

EXTRA

Many useful, advanced options are available with AdWords Editor. For example, with a simple click of a button, the program displays duplicate keywords that you are unaware of and provides the functionality to easily delete them. Duplicate keywords compete against one another and drive up the cost of your campaigns.

Another important feature of AdWords Editor is its capability to download complete exports of your AdWords account. This makes it easy to keep backup copies of your account information. If you chose to download your account monthly, you can always import the backup copies of your campaigns if they were performing better in the past.

Optimize Your Account

To get the most out of your PPC account, you should monitor your account daily. From keyword bids to ad copy, every aspect of a campaign needs to be monitored and tweaked to perform at an optimal level. In addition, you should actively take steps to grow your account as part of your ongoing account-optimization strategy.

Increasing bids is the quickest way to increase the number of clicks your ads receive. When you click a campaign in your AdWords account, you see a list of your ad groups and the average position of each group. Keep in mind that an ad group that has an average position of 12 or higher does not appear on the first page of the search results.

Optimize Your Account

Review Ad Position

1 Navigate to http://adwords.google.com/d/AdPreview.

2 Enter one of your keywords in the search box.

3 Click Preview.

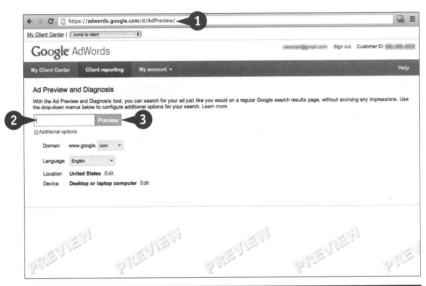

Ⓐ Examine your ad's placement.

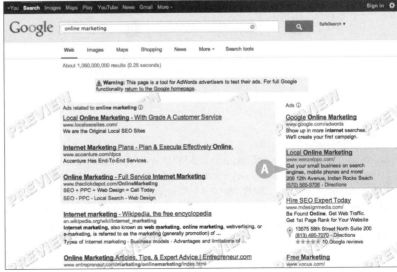

Optimize Ad Position

Note: *To complete the following steps, you must log in to your AdWords account.*

1 Click the Keywords tab and enter the same keyword into the search box.

2 Click Search.

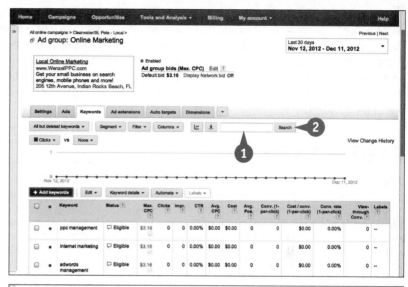

The keywords not containing your search phrase are filtered out.

3 You can edit the bids, edit or add new ad copy, and change match options as necessary to optimize your ad.

Note: *See the previous task to edit your ad using AdWords Editor.*

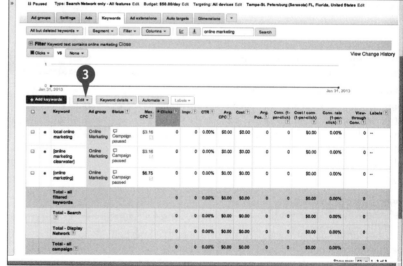

EXTRA

On-site optimization is one aspect of PPC marketing that is sometimes overlooked. This is where your SEO efforts coincide with your PPC efforts. The more relevant Google determines your site to be for a particular keyword, the less, on average, you are charged per click.

An optimized landing page results not only in lower prices on Google AdWords but also in a higher conversion rate. When customers are directed to your site through a paid advertisement, you should direct them to the page most relevant to the keyword that was searched. The fewer times potential customers have to click to navigate your site, the more likely they are to make a purchase.

An Introduction to Quality Score Optimization

In early 2007, Google announced the addition of *Quality Score* to its AdWords pay-per-click, or PPC, platform. Google introduced Quality Score to ensure that those advertisers with the most relevant PPC campaigns rank highest within the Google-sponsored results listings. In the past, advertisers willing to pay more for each click could rank as high as they chose for just about any keyword they wanted. This led to those advertisers with the highest budgets and risk tolerance monopolizing the sponsored results; those with limited budgets and less risk tolerance were left behind. Google's introduction of Quality Score is a sign that Google is interested in serving advertisements that lead to the most relevant search results and overall user satisfaction.

View Your Quality Scores

Other major search engines, including Microsoft's Bing, have followed Google's lead by introducing quality-based PPC search algorithms. This algorithmic shift within the PPC industry has caused much concern on the part of advertisers who previously were able to gain top placement almost solely based on a willingness to pay more than the competition. Now, in order to succeed, advertisers must approach PPC advertising differently, optimizing the Quality Score factors that Google and others use when ranking PPC ads.

Quality Score-based algorithms take into consideration numerous ranking factors, including the overall quality of your landing page, structure of your ad groups and campaigns, click-through rate (CTR), ad copy, and keyword bid, among other things. One of the major benefits of a high Quality Score is a lower overall cost-per-click (CPC), which leads to a lower cost-per-conversion across the campaign. In addition, those ads with higher Quality Scores tend to be ranked higher, on average, regardless of how much an advertiser specifies as a maximum CPC.

Optimize Your Quality Scores

There are some simple and complex methods you can use to optimize your PPC account and generate higher Quality Scores. Structuring your account properly is the first, and most important, step of Quality Score optimization. Other steps include the quality of the landing pages and the effectiveness of the ad copy.

Test Ad Copy

One of the most important things to do when optimizing an online marketing campaign is to test and retest all your Quality-Score-optimization strategies. There are limitless tests you can perform on your ad copy, and you can monitor the results using the various free tools that Google provides. See Chapter 11 for more information on writing effective ad copy.

Utilize Ad Extensions

You can further optimize your PPC ads by adding the latest ad extensions to your ad groups. Ad extensions enable you to include additional information, such as locations, phone numbers, and sitelinks, without affecting the character limits for your ad text. Displaying this supplementary information on your PPC ads can mean the difference between a customer clicking your ad or your competitor's ad.

Test Ad Copy with Advanced Keyword Insertion

By merely inserting your keywords dynamically into your ad copy, you can dramatically increase the clicks your ads receive. Various options are available to you within the AdWords platform, each with different benefits and drawbacks. The only way to decide which one works best is to test each one while monitoring the effect each has on your account.

Using Display Network Targeted Campaigns

Different types of networks are available to AdWords advertisers as well as different methods of displaying and monetizing ads each network presents. The Google Display Network is one of these channels; it allows you to display your ad on many different websites with something in common with your product. In this chapter, you learn how to utilize this avenue and become successful outside the search results.

Using Placement-Targeted Campaigns

Placement-targeted campaigns are similar to campaigns on the Google Display Network, but allow you more control over which sites your advertisements are shown on and where on those sites your ad can appear. By learning the differences between networks, you can intelligently decide which method is right for you and your product.

Install Remarketing

Some advanced techniques that previously required expensive software and advanced coding knowledge are now offered for free through your Google AdWords account. One of these techniques is called *remarketing* and it allows you to serve ads directly to customers who have already visited your site. Learning how to target your marketing effort using this information is invaluable.

Optimize Your Landing Pages

This chapter shows you how to study the pages you are driving customers to, the *landing pages,* and see how certain aspects of these pages influence customers to make purchases or navigate further into your site. Everything from color to font size comes into play when potential customers visit your site, and understanding how to measure and achieve success is key to improving your Quality Score and making the most out of every advertising dollar you spend.

After you understand how deep you can dive into your online campaigns, you are armed with the knowledge you need to control the traffic available to your website and achieve the greatest return on investment possible. The tools to marketing success are completely at your fingertips in the online world, and knowing how to use those tools is a large part of the battle. If you are aware of what is possible, there is nothing holding you back from making the most out of every dollar you spend online to advertise your website. As the visibility of your site grows through these paid platforms, free publicity often results from the increased exposure, and you see your SEO efforts blossom as a result.

If there is one thing you should take from this chapter, it is this: The best thing you can do for your PPC campaign is to remember your ABTs; that is, **a**lways **b**e **t**esting.

G oogle defines Quality Score as "an estimate of how relevant your ads, keywords, and landing page are to a person seeing your ad." Relevancy is very important to Google. The reason that most people continue to use Google to search the Internet is because Google provides the most relevant search results. To ensure that

their advertisers also focus on relevancy, Google created Quality Score and began rewarding advertisers whose ads, keywords, and landing pages provide the best experience to their users. Google rewards these advertisers by placing their ads at a higher position for a lower CPC than their competitors.

View Your Quality Scores

1 Navigate to https://adwords. google.com and sign in to your AdWords account.

2 Click a campaign, and then click the ad group that you want to optimize.

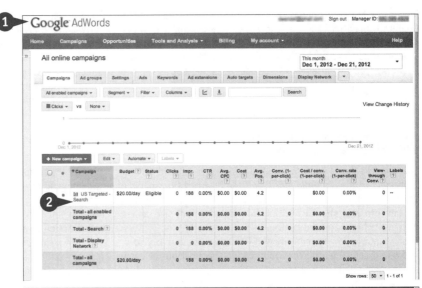

3 Click Columns and select Customize columns.

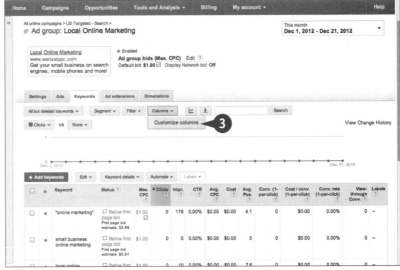

④ Navigate to the Attributes
section.

⑤ Click Add next to the Qual. score
attribute

Note: *You can arrange the order of
the columns in this window. Moving
the Qual. score column close to the
keyword is helpful.*

⑥ Click Apply.

Ⓐ Each keyword's Quality Score
appears.

EXTRA

Building up a good Quality Score can take some time. There are some aspects of Quality Score that advertisers
cannot control, such as the historic performance of a keyword across all AdWords campaigns. Certain keywords are
flagged with a low Quality Score as soon as they are added to an account and there may be nothing you can do to
improve it. Other keywords can take up to 90 days to achieve their maximum Quality Score and lowest CPC.
Remember that the score is just a guideline and some profitable keywords may never achieve a 10/10, so do not
give up on them.

OPTIMIZE YOUR QUALITY SCORE

The more specific your ad groups, the more specific your ad copy can be for those ad groups. This increases keyword-to-ad copy relevancy and in turn can raise CTRs. If you sell basketball shoes, create an ad group called Basketball Shoes, and within that ad group only have keywords that are directly related to the basketball shoes you sell. You can get even more specific and create ad groups for every brand of basketball shoes you sell. The more specific the ad groups, the more specific you can make the ads contained within those ad groups.

The synergy between the keyword, ad copy, and landing page within ad groups is something you can control and optimize to increase Quality Score.

Optimize Your Quality Score

① Navigate to https://adwords.google.com and sign in to your AdWords account.

② Click a campaign, and then click the ad group that you want to optimize.

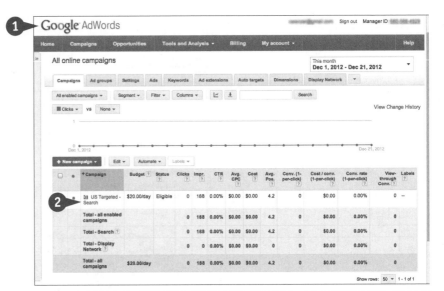

③ Hover your mouse pointer over a keyword's status icon.

Ⓐ Notice that your Quality Score is based on three main criteria: Expected clickthrough rate, Ad relevance, and Landing page experience.

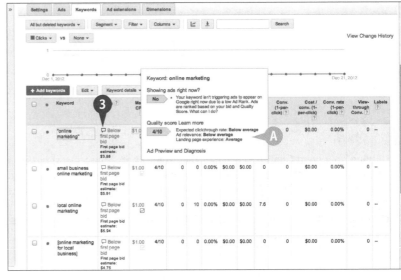

Note: *Expected clickthrough rate and Ad relevance tend to go hand in hand. If either is below average, you probably need to optimize your ad copy.*

④ Click the Ads tab and investigate your ad copy.

Ⓑ Does the ad headline include the keyword?

Ⓒ Does the ad description also contain some variation of the keyword, a value proposition, and a call to action?

Ⓓ Is the display URL and landing page the best possible match for the keyword and ad copy?

Note: *Ensuring that your keywords, ads, and landing pages are all in agreement and that your website loads quickly are the best ways to improve your Quality Score.*

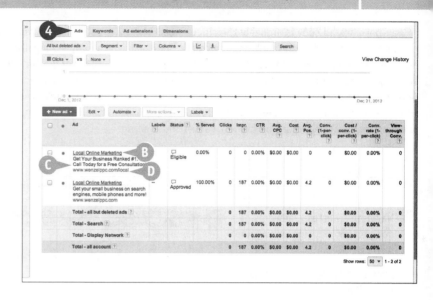

EXTRA

If a keyword does not seem to be performing well for you, do not necessarily give up on it immediately. Try creating a new, more specific ad group for that keyword and other keywords like it. Write new ad copy with that keyword in the text. You might even want to go as far as creating a new page on your website that revolves around that term.

Another easy way to ensure your campaigns are well optimized is to look at the number of specific pages that make up your website. A campaign that is correctly Quality-Score optimized should have at least one ad group for each page within the site. For example, if your web page is made up of ten separate pages, your PPC campaign should have at least ten different ad groups within it.

Study the structure of your site and create your campaign structure with that in mind. Suppose you have a site dedicated to shoes, and within that site you have a page for tennis shoes, basketball shoes, and running shoes. Consider creating a PPC campaign called Shoes and ad groups within it called Tennis Shoes, Basketball Shoes, and Running Shoes.

Pay-per-click ad copy is arguably the single most important aspect of the AdWords campaign. Your text ads directly compete with those of your competitors, and someone searching for a product or service like yours in Google quickly scans all the ads on the search results page to find the message that is the best match. You might have the most relevant keywords and highest converting landing pages in your industry, but if a customer does not find your ad copy compelling, that person may never even visit your site. Long after you have perfected your keywords, bids, and website, you will still be finding ways to optimize your ads, improve their click-through rates, and stand out from the competition.

Test Ad Copy

1 Navigate to https://adwords. google.com and sign in to your AdWords account.

2 Click a campaign that you want to optimize.

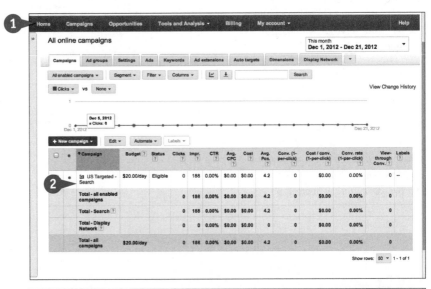

3 Click the Settings tab.

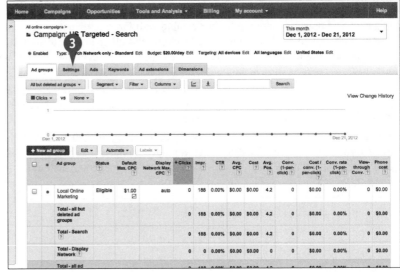

4 Scroll down to the Advanced settings section and expand the Ad delivery section.

Note: *If you do not see Advanced settings, you may need to adjust your campaign type to include All features at the top of the Settings page.*

5 Click Edit, and choose the Rotate Evenly setting so that your ad reports consist of consistent, even results. Click Save.

6 Click the Ads tab.

A Always run more than one ad variation in each of your ad groups. Try to choose one variable, such as the headline text or call to action, and keep the rest of the ad identical. After a few days, you will be able to tell which variable sends the most clicks or sales. Pause the less effective ad and create a new variation to test.

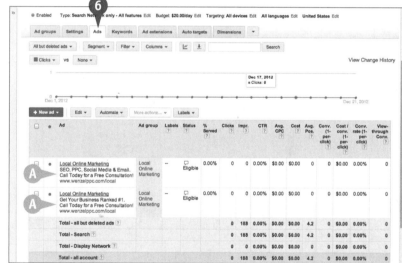

EXTRA

Your competitors can often provide some excellent advice for improving your ads without them even knowing it. Try testing different ad variations based on the other ads that appear when you search for one of your keywords. If your competition offers free shipping, so should you. If they claim to be "authorized" or the "official store," see what you can do to gain the same credentials. On the other hand, you may want to try to do what the competition is not doing. If none of the other ads on the page offers a coupon code, offer one yourself. Always remember that Internet shoppers are looking for the best deal.

UTILIZE AD EXTENSIONS

Google AdWords accounts are continually being updated and enhanced with new features. One easy and important way to stay ahead of your competition and increase the Quality Score of your ads is to implement any new features as soon as they become available. One of the main areas where new features are constantly popping up is called ad extensions. These extensions allow advertisers to add more information about their businesses, such as addresses and phone numbers. Advertisers also have the option to add sitelinks to their ad copy, which allows potential customers to navigate directly to a page on the advertiser's site that they determine is the most relevant page for their needs.

Utilize Ad Extensions

1 Navigate to https://adwords. google.com and sign in to your AdWords account.

2 Click a campaign.

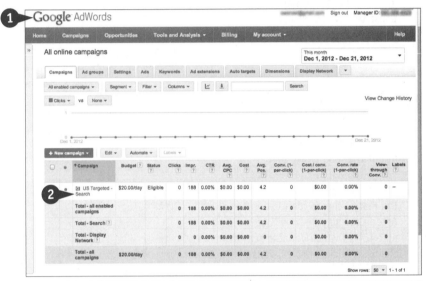

3 Click the Ad extensions tab.

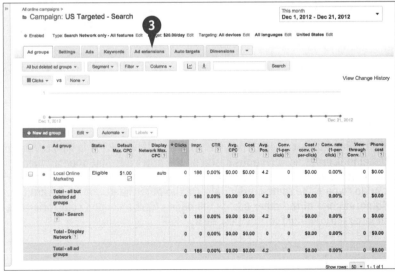

4 Choose Location Extensions in the View drop-down list.

5 Scroll down to Manually entered Addresses and click New Extension.

6 Choose Create new extension and fill out the required information.

7 Click Save.

8 Choose Sitelinks Extensions in the View drop-down list.

9 Choose Create new extension and fill out the required information.

Note: *Try to create sitelinks that will highlight all that your site has to offer as well as feature the most commonly visited pages. Creating a sitelink for customer support helps your customers get the information they need quickly while creating a sitelink for your top-selling product may alert customers to a section of your site that they would not visit otherwise.*

10 Click Save.

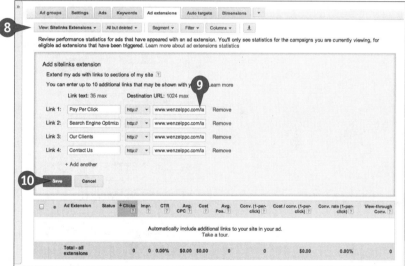

EXTRA

Remember to return to the Ad extensions tab to get detailed reporting on the performance of your ad extensions and to optimize and test based on the data you find. For example, if you have four sitelinks that you have created for your ads, you can examine their performance and determine whether a sitelink click resulted in a sale or a lead. If you notice that a particular group of sitelinks is not getting any clicks, try something different. If you notice that clicks on sitelinks are resulting in leads, try creating similar sitelinks for your other ads. There is no limit to how many extensions you can create, but you can only run one at a time.

TEST AD COPY WITH ADVANCED KEYWORD INSERTION

You can use the {keyword} parameter to automatically populate ad copy with the keyword that triggered the display of the ad. This can increase CTRs and directly influence keyword Quality Scores. There are advanced methods to format the {keyword} parameter that change the appearance of the dynamically inserted text.

By capitalizing the "K" and the "W," you can have the AdWords platform automatically format your keyword into proper case. For example, the headline {KeyWord:Shop Here} displays the text "Basketball Shoes" when the keyword "basketball shoes" is searched for.

Test Ad Copy with Advanced Keyword Insertion

1 Navigate to https://adwords. google.com and sign in to your AdWords account.

2 Click a campaign, and then click the ad group that you want to optimize.

3 Click the Ads tab.

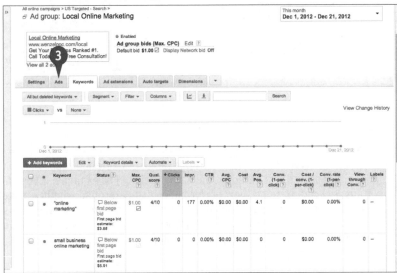

④ Choose New ad ➔ Text ad.

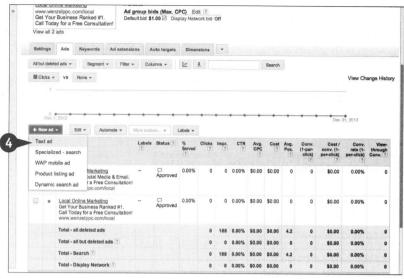

⑤ Enter the {KeyWord:} parameter into any line of the ad; for example, {KeyWord: Local Online Marketing}.

Note: *If the keyword that triggered the ad has too many characters to fit in the designated spot, or if the keyword is trademarked and restricted from appearing in ad copy, Google displays the alternate text that you provide within the brackets.*

Ⓐ View the ad preview to ensure you have done this correctly.

⑥ Click Save ad to save your ad.

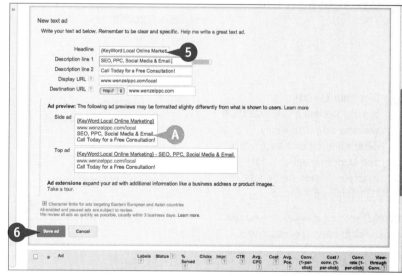

EXTRA

As mentioned throughout this chapter, one of the major factors affecting Quality Score at the text ad level is the CTR. Using the keyword insertion techniques discussed in this task can significantly increase the rate at which customers click your ads.

One of the major benefits of a high CTR is that as your Quality Score increases, keyword and ad combinations become eligible to appear above the organic search results. These top ad positions receive most of the PPC traffic for any given keyword or phrase. If your ad achieves a top position, the CTR is likely to receive a significant boost, again leading to more page views and more conversions.

Within the AdWords platform are various networks to which you can target your campaigns. One of these networks is called the *Display Network*. Display Network targeted campaigns allow you to place your ads on other websites, where they will appear as image ad banners or as text ads. Display Network targeted campaigns are perfect for advertisers who are looking to increase brand awareness, announce a big sale or event, or even advertise their products or services on major Google properties such as YouTube and Gmail. When creating Display Network targeted campaigns, remember that they are a completely different animal and should be kept separate from Search targeted campaigns.

Using Display Network Targeted Campaigns

1 Navigate to https://adwords. google.com and sign in to your AdWords account.

2 Click New campaign.

3 Click Display Network only.

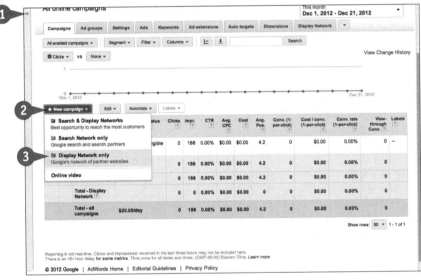

4 Give your campaign a descriptive name that will allow you and others to easily determine the campaign's focus and targeting options; for example, "Brand Awareness – USA Targeted – Display."

Note: *If you are a beginner, you can use the default campaign settings. You can always come back and adjust things later.*

5 Select the location your campaign is going to target, the default maximum bid for each keyword, and your daily budget.

Note: *These options will vary greatly depending on your product/service, geographic area, and budget. Start conservative and adjust as needed.*

6 Scroll down and click Save and continue.

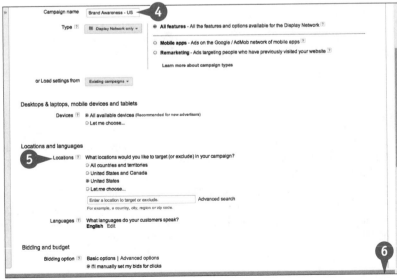

7 Name your Ad Group. Remember to be descriptive.

8 Choose a Default bid. $1 is a good place to start.

9 Select the Display Keywords option.

10 Enter a few keywords that describe the type of site you are targeting. For example, on a web page that includes brownie recipes, AdWords might show ads about chocolate brownies or dessert recipes.

11 Click Save and continue.

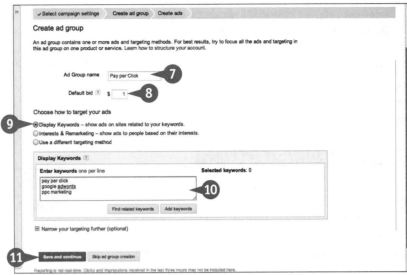

12 Create an ad by choosing an image and filling out the required fields.

A There are four types of ads you can create. An image ad is a graphic that you upload to Google. A text ad is similar to the ads you create for the Search Network. The Display ad builder guides you through the simple process of creating a banner ad based on Google's templates. Finally, a Video ad allows you to upload a video that will play when users click it.

13 Click Save ads.

EXTRA

Campaigns on the Display Network run the risk of overspending at a moment's notice. For example, your ad may be displayed on a site that normally receives about 100 unique visitors per day. An ad on this site may only cost you a small amount of money every day; however, if this website suddenly generates a large amount of press when it is featured on a major news website such as Reddit or in a national magazine or newspaper, the traffic coming to the site could increase dramatically. On the Display Network, a 25-cent daily ad spend can turn into $250 overnight. To avoid this type of overspending, be sure to set strict budgets on your Display Network campaigns.

USING PLACEMENT-TARGETED CAMPAIGNS

Placement-targeted campaigns are another type of Display Network targeted campaign. A placement-targeted campaign lets you choose specific sites on which to advertise.

You can choose which sites you want your ads to appear on in two ways. The first way is to name the specific site you want to advertise on. If you are browsing the web and

come across a site that you think your target customers might be viewing, check to see whether the phrase "Ads by Google" appears anywhere on the site. If it does, you can choose this site for your placement-targeted campaign.

The second way you can target your campaign is to use the data from your keyword-targeted display campaigns to find sites that perform well for you.

Using Placement-Targeted Campaigns

① Navigate to https://adwords. google.com and sign in to your AdWords account

② Click New campaign.

③ Click Display Network only.

④ Give your campaign a descriptive name that will allow you and others to easily determine the campaign's focus and targeting options; for example, "Brand Awareness – USA Targeted – Display."

Note: *If you are a beginner, you can use the default campaign settings. You can always come back and adjust things later.*

⑤ Enter the location your campaign is going to target, the default maximum bid for each keyword, and your daily budget.

Note: *These options will vary greatly depending on your product/service, geographic area and budget available. Start conservative and adjust as needed.*

⑥ Scroll down and click Save and continue.

7 Name your Ad Group. Differentiate your placement-targeted ad groups from other display ad groups.

8 Choose a Default bid. $1 is a good place to start.

9 Select Use a different targeting method and select Placements.

10 Enter the placements you have chosen to target.

Note: *You can also search for placements based on keywords or by entering a similar website.*

11 Click Save and continue.

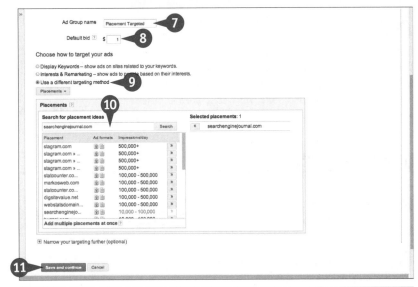

12 Create an ad by choosing an image and filling out the required fields.

A There are four types of ads you can create. An image ad is a graphic that you upload to Google. A text ad is similar to the ads you create for the Search Network. The Display ad builder guides you through the simple process of creating a banner ad based on Google's templates. Finally, a video ad allows you to upload a video that will play when users click it.

13 Click Done.

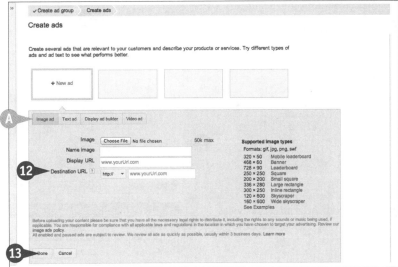

EXTRA

Placement-targeted campaigns offer you an option that keyword-targeted campaigns do not: the ability to reach out to a new demographic that you are otherwise unable to target by bidding on keywords. Because of the way the Google Quality Score algorithm works, if you try to bid on a keyword that does not directly relate to the content of your site, you are slapped with a high CPC and risk the chance of your ad not appearing at all. This makes thinking outside the box difficult. Placement targeting allows you to choose any site that you think might be a worthy platform for your product, which makes it an excellent tool for branding campaigns.

INSTALL REMARKING

marketing is a feature that lets you reach people who have previously visited your site, and show them relevant ads when they visit other sites on the Google Display Network. For example, when people leave your site without buying anything, remarketing helps you connect with these potential customers while they browse other websites. You can even show them a compelling message or offer that will encourage them to return to your site and complete a purchase.

You add a piece of code (a remarketing tag) to all the pages of your site. Then, when shoppers come to your site, they will be added to your remarketing lists. You can later reach out to these potential buyers while they browse other websites.

Install Remarketing

1. Navigate to https://adwords.google.com and sign in to your AdWords account.

2. Hover your mouse pointer over the gray sidebar on the left of the screen until it expands.

3. Click Shared library.

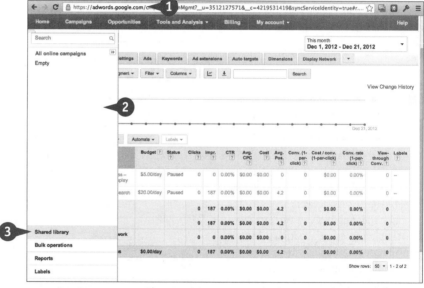

4. In the Audiences box, click view.

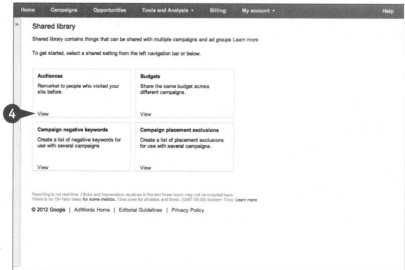

⑤ Click Set up remarketing.

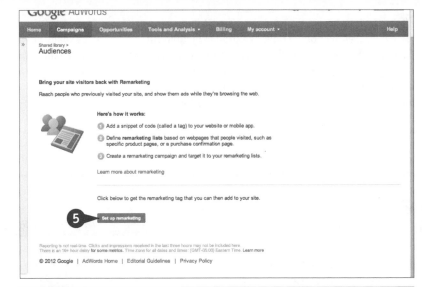

⑥ Select and copy the remarketing code.

Paste the remarketing code at the bottom of all the pages on your website, right before the `</BODY>` tag.

⑦ Click Continue to create specific lists for the various sections of your site. For example, if you have a page on your site that captures leads, you may want to create a specific remarketing list that targets all visitors who did not already complete the form.

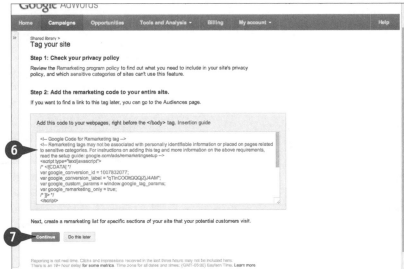

EXTRA

If you decide to install the Google remarketing code on your website, Google requires that you inform your website visitors that they are anonymously being tracked by including a privacy policy somewhere on your website where it can easily be found. Including this information is important both legally and in building trust between you and your website visitors. If you would like more information on privacy policies and the information that Google suggests that you include in your own, visit http://support.google.com/adwords and search for "information to include in your privacy policy".

OPTIMIZE YOUR LANDING PAGES

The landing page onto which you drop a searcher who has clicked one of your ads is extremely important. First, be sure that the landing page accurately pertains to the keyword that leads to it. If searchers are dropped on a page that has nothing to do with the term they were looking for, chances are they will feel tricked and navigate away immediately. Next, you need to be sure that the web page loads quickly. If the landing page takes a long time to load, chances are good that visitors will change their minds and navigate away from the site before they see what you have to offer.

Optimize Your Landing Pages

1 Navigate to https://adwords. google.com and sign in to your AdWords account.

2 Click the Tools and Analysis menu and select Google Analytics.

3 Click Content.

4 Click Experiments.

5 Enter the URL for the page you want to improve.

6 Click Start Experimenting.

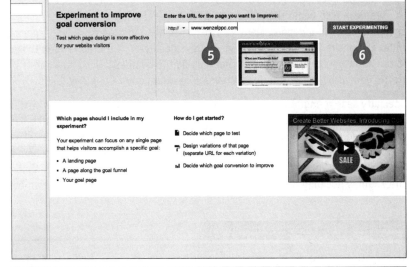

7 Name your experiment.

8 Identify the pages you want to test.

9 Click Save & Next to finish the process.

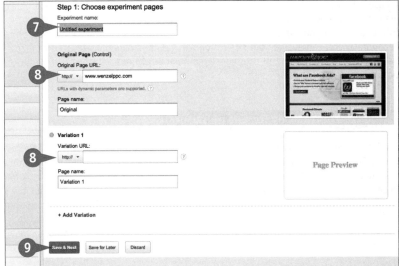

EXTRA

The landing page is one of the most discussed aspects of Internet marketing. The number of tests and tweaks you can perform is almost limitless. Every single factor comes into play and can influence the overall conversion rate for your campaign drastically. You first need to consider if you have chosen the right page. As an alternative to the Google Website Optimizer, consider a series of your own simple *A/B landing page tests*. This term is used to describe sending an equal amount of traffic at equal increments throughout the day to two landing pages. This type of test shows you which page is driving more conversions and which page is causing your potential customer to shop elsewhere.

After you have optimized your website for Google, you can sit back and catch your breath for a short time; however, you can also begin the process to drive even more traffic to your website using methods to optimize for image search, shopping search, and more. Many websites specialize in organizing very specific types of websites rather than trying to index the entire Internet. Getting your site exposure on these more targeted search engines can result in extra traffic, or it can allow you to target a niche that may be too competitive to rank for in the major search engines. The incremental traffic gained by optimizing for search engines outside of Google will allow you to stand out from the competition.

Specialty search engines cater to specific users by indexing only content within a specific area or niche. For example, some of the most useful specialty search engines allow web users to search blogs, images, auction sites, social bookmarks, or classified ads. Although you can use Google to search for practically any kind of information, using specialty search engines allows you to minimize nonrelevant search results, as well as become part of the community that is typically associated with niche engines. People who use search engines such as Technorati, eBay, and Shopping.com tend to use the engines not only to search for information but also to submit their own blogs or products.

Optimize Blog Posts for Technorati

Technorati is an example of a specialized search engine. It focuses mainly on blogs and allows users to search only for websites that have blogs about the specific topic they are interested in. If you can get your blog to rank high on Technorati, you can ensure your site's blog will get hundreds of new readers every day and in turn boost the number of links pointing to your website.

Unlike leading search engines such as Google and Bing that attempt to index the entire web, Technorati indexes only blogs. Technorati is the world's first and largest blog search engine. Technorati publishes a popular daily list of the top 100 blogs located at http://technorati.com/blogs/top100.

Optimize Your Images for Google Images

Google Images returns only images when a user enters a search query. This platform allows anyone searching for pictures to quickly browse and download images from all over the web. Recently, Google began showing select image results as part of its main search results. As a result, getting your images ranked by Google Images can result in significant supplemental website traffic beyond traditional search-engine marketing.

You can increase your rankings in Google Images in several ways. For example, make sure that the keyword you want the image to rank for is in the same table cell as the image. Another tip is to put the keyword above or below the image using a <div> or floating <div> tag. You should also place the keyword in the alt image tag, the image name, and the image meta file summary. Finally, and most important, make sure you include the keyword in the same paragraph as the image.

Increase Exposure on Ask.com

Ask.com was originally known as Ask Jeeves and allowed users to get answers to everyday questions phrased in natural, everyday language. In other words, the phrase "Who is the president of the United States?" would return results that answered that question. The need for this oversimplified search engine diminished as everyday users became more web savvy

and comfortable with the way that search engines like Google and Yahoo work. In February 2006, the Jeeves character was discontinued and the engine rebranded as Ask.com. Although Ask has faded in popularity over time, it continues to be one of the top five most popular search engines in the United States.

Improve Your Ranking on Bing

Bing is the search engine of Microsoft Corporation and was released in 2009 to replace Microsoft's predecessor search engines Live Search, Windows Live Search, and MSN Search. Bing is becoming an increasingly serious competitor to Google as both a stand-alone search engine and also because of a licensing partnership it has to power Yahoo's search technology.

The combined Yahoo-Bing search partnership represents roughly 26% of all U.S. searches, while Google continues to dominate with nearly 70% of all U.S. searches. Ranking well on Bing requires a similar approach to Google; however, unique Bing features, such as related searches, allow you to tailor your SEO efforts to improve your rankings on Bing.

Using Shopping Engines to Drive Traffic

Comparison shopping engines have become one of the most popular places for web users to compare prices and shop for products online. These engines specialize in giving consumers all the information they need to make thrifty purchases from online merchants. Shopping.com, PriceGrabber, Shopzilla, and BizRate.com are all favorite destinations for Internet shoppers, and if your site offers a product, be sure to get it listed on one or more of the leading comparison engines.

Keep in mind that getting your products listed on the leading comparison shopping engines is not free. The vast majority of comparison engines charge you to list your products on a cost-per-click (CPC) basis. You must pay a percentage of any sales referred for every user sent to your website by each comparison engine.

Produce Sales with eBay Auctions

eBay is the number-one name in online auctions. eBay allows users to compete to buy and sell new and used items. Some people have made a full-time job out of this practice. If you know how to get exposure for your products on eBay, you are well on your way to becoming one of those people who count the auction site as a never-ending source of revenue.

Using Craigslist to Drive Traffic

Craigslist is the ultimate site for advertising your products locally. Whether you are looking for a job, an apartment, or a new family pet, Craigslist has a listing for it. With more than 700 local sites in 70 countries, Craigslist can deliver highly targeted traffic for free.

Technorati works similarly to the way that other search engines work in that it uses the number of links pointing to a blog to track its popularity. To rank high on Technorati, you must participate regularly in the blogging community. If you read an article on someone else's blog that you think is well written, post a link to it on your blog; someday that blog's author may return the favor. You should also become a Technorati member and make friends on the site. Users on Technorati can declare your blog a "favorite" and help you rank higher for the key topics you write about.

Optimize Blog Posts for Technorati

1. Navigate to www.technorati.com.

2. Click Join to create a Technorati profile.

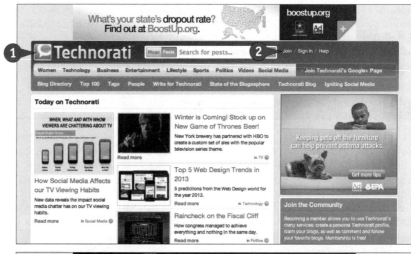

3. Fill out the form to create a profile.

④ Scroll down to the section titled My claimed blogs, enter your URL, and click Claim.

⑤ Enter details and profiles associated with your blog.

After you file your claim, Technorati sends you an e-mail with a token that you need to enter in your account area before approving your blog.

Note: *One way to ensure that you are appearing in the Technorati results is to tag every blog entry with descriptive keywords. You should also keep in mind that many items are ranked by the date posted, so be sure to update often.*

EXTRA

It is not always easy to think up new and interesting topics to blog about. If you want to get more traffic to your blog and need fresh ideas, navigate to Technorati's keyword tag page, located at http://technorati.com/tag, and look at the most popular tags over the last month. Tags represent keywords or short phrases that writers assign to articles to describe or identify the content and are a great indicator of what is hot in the blogosphere. If any of these popular searches relate to the focus of your blog, you should come up with a short article that you can tag with the same keyword.

OPTIMIZE YOUR IMAGES FOR GOOGLE IMAGES

You can do a number of things to increase your rankings in Google Images. First, include a keyword in the same table cell as the image. Second, make sure that your image's filename describes the image. Third, put the keyword above or below the image using a `<div>` or floating `<div>` tag. Fourth, the keyword should be in the alt image tag, the image name, and the image meta file summary. Finally, include the keyword in the same paragraph as the image. This is an example of a well-formatted image:

```
<div style="float:right"><img src="image/
  keyword.jpg" /><br>keyword, text, text,
  text, keyword, text, text, text, keyword,
  text, text, text, keyword.</div><p>text</p>
```

Optimize Your Images for Google Images

1 Open the source of your website in Notepad.

2 Locate an image.

```
Padding: 0;
Margin: 0; }
STRONG {
Font-size: 15px;
Font-family: Arial, Verdana, sans-serif;
Color: black; }
-->
</STYLE>
<TITLE>Creating Pages</TITLE>
<META HTTP-EQUIV="Content-Type" CONTENT="text/html; charset=utf-8">
<META NAME="description" CONTENT="Creating search-engine optimized Web pages is the core effort of a succe
marketing campaign.  This page will detail a numer of on-site factors that should be taken into considerat
Web pages.">
<META NAME="keywords" CONTENT="file names,title tags,meta description tag,meta keywords ta
modifers,creating links,validating HTML">
<META NAME="robots" CONTENT="index,follow">
</HEAD>

<BODY>
<img src="images/header.gif" alt="Chapter 3 Logo" width="500" height="100">
<H1>Introduction </H1>
<P>
Creating search-engine optimized web pages is the core effort of a successful internet marketing campaign.
technical on-site factors such as adding correct file names, title tags, meta description tags, meta keywo
robots tags is crucial to making sure the search-engine spiders can determine the relevance of your Web si
your content with header tags and other text modifiers allows you to stress the main ideas and topics that
```

3 Using a `<div>` tag, put the keyword above or below the image.

```
Padding: 0;
Margin: 0; }
STRONG {
Font-size: 15px;
Font-family: Arial, Verdana, sans-serif;
Color: black; }
-->
</STYLE>
<TITLE>Creating Pages</TITLE>
<META HTTP-EQUIV="Content-Type" CONTENT="text/html; charset=utf-8">
<META NAME="description" CONTENT="Creating search-engine optimized Web pages is the core effort of a succes
marketing campaign.  This page will detail a numer of on-site factors that should be taken into considerati
Web pages.">
<META NAME="keywords" CONTENT="file names,title tags,meta description tag,meta keywords tag,meta robots tag
modifers,creating links,validating HTML">
<META NAME="robots" CONTENT="index,follow">
</HEAD>

<BODY>
<div><img src="images/header.gif" alt="Chapter 3 Logo" width="500" height="100"><br />Chapter 3 Logo File</
<H1>Introduction </H1>
<P>
Creating search-engine optimized web pages is the core effort of a successful internet marketing campaign.
technical on-site factors such as adding correct file names, title tags, meta description tags, meta keywor
robots tags is crucial to making sure the search-engine spiders can determine the relevance of your Web sit
your content with header tags and other text modifiers allows you to stress the main ideas and topics that
```

4 Insert the keyword into the alt image tag, image name, and image meta file summary.

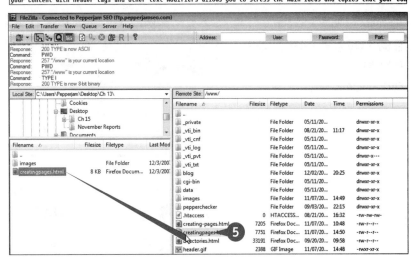

```
Padding: 0;
Margin: 0; }
STRONG {
Font-size: 15px;
Font-family: Arial, Verdana, sans-serif;
Color: black; }
-->
</STYLE>
<TITLE>Creating Pages</TITLE>
<META HTTP-EQUIV="Content-Type" CONTENT="text/html; charset=utf-8">
<META NAME="description" CONTENT="Creating search-engine optimized Web pages is the core effort of a successful int
marketing campaign.  This page will detail a numer of on-site factors that should be taken into consideration when
Web pages.">
<META NAME="keywords" CONTENT="file names,title tags,meta description tag,meta keywords tag,meta robots tag,header
modifers,creating links,validating HTML">
<META NAME="robots" CONTENT="index,follow">
</HEAD>

<BODY>
<div><img src="images/header.gif" alt="Chapter 3 Logo" width="500" height="100"><br />Chapter 3 Logo File</div>
<H1>Introduction </H1>
<P>
Creating search-engine optimized web pages is the core effort of a successful internet marketing campaign.  Taking
technical on-site factors such as adding correct file names, title tags, meta description tags, meta keyword tags,
robots tags is crucial to making sure the search-engine spiders can determine the relevance of your Web site.  Opti
your content with header tags and other text modifiers allows you to stress the main ideas and topics that your con
```

5 Save the changes and upload the source to your web server.

Your image is now optimized for Google Images.

EXTRA

Another factor to consider when optimizing for Google Images is the size of the images you are displaying. Recommended image sizes are as follows:

- Small: 150×150 or smaller
- Medium: Larger than 150×150 and smaller than 500×500
- Large: 500×500 and larger

You should also keep an eye on the traffic that Google Images sends to your site. If a particular image search is sending the wrong kind of traffic to your site, try to monetize that traffic or redirect it to another web page. For example, you can add Google AdSense next to the image on the page receiving the traffic. However, you should not optimize images that are unrelated to the content of your site.

INCREASE EXPOSURE ON ASK.COM

In 2007, Ask relaunched with a simplified interface and a customized results page based on the type of search being conducted. Although Ask has faded in popularity, Ask.com is the #4 search engine, behind Google, Yahoo, and Bing, and ahead of AOL.

One strategy for optimizing your Ask.com ranking is to include as many different forms of content as possible on your site. When a keyword is searched for on Ask.com, the user is presented with multiple forms of media relating to that term. Include an image, video, news article, and blog post along with your regular content and you may be able to appear in multiple sections of the Ask.com results.

Increase Exposure on Ask.com

1 **Navigate** to www.ask.com.

2 **Enter** a keyword related to your business.

3 **Click Find Answers.**

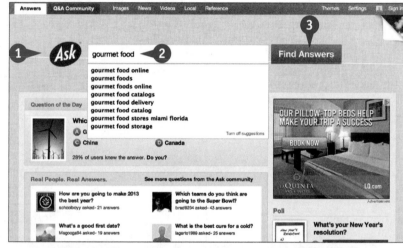

A **Note** the Ask sponsored results. Unlike Google and Bing, Ask incorporates sponsored listings into the actual search results, which provides you with greater control where you appear in Ask search results.

4 **Click Images.**

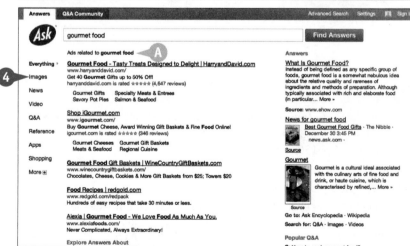

B Note the various images. Incorporating optimized images into your website is a good strategy for getting ranked on Ask.com and other major search engines.

5 Click Video.

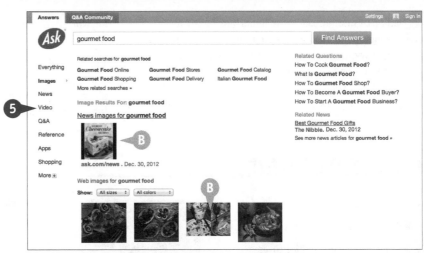

C Note the various videos. Submitting optimized videos to video-sharing websites like YouTube and incorporating those videos on your website are good strategies for getting ranked on Ask.com and other search engines.

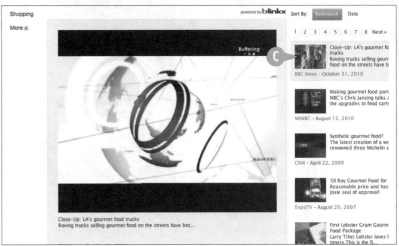

EXTRA

Ask.com runs sponsored ads at the top of its organic search results through a search partnership with Google AdWords. Therefore, if you want to place search ads on Ask.com, you must do so by opting into Google's Search Network, which includes Ask.com, AOL, and others.

Ask is consistently a top ten website, according to ComScore Media Metrix. In December 2012 Ask averaged 104 million visitors, and was the eighth most-visited site. Ask.com offers advertising opportunities located at www.ask.com/products/display. For instance, you can sponsor the Ask.com Question of the Day. In addition, you can place different types of graphical advertisements on Ask.com.

IMPROVE YOUR RANKING ON BING

Similar to Google, the most important factor for improving your organic search ranking on Bing is to build your website authority through link building. See Chapter 8 for more information on building links. The more quality links that point to your website, the more likely it is that you will rank high for your target keywords. Other standard SEO tactics, such as optimizing your title and description meta tags, as well as writing compelling,

keyword rich content, lead to better search rankings on Bing.

Images, videos, and local search are especially important to ranking well on Bing. Make sure you optimize images with alt tags and tag videos with descriptive keywords. With local search, make sure your company is listed as part of Bing Maps, located at www.bing.com/maps.

Improve Your Ranking on Bing

Learn How to Use Bing

1 Navigate to www.bing.com.

2 Type a keyword related to your business.

3 Click the Bing search icon.

Ⓐ Note that the Bing Map is part of the basic search results. On some queries, local results will also be included as part of the results.

Ⓑ Note the related searches. Related searches provide you with specific keywords for which you will want to optimize your website.

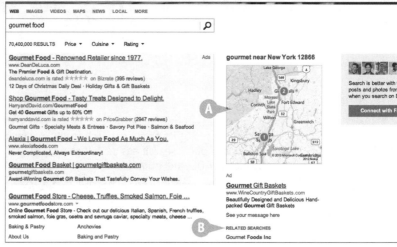

Add Your Business to Bing Maps through the Bing Local Listing Center

1. Navigate to www. bingbusinessportal.com/ BusinessSearch.aspx.

2. Fill in the requested information about your business.

3. Click Add new listing to verify that your company is not already part of Bing's Local Listings.

4. Type your phone number and the characters displayed in the image.

5. Click Ok.

Note: Your listing requires that you have a Microsoft Live account before completing the claiming process for your location.

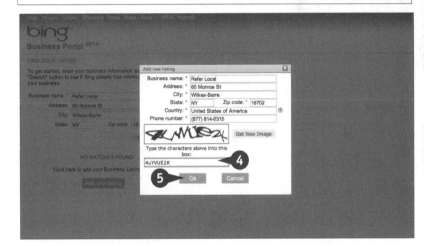

EXTRA

An increasingly popular and important part of the Bing search engine is Bing Shopping, located at http://advertise. bingads.microsoft.com/en-us/search-advertising/bing-shopping. Unlike other shopping comparison engines, such as Shopping.com and Shopzilla, Bing Shopping works on a cost-per-acquisition (CPA) model, not a CPC model. As a result, click fraud is eliminated and bid management tools are unnecessary, which means you can effectively maximize and manage your return on investment.

USING SHOPPING ENGINES TO DRIVE TRAFFIC

Most current comparison shopping engines accept *product feeds* from online retailers and allow users to search and sort these lists by various criteria. A product feed is a file, typically in a CSV or Excel format, that contains information about the products listed on your site. Some popular engines today are Shopping.com, Shopzilla, Bing Shopping, and PriceGrabber. Also, some search engines have added a separate vertical to their engines that allows shoppers to search only products; Google's is named Merchant Center and is located at www.google.com/merchants. The pricing structure allows retailers to submit and list products for free and then charge advertisers either by the click or by taking a commission of every sale made through the engine.

Using Shopping Engines to Drive Traffic

1 Navigate to www.google.com/merchants.

2 Sign in using an existing Google account or create a Google account.

Once you are logged into your account, navigate to view all feeds on the Google Merchant Center dashboard.

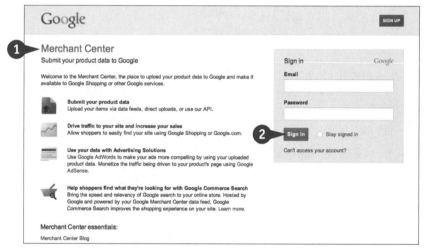

3 Click New Data Feed.

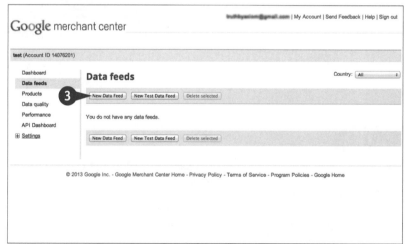

④ Select a target country.

⑤ Select a format.

⑥ Provide a data feed filename.

⑦ Click Save changes.

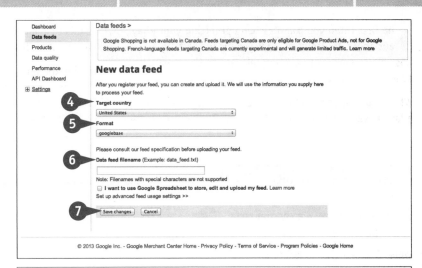

⑧ Click Manual upload and follow the steps to upload your product feed from your computer to the Google Merchant Center.

After you have uploaded it, your product feed is available on Google Shopping.

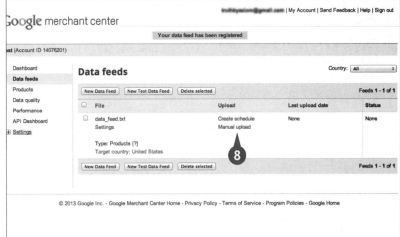

EXTRA

The first thing you should do to optimize your product list for comparison engines is to fill in every product attribute that you can. Most shopping engines provide you with these attributes when you download their product feed templates. By filling out all the fields provided, you increase your click-to-purchase ratio. You should also remove low inventory items and products with poor sales. Not all comparison engines provide product feed templates.

You should have proper tracking in place so that you can evaluate the success of your comparison shopping campaigns. Finally, make sure that you have at least 50 words or more of text to describe each product in your feed.

The first thing you can do when optimizing your eBay auction is to use as many keywords in the title as possible to make your auction relevant to the most user searches possible.

When you post your auction is also important. Most people use **eBay** between 8:00 p.m. and 10:00 p.m. Posting your auction at this time ensures that the most people will see what you have to offer. Sunday is also a high-traffic day for eBay.

Finally, the photos you post of your auction item are probably the most important aspect of your eBay auction. Websites like Photobucket allow you to host photos for free and provide you with code to cut and paste right into your auction.

Produce Sales with eBay Auctions

1 Navigate to www.ebay.com and sign in to your eBay account.

Note: *Click Register to create an eBay account if you do not already have one.*

2 Click Sell and select Sell an item from the drop-down list.

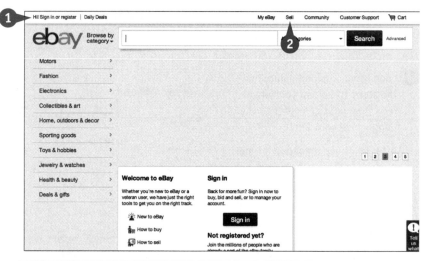

3 Use the search tool or click Browse categories to find a relevant category to list in.

4 Click Continue.

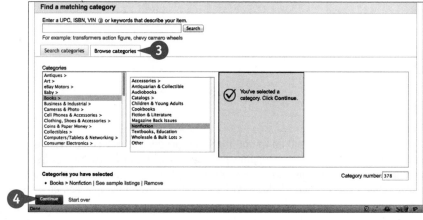

5 Add a title to your listing.

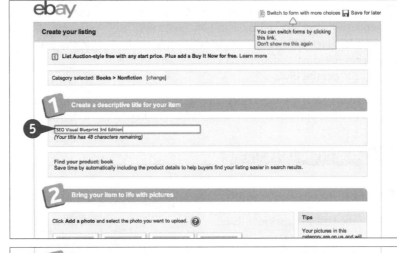

6 Add a picture to enhance your listing.

7 Describe the item you are selling.

8 Scroll down to enter payment and complete auction details.

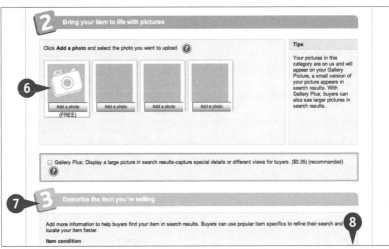

EXTRA

One of the easiest things you can do to optimize your eBay auctions along with any other content you post on the web is to use proper spelling and grammar. Be sure you spell-check everything you post online; you may even want to have someone else proofread your material. Another rule of etiquette is to avoid using CAPS as much as possible.

Also, as with everything this chapter has discussed, become part of the community. Create a profile and keep it up to date. If you purchase items from other eBayers, be sure to leave them feedback. If customers are happy with the service you have provided, be sure to ask them to post feedback about their experience.

USING CRAIGSLIST TO DRIVE TRAFFIC

Posting ads on Craigslist regularly can greatly help your website get indexed by search engines, which can result in more traffic for your website. Keep in mind that whenever you post anything on Craigslist you should include your website URL.

For your actual post, the same rules apply that apply to your onsite HTML optimization, as discussed in Chapter 3.

Use H1 and H2 headings for the most important keywords. You can also bold anything important within the body text of the post.

Craigslist posts expire after a limited time. Therefore, if your listing was not successful, you should repost it once it expires so that Google and other search engines continue to index and list it in their search results.

Using Craigslist to Drive Traffic

① Navigate to your local Craigslist.

② Click the Post to classifieds link.

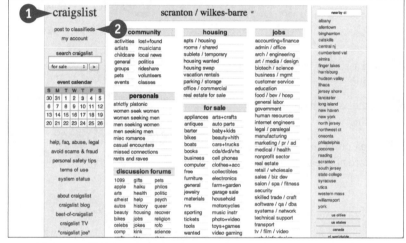

③ Choose the appropriate posting type for your site.

④ Click Continue.

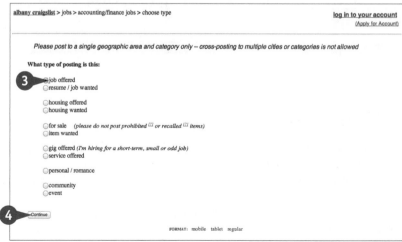

5 Choose the appropriate category.

6 Fill in all the required fields using the techniques described in this task.

7 Click the anonymize button if you would like to be contacted via e-mail with questions about your listing.

Note: *The anonymize button masks your actual e-mail with a craigslist. org e-mail to protect your identity and minimize spam.*

8 Click Continue.

Your Craigslist post is now live.

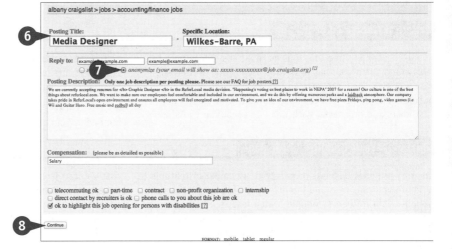

EXTRA

Although Craigslist can be a useful source of traffic to your website, you must understand and adhere to the Craigslist terms of service or risk having your website and listings banned from using the service. For example, do not post too many listings at once, and avoid posting multiple times in the same category. In addition, you should place your listings in the most appropriate category related to your product; you should not use multiple aliases attached to the same website.

When you make your post, remember to select the option that prevents people from seeing your e-mail address. You do not want Craigslist members e-mailing you directly or automated spambots picking up your address.

An Introduction to Local Search

Although search-engine optimization (SEO) best practices have not changed much over the last several years, there have been a number of significant structural changes made by search engines that require you to tailor your SEO efforts. For example, in October 2010, Google began displaying blended search results for local businesses. Blended local search results include a snippet of text about the business along with links to your business website and your Google+ Local Page. Google also displays the number of reviews and average ranking you receive from your Google+ Local Page. As a result you need to optimize your website, as well as your Google+ Local Page, for search results.

A number of other important factors influence the success of your local search marketing efforts. One of the primary signals that search engines like Google look at is your engagement on social media sites such as Google+ Local, Facebook, and Twitter. In fact, websites such as Klout have emerged that provide a measure of social influence to provide a score of how authoritative a person is in social media. Similarly, search engines look at social signals such as the number and quality of reviews you receive on Google+ Local and other sites and the amount of engagement you receive from your followers as measures of your authority for search-engine ranking purposes.

Search engines also look at how many, and the quality of, links that point to your website. One way to increase the number of links you have for your website is to make sure you are listed in local online business directories such as Local.com and ReferLocal.com.

Create a Google+ Local Page

Google+ Local is a free tool that makes it easy for people to review and share your business with friends and around the web. Google+ Local provides an interactive page of your business and allows you to easily connect with existing customers and prospects. With Google+ Local you can share pictures and videos of your business and interact with customers and fans through a conversation wall similar to Facebook's Timeline.

Google+ Local is becoming an increasingly significant tool for improving your overall SEO performance.

Optimize Your Google+ Local Page

Google+ provides business owners with a number of features to promote your business and improve your SEO. For instance, Google+ data influences Google search results. In this way Google hopes to encourage business owners and webmasters to actively engage with Google+ and the Google.com search engine. In addition, Google+ functions similarly to Facebook in that you can leverage friend connections and social sharing to drive traffic to your business. The key to maximizing the SEO benefits of Google+ is to actively engage with the platform. In this way you will grow your following, while also providing Google with many positive signals about you and your business.

Leverage Reviews to Increase Your Local Search Ranking

How many reviews do you have on Google+ Local? One of the most important factors Google uses to determine relevance and authority when ranking websites is the number and velocity of consumer reviews a website receives. While you can get reviews for a number of places, including Yelp, Merchant Circle, and Foursquare, it is most important to receive reviews on your Google+ Local Page because you will rank better on Google.

Optimize Your Website for Local Search

For local search purposes, it is important to consider SEO tactics that reflect your specific geography. For example, when optimizing for local search, make sure to place your business contact information in the footer or header of each page. Adding your geographic information ensures that search engines identify your content with a specific geographic location.

In addition, if you sell a product or service that is targeted or limited to a specific geographic location, you should add geographic information such as a city, state, and zip code to the title and meta description tags for each relevant page of your site.

Maximize Social Media Ranking Factors

Social media continues to play an increasingly important role across all forms of digital marketing, including local search. Social media signals, such as the number of followers you or your business has on sites like Twitter, Google+, and Facebook, are an important ranking factor considered by search engines like Google. Keep in mind that it is not enough to just grow your following; you must also focus on acquiring followers who have social influence. Your level of social media engagement is another signal search engines consider. The more engaged your business is on sites like Facebook and Google+, the more likely that engagement will have a positive influence on your search rankings.

Eliminate Negative Ranking Factors

Negative ranking factors include inaccurate or inconsistent location information across the web, the presence of multiple Google+ Local listings with the same information, a failure to confirm ownership of a Google+ Local Page, and inaccurate category associations on Google+ Local. Google considers other factors negative, such as low numerical ratings and negative sentiment in Google+ Local reviews, as well. Negative ranking factors have a detrimental impact on your local search ranking and should be avoided.

Consider Offsite Ranking Factors

For local SEO purposes, the quantity and quality of inbound links is an equally important ranking factor for your business website and Google+ Local listing. However, Google considers the *quality* of inbound links more important for ranking purposes than the *quantity* of inbound links. For local listings such as Google+ Local, anchor text is also a very important offsite ranking factor. When link building for your Google+ Local listing, you should make sure that you use a variety of product/service and location keywords, and that your business name is in the anchor text of inbound links.

Get Listed on Local.com

Local.com offers a basic free listing that includes your business name, address, website URL, and contact information. Local.com also offers a paid premium listing, which includes your business logo and enables you to upload pictures and videos related to your business.

Getting listed on local business directories like Local.com is one of the primary ways to improve your local SEO. Typically, the more directory listings and the higher the quality of the directory, the more influence the listing will have on your search marketing efforts.

Get Listed on ReferLocal.com Business Pages

ReferLocal.com is a leading local e-commerce website that maximizes its reach through partnerships with local newspapers, radio stations, and television broadcast companies in various parts of the United States. ReferLocal Business Pages gives you the ability to profile your business and easily upload pictures, coupons, and videos. In addition, ReferLocal allows you to integrate your Facebook Business Page profile into your ReferLocal Business Pages, thereby helping you generate more Facebook likes from ReferLocal members and cross-publish your Facebook posts.

CREATE A GOOGLE+ LOCAL PAGE

Google+ Local, formerly Google Places, makes it easy for people to review and share your business with friends and around the web. Google+ Local provides a hosted, interactive profile page of your business at https://plus.google.com. With Google+ Local you can easily upload pictures and videos of your business and interact with

customers and fans through a conversation wall similar to Facebook's Timeline.

Google+ Local Pages are free and are becoming an increasingly significant tool for improving your overall SEO performance. Make sure that all the information you provide Google is accurate, current, and consistent across the web.

Create a Google+ Local Page

Note: *Google+ boasts more than 250 million active members and is the social network of Google.*

① Navigate to https://plus.google.com/pages/create and sign in to your Google account.

② Click Local Business or Place.

③ Select the country or location of your business from the drop-down list.

④ Enter your primary business phone number.

⑤ Click Locate. Google automatically locates your business or prompts you to provide more information.

⑥ Click the Change cover photo link to add or change your cover photo. A copy photo should include a picture of your business, product, or staff.

⑦ Click the Change profile photo link to add or change your business logo.

Ⓐ Click the Introduction, Hours, Contact info, Website, and Address sections to provide accurate, up-to-date information about your business.

⑧ Click Done editing once you have added all the necessary information about your business.

⑨ Click Photos to add images to your Google+ Local Page.

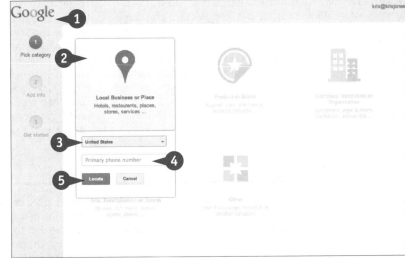

10 Click Upload New Photos to add images from your computer to Google+.

11 Click Videos and follow the steps to add video to Google+.

Note: *Adding images and video significantly increases the credibility of your business and provides opportunities for Google+ members to learn more about your business and to interact with your Google+ Local Page.*

12 Click the Home icon to go to your conversation page.

B Start a conversation with your followers by posting an update or sharing an image or video.

Note: *You can update your customers and prospects with information about your business, including special deals, holiday hours of operation, or anything interesting about your business.*

C Click Share to make your post viewable to your followers.

D A feature of Google+ is Hangouts. Hangouts allows you to easily start a video conversation with your friends and customers. Video Hangouts are a powerful feature for engaging with customers and prospects.

EXTRA

Similar to other social networks such as Facebook and Twitter, Google+ requires that you promote your page to increase your followers. You can link to your Google+ profile page from your website or in an e-mail signature, and promote the page as part of any advertising you currently do to promote your business. The more targeted followers you accumulate, the more beneficial Google+ will be to your business.

Note that you are providing Google with numerous signals about your business by having a Google+ page. Therefore, make sure you keep best practice SEO principals in mind when posting and be sure to engage with as many Google+ features as possible.

OPTIMIZE YOUR GOOGLE+ LOCAL PAGE

Google+ provides business owners with a number of features for improving their SEO. Google has publicly disclosed that they may use Google+ data to influence Google's search results. In this way Google hopes to encourage business owners and webmasters to actively engage with Google+ and the Google.com search engine. The benefit to you as a business owner is that by simply using Google's tools, such as the Google +1 feature, and

encouraging your customers and fans to do the same, you are actively engaging in practices that may improve your search rankings.

The key to maximizing the SEO benefits of Google+ is to actively engage with the platform. In this way you will grow your following, while also providing Google with many positive signals about you and your business.

Optimize Your Google+ Local Page

Follow Your Google+ Local Page

1. Navigate to https://plus.google.com.

2. Type the name of your business into the Google+ search bar.

3. Select People and pages from the drop-down list.

4. Click the search icon and results for your search appear.

Ⓐ Locate your business among the search results.

5. Click the Follow button to follow your business. Once you follow your business, all posts made on your Google+ Local Page appear within your personal conversation feed.

6. Click the Google+ button to recommend your Google+ Local Page on your personal Google+ page.

Add Links to the About Section of Your Profile

1. Navigate to your Google+ Local Page, click your profile, and then click Edit Profile.

2. Highlight the text that you would like to hyperlink and click Link.

3. Click Save.

Add Custom Links to your Profile Page

Note: *Google allows you to link out from your Google+ Local Page to other websites in a special section on your profile called Links.*

1. Click Add custom link.

2. Enter the name of your link and the URL.

Note: *You should use this section to link to important sections of your website; your business profiles on sites such as Facebook, Twitter, and Yelp; and other websites that provide useful information about your business.*

3. Click Save.

Follow Google+ Members with Similar Interests

Note: *Once way to grow your audience is to join Google+ communities focused on topics related to your business.*

1. Navigate to your Google+ Local Page and click the Communities icon.

A. Discover communities to join from the list of suggestions or perform a search.

2. Enter a keyword related to your business and join relevant communities.

Note: *Once you join a community, you will be able to scroll over the profile images of existing community members. When you scroll over a profile image, you will be given the opportunity to follow the member and begin the process of building your following.*

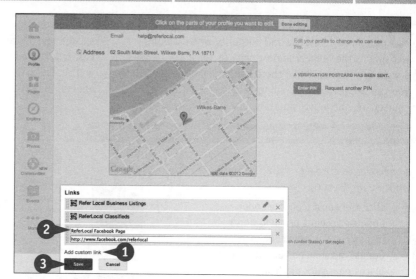

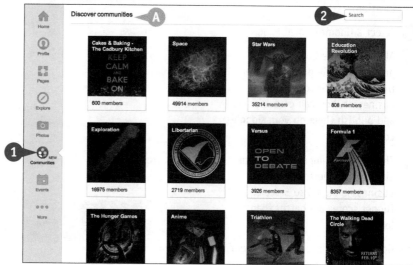

EXTRA

The Google +1 button is a powerful Google tool integrated into most Google products, including Google+, that allows you to easily share and endorse links and specific content you like on the web. When you +1 something, it is shared on Google+ and appears as a social feature within the Google search results. The Google +1 button is a powerful way to build and communicate authority and is one of the most talked about Google features within the SEO community. Many believe that the greater the number and quality of +1's for a website, the higher its ranking.

LEVERAGE REVIEWS TO INCREASE YOUR LOCAL SEARCH RANKING

One of the most important factors Google uses to determine relevance and authority when ranking websites is the number and velocity of consumer reviews a website receives. While there are a number of places you can get reviews, including Yelp, Merchant Circle, and Foursquare, the most important place to receive reviews

to help you rank higher on Google is on your Google+ Local Page. Therefore, you should encourage your existing customers or clients to submit reviews on your behalf, and you should actively promote your Google+ Local Page to the general public.

Leverage Reviews to Increase Your Local Search Ranking

Learn the Google+ Local Review and Rating System

1. Click the Local icon from your Google+ account or navigate to https://plus.google.com/local. Google recommends Google+ Local places near your physical location.

2. Select a Google+ Local Page.

A Along with the Google+ Local product, Google promotes offers from specific Google+ Local businesses. You can create offers and publish them on your Google+ Local Page.

B The Google commenting system allows consumers to rate businesses on a 0 to 3 scale. Higher scores are better than lower scores.

C Google prominently displays your reviews and overall rating.

D This business properly uses a local number. For local search purposes, make sure to provide Google with a local landline phone number.

E This merchant has uploaded multiple images of its business. It is highly recommended that you upload pictures to drive user interaction on your Google+ Local Page.

3. Click Write a review.

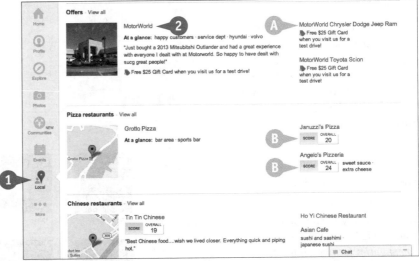

Write a Google+ Local Review

① Rate the business based on quality, appeal, and service.

② Describe your experience with the business.

③ Click Publish.

Note: *This is a similar process to what your customers will see when rating and reviewing your business. When you ask a customer to write a review and rate your business, you may want to provide a description of how to locate your business and how Google's review system works.*

Ⓐ Your review appears.

Ⓑ Note that as a Google+ Local Page owner, you can respond to the reviews and ratings provided about your business. It is important to connect with your customers regardless of whether they provide a positive or negative review.

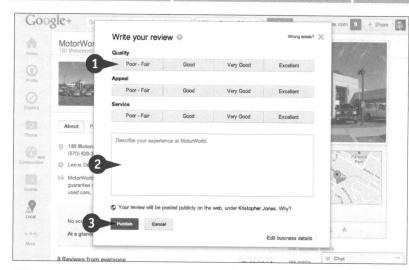

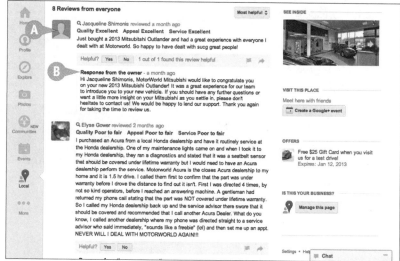

EXTRA

Google blends local search results for Google+ Local listings with rankings for your actual website. Therefore, when someone types in your brand or triggers your Google+ Local listing or website listing in a Google search result, the viewer sees a result that includes links to both your Google+ Local Page and your website. Google also displays a snapshot of the number of reviews you have received, along with your overall rating if you have one, as part of its local search results.

The importance of creating and optimizing your Google+ Local Page cannot be overstated. Google+ provides powerful tools that allow you to connect and engage with your audience, and when your Google+ Local Page is optimized properly, you get higher search-engine placement on Google.

OPTIMIZE YOUR WEBSITE FOR LOCAL SEARCH

When you are optimizing your business website for local search purposes, it is important to consider SEO tactics that reflect your specific geography. For example, when you optimize for local search, make sure to place your business contact information in the footer or header of each page. Adding your geographic information ensures that search engines identify your content with a specific geography.

In addition, if you sell a product or service that is targeted or limited to a specific geographic location, you should add geographic information, such as the city, state, and zip code, to the title and meta description tags to each relevant page of your site. An example of a local search-optimized title tag would be "ReferLocal.com – Limited Time Daily Deals in Scranton, Pennsylvania 18503."

Optimize Your Website for Local Search

Add Geographic Information to Your Website Header or Footer

Note: *Adding contact information, including the city, state, and zip code, to the header or footer of your website provides important geographic information to Google and other search engines about your location for local search ranking purposes.*

1. Navigate to www.belt-law.com.

2. Observe the local search-optimized header of the Belt Law Firm website, including relevant geographic information.

Ⓐ Adding a Contact Us link to your website allows you to provide additional ways for prospective customers to contact you. Just because you add contact information to your header or footer does not eliminate the best practice of also having a Contact Us form.

3. Navigate to www.allied-services.org.

4. Observe the local search-optimized footer of the Allied Services website, including relevant geographic information.

Note: *Adding a local phone number to your header or footer provides search engines with additional information they can verify on your location.*

Optimize URLs and Meta Tags for Local Search

1. Navigate to http://referlocal. com/local/motorworld-auto- group-150-motorworld-dr- wilkes-barre-pa-18702.

2. Observe that the URL is search-engine optimized for local search and includes the business name, address, and zip code of the business listing.

A Note that this page also includes the business name, address, and zip code. Although this may seem redundant, URL and page content are two separate cues that search engines like Google use to determine location and page relevance for specific keyword rankings in local search.

3. Right-click the page to view the page source. The page's HTML appears.

B Observe a local search-optimized meta title tag, which includes the business name, address, and zip code.

C Observe a local search-optimized meta description tag, which includes the business name, address, zip code, and a general description of the business.

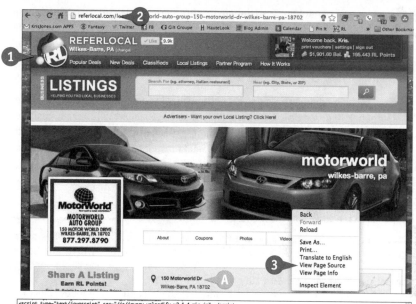

EXTRA

Note that you do not need to optimize all your content for local search. For example, you may be a local business but have products or services with a geographic reach beyond your primary place of business. If you conduct some or all of your business outside of a specific geographic region, you have at least two options to consider. First, you can tailor your content and page information to reflect the specific geographic region you are targeting at the product or service level. Second, you can remove specific geographic information from your URL, meta tags, and content on a page-by-page basis.

MAXIMIZE SOCIAL MEDIA RANKING FACTORS

As covered in Chapter 10, social media continues to play an increasingly important role across all forms of digital marketing, including local search. In fact, social media signals, such as the number of followers you or your business has on sites like Twitter, Google+, and Facebook, appear to be an important ranking factor search engines like Google consider. Keep in mind that it is not enough to just grow your following; you also must focus on acquiring followers who have social influence. Innovative technologies such as Klout and Kred provide measures of social influence.

Level of social media engagement is another signal search engines consider. The more engaged your business is on sites like Facebook and Google+, the more likely that engagement will have a positive influence on your search rankings. Because of the increasing influence of social media on customer service and lead acquisition, you should consider hiring a dedicated social media manager or outsource social media responsibilities to a knowledgeable professional. It is highly likely that over time social media signals will become as important as more traditional SEO signals, such as links and title tags.

Acquire Followers with High Klout Scores

Klout is a free service that measures social media influence by analyzing factors such as the size of a person's social network and the level of engagement by others with the person's content. Scores range from 1 to 100, with higher scores corresponding to a higher assessment by Klout of the breadth and strength of a person's social influence. To maximize your efforts when building your following on sites such as Facebook, Twitter, and Google+, you should use Klout to identify social media influencers with scores above an average of 40. One of the best ways to get social media influencers to follow you is to follow them first and engage with their content frequently by sharing it with your social networks.

Prune Your Followers

As discussed in Chapter 10, using Twitter Search, located at https://twitter.com/search, to identify people that you share personal or professional interests with is a strategic way to grow your following. However, not everyone you follow will follow you back and some of the people whom you follow may not actively engage with social media. Since your goal with leveraging social media for SEO is to maximize both the quantity and quality of your social media following, from time to time you should remove people from your social network who have minimal social influence or who rarely or never engage with your content. Keep in mind when pruning followers to remove those with lower social influence first.

Install Google +1's Widgets on Your Website

Google allows users to easily vote on content they like by clicking a +1 button. One strategy to leverage Google's +1 system to improve your SEO and generate more website traffic is to install a +1 widget at the top of your home page to encourage your visitors to +1 your website. The number of +1's your website receives directly influences search rankings. Another strategy to leverage Google's +1 system is to install a +1 button next to all your shareable content. When one of your visitors clicks the +1 button, the system automatically shares the content on the Google+ page of the person who clicked the button. Installing +1 buttons is the most effective way to leverage Google+ to increase your website search rankings. Learn more about installing Google +1 widgets on your website at https://developers.google.com/+/plugins/+1button.

Install Facebook Like and Twitter Tweet Buttons on Your Website

Similar to Google+, both Facebook and Twitter offer widget technology to allow you to easily increase your social media following and make your website content shareable. Facebook's Like button widget, located at http://developers.facebook.com/docs/reference/plugins/like, allows you to easily install a Like button at the top of your website and next to any content that you would like to make shareable. Note that share buttons are particularly useful for e-commerce sites because they allow your visitors to easily share products they like with their social media following. Twitter's Tweet button, located at https://twitter.com/about/resources/buttons, provides you with multiple options for growing your followers and increasing the distribution of your content through Twitter sharing. You will generate more website traffic and improve your SEO by installing Google+, Facebook, and Twitter widgets on your website.

Hire a Dedicated Social Media Manager

The increasing importance of social media on search-engine rankings cannot be overstated. In addition to influencing search-engine rankings, social media also allows you to provide real-time customer support and to answer questions or concerns prospective customers have about your business. Because of the widespread growth and popularity of social networks like Facebook and Twitter, it is not acceptable to not have an active social media strategy for your business. One primary reason that you should leverage social media is to manage your online reputation. By having someone from your company involved in managing your social media presence daily, you will be in a much better position to quell any negative sentiments that may arise about your product or service.

Sign Up for Leading Social Media Networks and Check-In Services

The three most important social networks for maximizing your search-engine ranking are Facebook, Twitter, and Google+. However, there are a number of newer or smaller social media platforms that you should also build a presence on and leverage to engage with your audience. For example, Foursquare is a social media platform that allows users to check-in to your location and share it with friends. Check-ins are a way to tell your social media followers where you are. Foursquare is particularly effective at driving people to specific locations because it allows you to post exclusive coupons or discounts to anyone who checks-ins at your location. The number of check-ins that your business has on social networks like Facebook and Twitter influences your search ranking.

Leverage Twitter Ads to Extend Your Reach on Twitter

Research from digital intelligence firm Compete shows Twitter followers are more than 60% more likely to visit your website and more than 50% more likely to make a purchase and recommend your company. Therefore, increasing your number of Twitter followers will not only benefit your SEO efforts but also improve your ability to attract new customers and convert existing customers. Most recently, Twitter released a product called Twitter Ads, located at https://business.twitter.com/advertise/start to help businesses generate more followers and to extend the distribution of specific tweets. Twitter Ads is a recommended tool for growing your followers on Twitter. Facebook offers a product called Facebook Ads, which is covered in Chapter 10, as a way to generate more Facebook likes, Facebook's equivalent of followers.

Add Your Social Media Profiles to Your Business Cards and E-mail Signature

Adding your social media profiles to your business cards and e-mail signature is an effective way to gain followers and to also demonstrate your commitment as a business owner to providing exceptional customer service. You should select names for your social media pages that are easy to remember and share. For example, if the name of your business is ReferLocal, you should name your Facebook page www.facebook.com/referlocal. Note that Facebook allows you to provide a name for your page that comes after facebook.com. Similarly, Twitter allows you to select an alias that comes after Twitter.com. For example, twitter.com/krisjonescom. Changing your alias for both Twitter and Facebook is located within the account settings area of your respective social network account.

Eliminate Negative Ranking Factors

Negative ranking factors include inaccurate or inconsistent location information across the web, the presence of multiple Google+ Local listings with the same information, the failure to confirm ownership of a Google+ Local Page, and noncompliance of category associations on Google+ Local. Google also considers low numerical ratings and negative sentiment in Google+ Local reviews negative factors. Negative ranking factors have a detrimental impact on your local search ranking and should be avoided. Note there are paid services, such as Yext (www.yext.com), that help you identify inaccurate or inconsistent location information about your website and help you fix it across multiple online directories, including Yelp, Foursquare, Superpages, and others.

Eliminate Negative Ranking Factors

Note: *Yext.com does not address all the potential negative factors associated with local SEO, but it addresses one of the most important — inaccurate or inconsistent location information.*

1 Navigate to www.yext.com.

2 Enter your business information.

3 Click Scan Now.

A Note the number of errors for this business across 219 online directories.

B Yext provides a list of each of its online directory partners with the status of your listing in each directory.

C Note that Yahoo is one of the most trafficked business directories online and this business is currently not found in the directory.

Note: *It is not necessary to pay for placement in every directory that Yext recommends. Instead, use Yext as a powerful tool to identify inaccurate or inconsistent location data and make changes where necessary. However, if you are not listed in a major directory such as Yahoo or Yelp, you should consider joining those directories through Yelp or individually at http://dir.yahoo.com and https://biz.yelp.com/claiming, respectively.*

4 Click Fix It All.

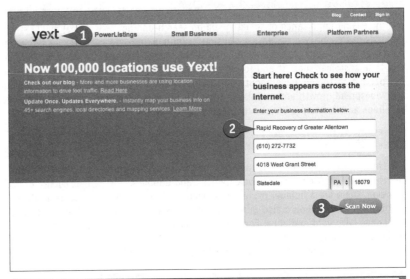

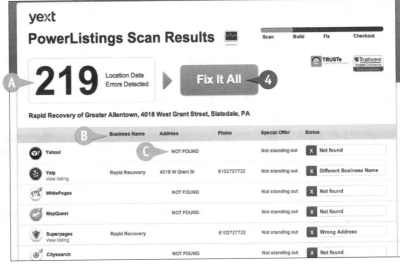

⑤ Complete all the basic information about your business. Note that this is the information you are telling Yext that you want to add to all your online directory listings.

Note: *Yext is able to only correct listings across its partner network. A comprehensive list of network partners is available at www.yext.com/network.html.*

Ⓓ Verify that your location data is accurate.

⑥ Scroll to the bottom of the page after providing your basic information and click Continue.

Ⓔ Review available directory options to fix or submit your local directory listing.

Ⓕ Click the View sample link to view what your listing would look like on Yahoo. Note that it costs $150 per year for a listing in the Yahoo Directory.

Ⓖ Click Fix Now to drop the Yahoo Directory listing in your shopping cart.

⑦ Click Review & Checkout if you made any purchases.

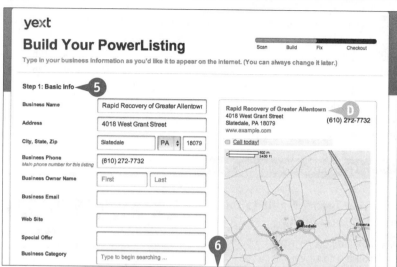

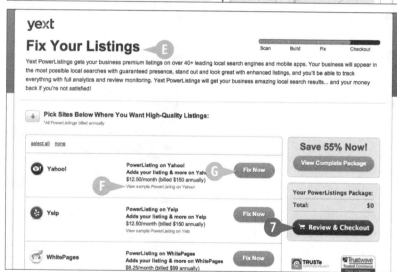

EXTRA

This section emphasizes that to avoid negative penalties by search engines such as Google it is critical you make sure that your location information across the web, including local directories and social networks, is consistent. At the same time it is also important to make certain that the way you represent your business outside of its location is consistent and accurate. For example, Google+ and others ask you to identify the most important category associations for your business. In this regard you need to make sure that the categories you select are accurate and do not misrepresent your business. Inaccurate category associations can have a negative impact on your search rankings.

CONSIDER OFFSITE RANKING FACTORS

The quantity and quality of inbound links is an equally important ranking factor for your business website and Google+ Local listing. However, for both your website and listing Google considers the *quality* of inbound links more important for ranking purposes than the *quantity* of inbound links. For local listings such as Google+ Local, anchor text is also a very important offsite ranking factor. When link building for your Google+ Local listing, you should make sure that you use a variety of product/service and location keywords, and that your business name appears in the anchor text of inbound links. The easiest way to control the variety of the anchor text for your Google+ Local listing is to link to the site using various anchor text from your other social network profiles, as well as from any other websites that you own.

Consider Offsite Ranking Factors

Link Your Twitter Profile to Your Google+ Local Profile

① Navigate to www.twitter.com and log in to your account.

② Click Edit profile from the Settings drop-down list.

③ Add your Google+ Local listing URL as your website.

④ Scroll to the bottom of the page and click Save changes.

Ⓐ Observe that your profile website now reflects a direct link to your Google+ Local Page.

Note: This would have been a great place to add target anchor text, but Twitter does not allow you to do so.

Link Your LinkedIn Profile to Your Google+ Local Profile

1 Navigate to LinkedIn.com and log in to your account.

2 Click the Profile link and follow the instructions for editing your profile.

3 Click the Edit Contact Info button followed by the Edit Website icon. A Websites box appears with the option to add new websites to your LinkedIn profile.

4 Select Other in the website classification drop-down list and enter the name of your Google+ Local Page and the direct URL.

Note: This example demonstrates setting up the link with anchor text reflecting the company name and location.

5 Click Save.

Ⓐ Observe your new LinkedIn profile link to your Google+ Local Page with your preferred anchor text.

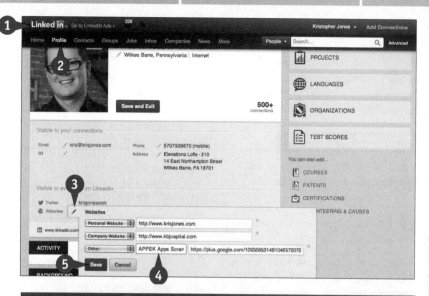

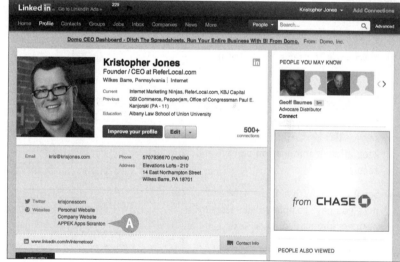

EXTRA

Structured and unstructured citation link types help you build links for local search optimization. Structured citation links are from local directories, data aggregators, and Internet yellow pages such as Yahoo, Yelp, Local.com, YP.com, and ReferLocal.com. Structured links tend to include similar information about businesses, and it is important to make sure location information across structured links is accurate and consistent. Unstructured citation links are those from websites such as newspapers and blogs. Build as many links as possible from high-quality structured and unstructured sites to your business website and Google+ page and whenever possible use location-based anchor text along with your company name.

GET LISTED ON LOCAL.COM

One of the most popular places to list your business is Local.com. Local.com offers a basic free listing that includes your business name, address, website URL, and contact information. Local.com also offers a paid premium listing, which includes your business logo and enables you to upload pictures and videos related to your business.

Getting listed on local business directories like Local.com is one of the primary ways to improve your local SEO. Typically, the more directory listings and the higher the quality of the directory, the more influence the listing will have on your search marketing efforts.

Get Listed on Local.com

1 Navigate to https://advertise.local.com.

2 Provide information for your business.

Note: *You should use the same business information, including the address and contact information, that you use for Google+ Local and other business directories or social networks.*

A Always use the same local landline phone number for all business directories. If your number changes, you should change it immediately on all your directory listings or use a service like Yext.com to help you keep all your information current and accurate.

3 Scroll to the bottom of the page and once you have completed all necessary business information, click Next.

B Observe your free listing as it will appear on the Local.com website. Click the edit link if information is incorrect.

4 Select a primary and an optional secondary category for your listing.

C Consider upgrading your listing for $49.95 per month. The added benefits include the ability to add videos and pictures about your business.

5 Scroll to the bottom of the page and click Next.

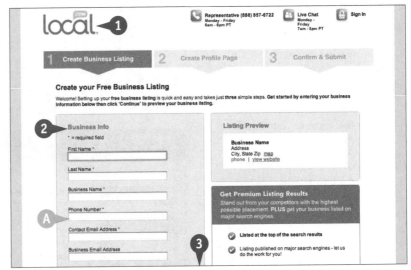

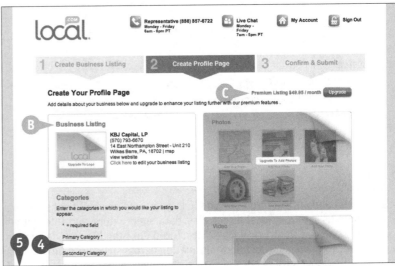

6 Click Confirm Listing.

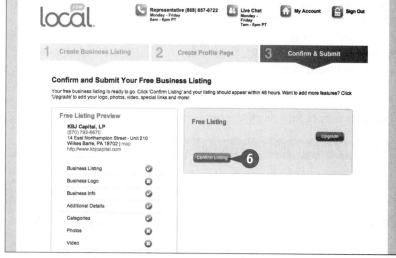

D Your listing is submitted.

Note: *Your listing is not yet live; it needs to go through at least two approval steps. First, click the link in your Local.com free listing confirmation e-mail to verify your e-mail. Second, you will receive a phone call from a customer support representative from Local.com on the business phone number you provided to verify your business information over the phone.*

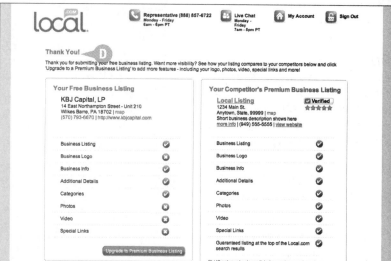

EXTRA

There are many benefits to getting your website listed in directories, including a more diverse link profile, qualified referral traffic, citations for different ranking algorithms such as local search, and the fact that it sends positive signals to Google and other search engines about your authority. In addition to local business directories like Local.com, you should consider several other directory types. Depending on your area of business, there is likely a niche directory for your specific industry. For example, trade organizations offer online directories of members. Not every directory link is right for your site. Be selective and do not go for every link out there.

Get Listed on ReferLocal.com Business Pages

ReferLocal.com is a leading local e-commerce website with millions of monthly visitors. One of the benefits of ReferLocal is that it partners with local newspapers, radio stations, and television broadcast companies in various parts of the United States to promote businesses that are featured on the platform. ReferLocal Business Pages, located at www.referlocal.com/local, provides you with the ability to list your website for a nominal monthly fee.

ReferLocal Business Pages offers you the ability to profile your business and easily upload pictures, coupons, and videos. In addition, ReferLocal enables you to integrate your Facebook Business Page profile into your ReferLocal Business Page, thereby helping you generate more Facebook likes from ReferLocal members and cross-publish your Facebook posts.

Get Listed on ReferLocal.com Business Pages

Get Listed on ReferLocal Business Pages

1 Navigate to www.referlocal.com/local.

2 Click Get Started Now and follow the steps to get listed on ReferLocal Business Pages.

Note: *ReferLocal Business Pages is a paid service but you can sign up for a free month by using coupon code* **WILEYSEO** *at checkout. Call (877) 814-6315 if you need assistance. The author of this book is the CEO and founder of ReferLocal.*

A As part of ReferLocal Business Pages, your website will be included in the ReferLocal search engine.

B Visitors to www.referlocal.com/local will be able to find your business through featured listings.

Add Photos to Your ReferLocal Business Page

1 Navigate to www.referlocal.com, sign in to your account, go to your listing page, and click the Photos tab.

2 Click Add More Photos.

A Note that ReferLocal members will earn points for sharing your ReferLocal Business Page on Facebook and Twitter, and to friends and family through e-mail.

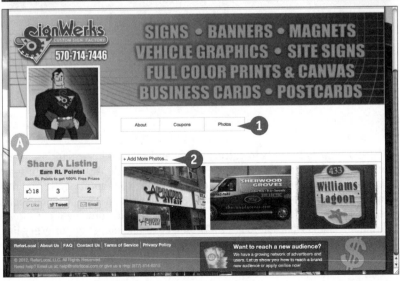

3 Click Upload Photo. A dialog box appears.

4 Select a photo to upload from your computer to your ReferLocal Business Page.

5 Add a photo caption to your photo. A photo caption will appear when someone scrolls over your image and may also be used by search engines to index your image.

6 Click Save Photo. Your image is now saved to your ReferLocal Business Page and will be viewable to users visiting your listing.

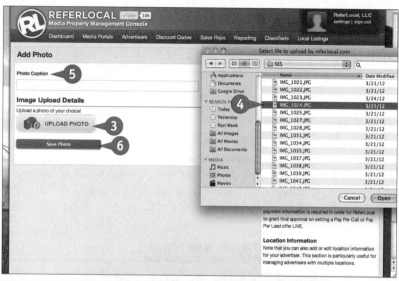

Edit Your ReferLocal Business Page

1 Scroll over your cover photo or business logo to make edits.

A Click the About, Coupons, Photos, or Videos tab to edit those portions of your page.

B Click Edit Listing Information to update basic information, including the URL, Facebook page, Twitter name, and location hours.

C Note that visitors to your ReferLocal Business Page can easily like your Facebook page or follow your business on Twitter.

D Your Facebook Business Page is integrated into your ReferLocal Business Page. Every time you update your Facebook page, it automatically updates on ReferLocal.

EXTRA

A primary benefit, beyond local SEO, of getting listed on ReferLocal Business Pages is you will grow your social media following in terms of more likes on Facebook and followers on Twitter. ReferLocal uses a points system modeled after the American Express points system to incentivize its members to be part of the social sharing process and to promote ReferLocal Business Pages. ReferLocal members earn points redeemable for rewards by simply liking and following a business on Facebook and Twitter.

An Introduction to SEO Tools and Plug-ins

Search-engine optimization (SEO) is often a tedious job and requires you to perform numerous tasks over and over. Fortunately, SEO tools enable you to save time and work more efficiently.

SEO tools have become increasingly popular because of the sheer amount of time they save you during the SEO process. For example, instead of browsing several different websites to research your information, you can view all the data right from one spot in your web browser. By using SEO browser plug-ins, you can quickly access a website's PageRank, its age, indexing and backlink information, and even mentions of it in the social media space. Plug-ins can generate a list of topically related websites that can serve as your gateway to the online community for any given topic.

The SEO plug-ins commonly used for WordPress have been created out of necessity. The standard installation of WordPress is by far the most popular blogging software; however, it does not support commonly known best practices for on-page SEO. For this reason, SEO-savvy developers have taken the time to produce powerful plug-ins that make doing SEO for your blog far more effective and efficient. From custom title tags to automatic sitemap generation, these plug-ins are a must for publishers using WordPress to publish content.

Using the Side-by-Side SEO Comparision Tool

Internet Marketing Ninjas' Side-by-Side SEO Comparison Tool is a useful tool for improving page optimization on top landing pages that you want to rank better in search engines for specific keywords relative to your competitors. This tool shows meta tag information for you and your competitors. It also shows keyword density information for you and your competitors for head phrases and tail phrases. *Keyword density* is the number of instances that a particular keyword appears on a web page, which may indicate whether you are over-optimized or under-optimized for a particular keyword you rank for or are targeting. This tool also shows the ratio of linked text to nonlinked text as well as internal linking information for the page on your website selected for analysis and each of your competitor's web pages.

Using the SEOmoz Browser Toolbar

The SEOmoz Toolbar for Chrome and Firefox is useful for quickly checking backlink data for web pages as your browse the web. This tool is part of the SEOmoz PRO Tools Suite. It can also be used to highlight links or text and includes an overlay to help you analyze the on-page components of a page as you browse the web. This tool is useful for on-the-fly analysis as you browse websites.

Using the SEO for Firefox Plug-in

Aaron Wall from SEO Book has created what is arguably the most useful and popular SEO browser plug-in to date, SEO for Firefox. This powerful tool displays vital technical information you need to assess a website's strength all in one place. By using search engines and other various application program interfaces, or *APIs,* SEO for Firefox offers a large amount of important data in seconds, saving you from having to go to multiple sources for that same data. This tool can save an immense amount of precious time for any Internet marketer and is a "must have" plug-in. SEO for Firefox lists a website's indexing information, backlink information, age, Google PageRank, listings in popular social media sites, as well as listings in large, powerful directories.

Check Page Performance Using the Load Time Speed Test Tool

In 2010, Google announced load time speed as a search-engine ranking factor. One useful tool for analyzing site performance is the free Internet Marketing Ninjas' Load Time Speed Test Tool. This tool includes load speed information, with a graph showing load times for various files. A unique feature of this tool is that it allows you to compare your site's load time against competitors.

Using the WordPress SEO Plug-in by Yoast

WordPress SEO is a WordPress plug-in created by Yoast to help easily solve some of the SEO issues created by WordPress. For example, the plug-in allows you to set templates for title tags and meta descriptions for all types of pages. WordPress SEO also makes it easy to set breadcrumbs and XML sitemaps. Additionally, Wordpress SEO allows you to easily edit your robots.txt, .htaccess files, and more.

Using the SEO Book Rank Checker

SEO Book Rank Checker is a useful free browser plug-in for quickly checking rankings for one phrase or multiple phrases in Google, Bing, and Yahoo. This tool also allows you to export ranking data to spreadsheets, so that you can easily combine this data with other data. This browser plug-in also allows you to toggle between Google US and Google UK and allows you to schedule rank check tasks.

Using the SEOTools for Excel Add-In

Excel is an essential component of any SEO toolkit. However, some routine SEO functions tend to be time-consuming. SEOTools for Excel by Niels Bosma is a free Excel add-in that provides useful functions for working with SEO and other web metrics directly in Excel. It includes features for SEO, traffic analysis, social media metrics, string manipulation, and more.

If your business is in a competitive search niche, make sure that the page that you want to rank competitive keyword phrases for is well optimized. The free Internet Marketing Ninjas Side-by-Side SEO Comparison Tool, located at www.internetmarketingninjas.com/seo-tools/seo-compare, helps you identify gaps in your on-page optimization strategy as well as on-page optimization tactics that competitors use to rank for your desired keyword phrases. The Side-by-Side SEO Comparison Tool also provides meta tags, keyword density, internal linking data, and markup of the page. By leveraging this tool, you can identify desirable competitor keywords and learn more about competitors' on-page optimization strategies.

Using the Side-by-Side SEO Comparison Tool

1 Navigate to www.internet marketingninjas.com/seo-tools/seo-compare.

2 Enter URLs you want to analyze and click Ninja Check.

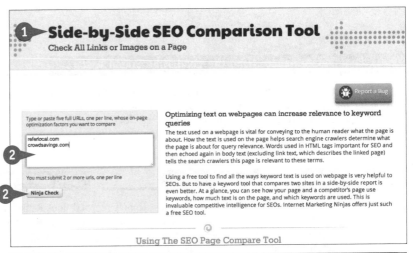

A Compare meta tag optimization and the persuasiveness of your meta tag copy against competitors.

Note the amount of linked text and nonlinked text on your page versus your competitor's page.

3 Scroll down.

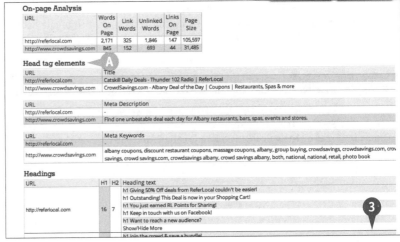

B In the section Keyword usage of non-linked words on-page, note keywords that appear. Evaluate how well you are optimized for keywords you are targeting. Also, note the distribution of two-word and three-word phrases included as part of your nonlinked text and your competitors' nonlinked text. You should strive for a good balance of head and tail terms in your content.

4 Scroll down.

C In the section internal linking structure, notice your internal linking structure compared to competitors'; especially note whether the number of pages that competitors link out to is much higher than yours. Overall, linking out generously from powerful pages on your site helps link equity to better spread across your website to deeper pages of your website.

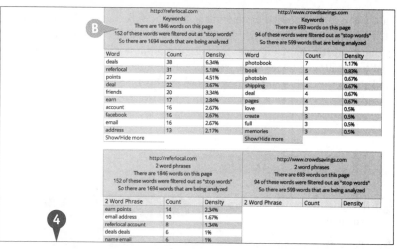

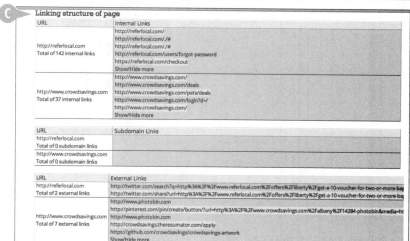

EXTRA

One thing to note as you analyze data from this tool is to see whether your page links out to internal redirects. Linking out to redirects has a negative impact on how link equity is distributed across your website.

Another thing to look at is the amount of linked text versus nonlinked text on a page. A higher amount of nonlinked text tends to do better than a lower amount of nonlinked text. Also, a combination of a low amount of nonlinked text and a high amount of linked text suggests *thin* content. Google is beginning to take an aggressive stance against thin site content and low-quality content.

In many cases, knowing basic on-page and backlink information is useful as you are browsing web pages to gather competitive intelligence. It is also useful for finding quality websites as target audiences for your content marketing efforts. The MozBar helps speed up this type of research.

One popular use for this tool is to easily compare backlinks alongside competitor pages. For example, if you are analyzing a competitor that ranks above you for a particular phrase, you can use the Side-by-Side SEO Comparison Tool discussed previously to analyze on-page features of the competitor page and use the MozBar to analyze backlinks.

Using the SEOmoz Browser Toolbar

1 Navigate to www.seomoz.org/ seo-toolbar.

2 Click a Mozbar download.

3 A Mozilla.org add-ons page opens. Click Download Now.

You will have to restart your browser to complete the installation.

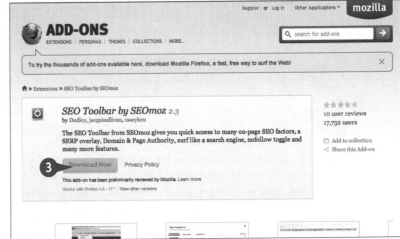

A Note that the SEOmoz Toolbar provides backlink data for both the page and domain.

4 Click the highlighter button to view and select highlight links and keywords options.

5 Click the settings button to view options for disabling CSS and JavaScript.

EXTRA

With the SEOmoz Toolbar, you have ability to highlight on a page. This robust feature gives you the ability to highlight followed links, no followed links, external links, internal links, and instances of any keyword you specify in your browser. When using this feature, identify links that have an unwarranted nofollow attribute applied to them, which is an instance of invalid usage of the nofollow link attribute. The nofollow attribute should only be used to prevent search engines from crawling pages that they cannot access, such as those that return 403 server responses, those which include content that cannot be read by search engines, or areas where third-party users may generate outbound links from your site.

SEO for Firefox gathers marketing data about a website and displays that data within your browser alongside the search results from Google or Yahoo. Because the data is provided to you alongside the actual search results, this extension allows you to check the most important statistics of a website before you even visit the domain.

SEO for Firefox provides a useful gauge for the number of backlinks a web page and website have, from several sources. The number and topical relevancy of a website's backlinks are two critical off-site SEO factors search engines use to determine ranking position in the organic search-engine results.

Using the SEO for Firefox Plug-in

1 Navigate to http://tools.seobook.com/firefox/seo-for-firefox.html.

2 Sign up for an SEO Book free account to gain access to the SEO Book suite of free tools.

3 Log in to your account and then click Download Now.

This prompts you to install the SEO for Firefox plug-in and restart Firefox.

A This plug-in displays an overlay of marketing data within Google search results.

④ To view additional features for this tool, click the SEO for Firefox icon in your browser.

⑤ Select Options from the drop-down list.

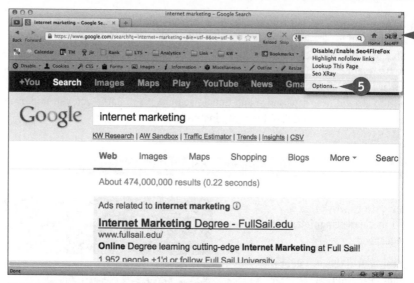

⑧ This interface allows you to select or hide which marketing data SEO for Firefox includes in the search engine results page overlay.

⑥ Select data options in the Mode column that you want to include or hide, and then open Google in a new tab to rerun the results with your new options set.

EXTRA

Be warned that the SEO for Firefox extension is resource intensive because it pulls data from multiple search-engine back-end systems all at once. For this reason, you should do your day-to-day surfing with the extension turned off, and use it only while you are doing market research. Setting the data to be retrieved "on demand" rather than automatically is another alternative.

SEO for Firefox has gone through multiple upgrades, so future upgrades and improvements are likely to occur. According to SEO expert Aaron Wall, more than 130,000 webmasters and Internet professionals are currently using the SEO for Firefox extension.

Quality indicators are starting to play a larger role for search engines. For example, Google now has gathered extensive user experience data from sources such as the Chrome browser and the Google Toolbar, in addition to traditional search logs. Site performance is both a factor for creating a good user experience and Google search-engine rankings. One useful tool for analyzing page performance is the Load Time Speed Test Tool. This tool shows performance data for any web page you select as well as performance data for your competitors' web pages. Knowing how your load time compares to competitors' is one way to identify whether performance optimization is an area you can improve upon for your website.

Check Page Performance Using the Load Time Speed Test Tool

1 Navigate to www.internetmarketingninjas.com/pagespeed.

2 Enter your URL and select the Single Page option.

3 Click Start Test.

4 Scroll down to the Full detail load speed information section. This graph provides insights into what is slowing load time down.

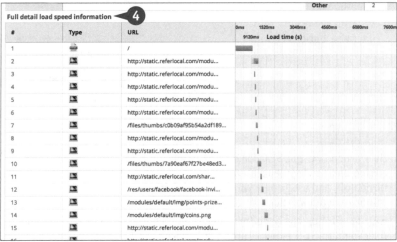

5 Scroll up to the top of the page and select the Compare Two Pages option.

6 Click Start Test.

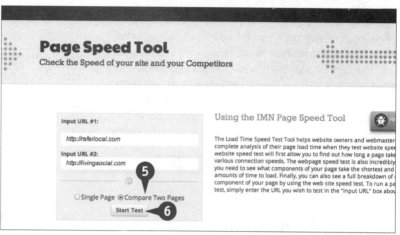

A View comparative results.

7 Select a detailed view of the result to drill down in greater detail using the Detail analysis buttons.

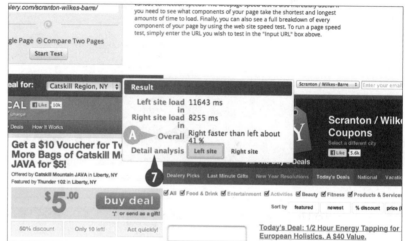

EXTRA

One way to improve load time speed at the website level is to optimize images. Keeping image sizes minimal helps load time and speed pages up for visitors on slow connections. One tool to assist you in optimizing images is Yahoo Smush.it at www.smushit.com/ysmush.it. If you are using WordPress as a CMS, consider trying the WordPress Smush.it plug-in at http://wordpress.org/extend/plugins/wp-smushit.

The WordPress SEO plug-in by Yoast, located at http://yoast.com/wordpress/seo for download, consolidates many features from other smaller WordPress SEO plug-ins into one bundle. This plug-in fixes SEO issues unique to WordPress and also has special options to help you better optimize your website. This plug-in also makes it easy to implement meta robots tags and the robots.txt and .htaccess files. The WordPress SEO plug-in is available for

free and enables you to easily manage your SEO efforts from the WordPress blog administration area.

Note that SEO WordPress plug-ins require you to customize each of your pages for SEO purposes prior to publication. Always make sure you are optimizing title tags and URL conventions to maximize your search-engine ranking.

Using the WordPress SEO Plug-in by Yoast

1 Navigate to http://yoast.com/wordpress/seo.

2 Click Download.

3 Log in to WordPress, scroll down the page, and under Plugins, click Add New.

4 Click the Upload link and upload the WordPress SEO plug-in files.

A Note that the WordPress SEO files need to be zipped before you upload them to WordPress. You will also be prompted to activate the plug-in once it is installed.

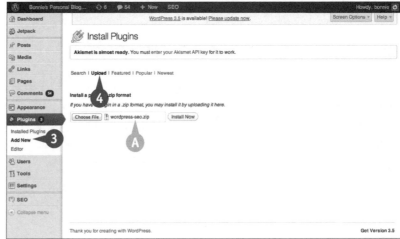

⑤ You can verify Google Webmaster Tools and Bing Webmaster Tools from the WordPress SEO dashboard, which is the first screen that appears after you activate the plug-in.

Ⓑ To view various settings and options for WordPress SEO, simply scroll down and select your feature of choice to customize by clicking on a sidebar text link under SEO.

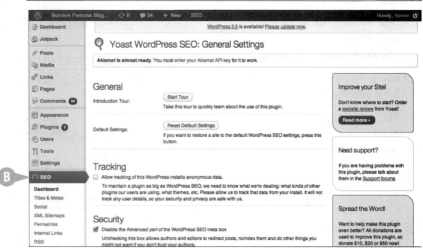

EXTRA

Depending on your marketing goals and requirements, you may want to append an add-on to the WordPress SEO plug-in. Yoast offers several add-on modules for the WordPress SEO plug-in. Currently, two add-ons are available, one for video SEO found at http://yoast.com/wordpress/video-seo and one for news SEO found at http://yoast.com/wordpress/news-seo. Also, Yoast is developing a Local SEO plug-in at the time of this writing. In the meantime, if local SEO is part of your online marketing strategy, consider trying the hCard WordPress plug-in at http://lautman.ca/hcard-wordpress-widget.

Rank checking is an essential SEO measurement metric. Measuring your rankings over time, in addition to **data** your analytics provides, gives you insight into your **overall** visibility in search engines and how well search **engine** traffic is converting for you. SEO Book has a useful **Firefox** plug-in for checking rankings for a keyword or

group of keywords in Google, Bing, or Yahoo. It also has several handy features, such as the ability to view Google UK rankings and to schedule rank checks. This rank checker is good for checking rankings live for yourself and your competitors.

Using the SEO Book Rank Checker

1 Navigate to http://tools.seo book.com/firefox/rank-checker.

2 Sign up for a free SEO Book account to gain access to the SEO Book suite of free tools.

3 Log in to your account and then click Download Now.

This prompts you to install the SEO for Firefox plug-in and restart Firefox.

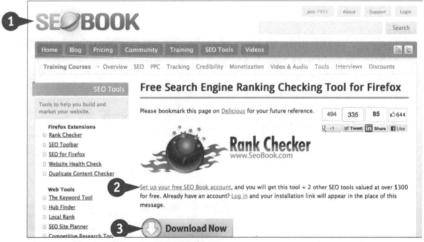

4 Enter the domain and the keyword you would like to check the rankings for.

5 Click Add.

6 Click Start.

Once you click Start, you are able to view ranking results from Google, Bing, and Yahoo.

7 Click the Add Multiple Keywords link.

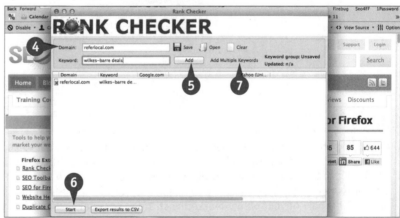

8 Write or paste keywords you want to find rankings for from your Clipboard.

9 Click Add.

Once keywords appear in the rank checker, click Close in the Add Multiple Keywords window.

10 Click Start to run the tool.

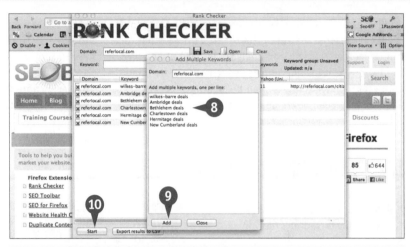

11 When SEO Book Rank Checker is finished running, click Export results to CSV to export the results.

EXTRA

The SEO Book Rank Checker is useful for small datasets and for cross-checking data from other sources. Google and Bing Webmaster Tools provide some information regarding your ranking positions. However, if you have a large custom list of keywords that you want to check rankings for, consider a premium solution. Advanced Web Ranking, found at www.advancedwebranking.com, is a very popular rank tracking solution. Also, SEOmoz provides a rank checker with the SEOmoz PRO subscription service at www.seomoz.org/rank-tracker.

Using the SEOTools for Excel Add-In

Microsoft Excel is by far the most versatile SEO tool in any Internet marketing toolkit. Data from other tools can be merged, parsed, and analyzed in a variety of ways to provide fresh insights. However, sometimes distilling the data that you need in Excel can be laborious. Luckily, Excel add-ins have been developed to make many Excel-based

SEO tasks easier. One great add-in to aid your research is the free SEOTools for Excel Add-in by Niels Bosma. This useful tool includes features for SEO and analytics, as well as helpful utilities you can use for a variety of purposes. However, note that this add-in only works for the Windows version of Excel.

Using the SEOTools for Excel Add-In

① Navigate to http://nielsbosma. se/projects/seotools/download.

② Click the download specific to your 32-bit or 64-bit version of Excel.

③ Open Excel.

④ Click the File tab.

⑤ Click the Options link.

6 Click Add-Ins in the sidebar menu on the left of the Excel Options widow.

7 On the Add-Ins tab, choose the Excel Add-Ins option from the Manage drop-down list and click Go.

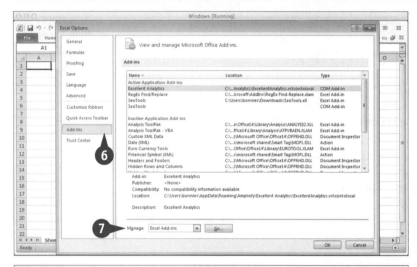

8 In the Add-Ins window, click Browse and locate the SEOTools add-in.

9 When the SEOTools add-in appears in the Add-Ins available list, select the check box next to it.

10 Click OK.

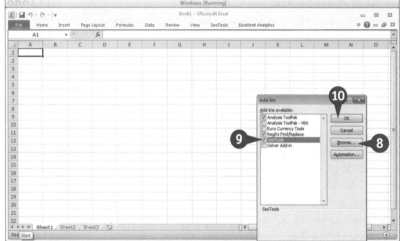

EXTRA

Several additional Excel add-ins are useful for SEO as well as broader Internet marketing functions. Three popular ones are the Excellent Analytics add-in, which can be found at http://excellentanalytics.com. SEO Gadget has also created several notable SEO extensions, including the Google AdWords API Extension for Excel at http://seo gadget.com/google-adwords-plugin-excel, and the SEOmoz Links API Extension for Excel at http://seogadget.com/ tools/links-api-extension-for-excel. All these tools make it easier to import data from other popular SEO tools into Excel and gain deeper insight into your SEO by being able to view and visualize data from diverse sources together.

Office

InDesign

Facebook

THE WAY YOU WANT TO LEARN.

HTML

Photoshop

DigitalClassroom.com

Flexible, fast, and fun, DigitalClassroom.com lets you choose when, where, and how to learn new skills. This subscription-based online learning environment is accessible anytime from your desktop, laptop, tablet, or smartphone. It's easy, efficient learning — on *your* schedule.

- Learn web design and development, Office applications, and new technologies from more than 2,500 video tutorials, e-books, and lesson files
- Master software from Adobe, Apple, and Microsoft
- Interact with other students in forums and groups led by industry pros

Learn more! Sample DigitalClassroom.com **for free, now!**

We're social. Connect with us!

facebook.com/digitalclassroom
@digitalclassrm

For more professional instruction in a visual format, try these.

All designed for visual learners—just like you!

Read Less–Learn More®
Visual®

978-0-470-59160-4

978-0-470-90432-9

978-0-470-55651-1

For a complete listing of *Visual Blueprint*™ titles and other Visual books, go to wiley.com/go/visual

Visual®
An Imprint of ⊕WILEY
Now you know.

Wiley, the Wiley logo, the Visual logo, Read Less-Learn More, and Visual Blueprint are trademarks or registered trademarks of John Wiley & Sons, Inc. and/or its affiliates. All other trademarks are the property of their respective owners.